For Michaes and June

with my best love —

THE EDGE OF MEANING

James Boyd White

THE
EDGE
OF
MEANING

The University of Chicago Press

Chicago & London

JAMES BOYD WHITE is the Hart Wright Professor of Law, professor of English, and adjunct professor of classical studies at the University of Michigan. He has written a number of books, including *Acts of Hope: Creating Authority in Literature, Law, and Politics* (1994), *Justice as Translation: An Essay in Cultural and Legal Criticism* (1990), *The Legal Imagination*, 2d ed. (1985), and *When Words Lose Their Meaning: Constitutions and Reconstitutions of Language, Character, and Community* (1984), all published by the University of Chicago Press.

The University of Chicago Press, Chicago 60637
The University of Chicago Press, Ltd., London
© 2001 by The University of Chicago
All rights reserved. Published 2001
Printed in the United States of America
10 09 08 07 06 05 04 03 02 01   1 2 3 4 5

ISBN: 0-226-89481-9 (cloth)

Library of Congress Cataloging-in-Publication Data

White, James Boyd, 1938–
    The edge of meaning / James Boyd White.
        p.   cm.
    Includes bibliographical references and index.
    Contents: Thoreau's Walden—Huckleberry Finn—The Odyssey—Reading Greek—Making meaning in the sentence—The Phaedrus—Frost and Herbert—The life of the law as a life of writing—The depth of meaning in Vermeer.
    ISBN 0-226-89481-9 (cloth : alk. paper)
    1. Literature—History and criticism.   I. Title.
    PN511.W59   2001
    809—dc21
                                                    00-012903

♾ The paper used in this publication meets the minimum requirements of the American National Standard for Information Sciences—Permanence of Paper for Printed Library Materials, ANSI Z39.48-1992.

TO GERDA SELIGSON

For flowing is the secret of things & no wonder the children love masks, & to trick themselves in endless costumes, & be a horse, a soldier, a parson, or a bear; and, older, delight in theatricals; as, in nature, the egg is passing to a grub, the grub to a fly, and the vegetable eye to a bud, the bud to a leaf, a stem, a flower, a fruit; the children have only the instinct of their race, the instinct of the Universe, in which, *Becoming somewhat else* is the whole game of nature, & death the penalty of standing still.

Emerson, *Journals*, 1855

CONTENTS

PREFACE

Though we have no very good way of talking about it, one of the deepest needs of human beings—perhaps of all our needs the one that is most distinctively human—is for what we in English call "meaning" in our experience. It is meaning that we seek to create through our cultures, those complex symbolic and expressive practices ranging from music to politics, football to religion, that occupy us so much of the time; and meaning, perhaps in a somewhat different sense, that each individual seeks as he or she works through the choices and possibilities of existence, trying to make them add up to something whole and coherent.

To say this will I hope make a kind of intuitive sense, but it is also plain that we are collectively not very clear about exactly what it is we point to in such uses of the word *meaning*. One way of putting it—which I know can be only the slightest of sketches, and which it is the aim of the rest of the book to complete—is to say that each of us constantly seeks to imagine the world, and the self and others within it, in such a way as to enable us to engage in coherent and intelligible speech, valuable and effective action. We want, that is, a way of imagining life as a whole, on which our own action and thought and speech, our own relations with others, can sensibly and effectively be based. How is this desire to be addressed, put to work, and connected with other desires and realities?

This book emerges from an interest in this question, which it explores by examining a series of texts and artefacts in which the author faces with particular intensity and richness the difficulties involved in this activity of the imagination. The works chosen range widely, from Thoreau's *Walden* to the paintings of Vermeer, from the *Odyssey* and Plato's *Phaedrus* to a modern law case. One of the points of this diversity is to make it easier for us to see, and begin to analyze, the process at work in all of them; another is to begin to show how different people, located in different cultural contexts and working in different genres, address in significantly different ways the possibilities and difficulties inherent in the process in which we are all engaged.

Let me now attempt a slightly fuller description of that process. I think that in each of us there is a part of our being that is the source of mental life and imagination; that, without our being wholly aware of it, in this part of the self we are constantly asking a set of questions about the world, of which the deepest is the question of meaning as I have defined it above, namely, whether we can find or make an adequate way of imagining the world, and the self and others within it; that to ask this question is to involve us in trying to respond to it, which in turn brings us to face the adequacies and inadequacies of the languages we are given to speak, of the cultures we inhabit, and the constraints imposed on us by nature as well; that our engagement with these questions is for the most part unconscious, but can be made the object of attention and thought, particularly through the careful reading and study of certain works of literature and other forms of art, including the art of law; indeed that to make us aware of this process and our own participation in it, and to teach us how to think about and criticize our own performances of it, is one of the central functions of art; and, finally, that we pursue these questions not alone but in relation to others, with whom we make real whatever we manage to learn. The process to which I am drawing attention is thus one in which we all engage, all the time, but do so for the most part outside the field of conscious awareness—it is a piece of that rich and complex life that takes place in the ocean of the mind, beneath the surface on which we consciously live. But it does manifest itself constantly in what we say and do; not explicitly, but in our performances with language and each other.

As my brief account suggests this process consists of a series of phases that fall into a kind of natural sequence; but they also overlap, one continuing or recurring in what we might think of as the domain of the other. One way to think about it would be to say that the stages I have identified mark a story of human life: we begin full of a youthful need and hope for coherence and understanding; we must soon confront the stubborn facts of culture and nature and language, including the ways in which these constitute forces that act on us, changing our ways of imagining the world; in the end we must find a way to live as expressive beings in a world full of constraint and limit, including on our own minds and imaginations; and the question is thus presented: How, by what art or arts, we can do so? How, that is, can we respond to the inevitable discovery that the coherence and unity that a side of us most deeply desires cannot in any simple way be attained?

This sequence of stages is in fact mirrored in the structure of this book. I begin with Thoreau's claim to have found a way to reimagine the world and himself, his language and his mind, in such a way as to make life an act of perpetual and joyful creation; then I turn to Huckleberry Finn, who is equally insistent on making sense of the world and himself, but is in the end incapable of comprehending the externally determined, inwardly validated, fact of race, which makes the most important event of his life, his friendship with Jim, unsayable; then I consider Odysseus, who must deal, not only once but twice, with fundamental changes in his culture, which require different ways of thinking and being, which he is, for the most part, remarkably able to achieve.

At this point I begin a new sequence, meant to bring the problem home to you as reader, me as writer: I look first at a piece of the ancient Greek language, for all of us foreign, trying to get some sense of the peculiar ways it works as a source of meaning in the world, at once enabling and restraining its user; then I examine some of the ways in which the possibilities and problems of meaning are present in what we call the sentence, the smallest unit of normal speech, with the idea of deepening our sense of the pervasiveness of the questions we are pursuing, including in Greek; then I turn to Plato's *Phaedrus,* perhaps as rich and challenging a treatment of the issues that concern us as any in Western literature, and do so with attention both to its Greek and to the kind of experience offered by its sentences.

Finally, in the last three chapters, I address some specific ways in which the questions I am pursuing, particularly as redefined by our reading of the *Phaedrus,* are addressed by minds working in three distinct genres and cultural contexts: in the religious or metaphysical poetry of Frost and Herbert; in the way a particular law case is put together, as a set of questions and responses; and in the paintings of Vermeer. The *Phaedrus* is the center of the book: everything before builds up to it, everything after builds upon it.

The readings that make up this book are, like any work of criticism, a piece of an intellectual autobiography. Certainly the works I have chosen are among those that have been of the deepest importance to my own life. They also happen to be drawn from what is often called the Canon, or the Western tradition of high culture. This presents a complex problem, for such texts are often invoked as though they represented universal human experience, sometimes as though they in some way supported a particular view of society and politics—patriarchal, imperialist, and inegalitarian. But I agree with neither of these positions. For me the interest of these works lies not in their universality but in their particularity, in the unique and revealing ways in which Thoreau, say, or Plato, or Herbert, engage in the larger process that is my subject. And, though this is not my major concern here, I certainly do not think that these works, separately or together, define a reactionary politics.

Yet the fact that they are all from what is perceived as the Western Canon does have its significance. Not because their authors are all "white," since that term in my view cannot sensibly be applied to Homer or Plato, nor even "European," and for much the same reason: Greece did not know "race" as we do and Europe did not then exist. And these writers are "dead" only if we fail to give them life. But they are all written by men, and I am a man, and this fact may lead some readers to think that I am working on the assumption, familiar enough in our world, that all experience is male experience, all thought male thought.

I can only say that this is not what I believe. I have chosen these works because of their importance in shaping my own mind and because of their value in illuminating the process that is my subject, and they naturally reflect the nature of my own education, both its limits and its virtues. Of course that education is not the only possible one but itself is partly shaped by my own social and cultural context, as a boy growing up to adulthood under privileged circumstances in New England in the forties and fifties, as a man living in and around universities ever since, in the West and Midwest, and as what we in America call a "white" person—though I should also add that it has been shaped as well by the nature of my own mind and personality. Other people speak from different positions, out of different experiences—this is true of those whose works are discussed here, true of those who share my formal education and social characteristics, and true also of each of the readers of this book—and it is ultimately in these differences that we live. My hope is that the reader will find it valuable to compare his or her experience with my own, on the understanding that whatever value this book may have will lie as much in the reader's sense of difference as in any perceived similarities, in felt dissonance as much as resonance.

Beyond Words

In the National Gallery in London I once saw a small painting showing a squat black boat, a little like a tugboat, heading upstream into the waves of a windy day and leaving behind it a large wake, reflecting the sky. If you were to see the painting yourself—I choose it partly because it is a minor one, not well known, thus not likely to live in your memory—what do you think you could say about your experience of it? Or take a picture you have seen, a self-portrait by Rembrandt, say, or the crows in the cornfields by Van Gogh, or perhaps the famous picture by Vermeer (to which we shall return in the last chapter) that shows a woman reading a letter, standing at a table with a map behind her and with light falling through a window from our left. What can you say about your experience of such a painting? Of course volumes have been written in efforts to describe and interpret and understand, and I will in fact do some of that myself in what follows. But I want to begin by drawing attention to the simple, obvious, though sometimes forgotten fact that nothing any of us can say will ever exhaust or fully express the experience of the painting. It cannot, for the painting has much of its life and meaning in the world beyond words, in the world of color and form and texture, the world of sensation and vision. Something similar could be said about music as well—it is its own world, not reducible to language—and about the physical world of nature too: What in the end can one say about a foggy morning on a rocky coast; the bright blue flowers on the edge of a midwestern country road; the stone smoothed by the waters of a river into a shape with form and balance?

One reason we turn to painting and music and nature is in fact to move, or to try to move, beyond the world of our languages. But even as we watch or look or listen, words, or potential words, flow through our minds, perhaps just below the level of consciousness, forming and shaping part of what we call experience. Sometimes we may seem to

lose ourselves completely in wordlessness, though this may be something of an illusion; but in any event we always return to the world of
words.

When we do, it is with a partial awareness of what we normally
occlude: that the way our languages present and shape the world is not
the only one; that they float as it were on a sea of experience they can
never wholly capture or reflect or express; that they are always imperfect or inadequate, sometimes false or misleading; and that we are
nonetheless implicated in them, indeed partly made by them. From this
realization we may turn once more to the immediacy, reality, and irreducibility of a field of grass on a summer afternoon or a cello suite by
Bach, away from the world of words.

Though it is of course composed of words, poetry paradoxically has
often much the same effect, carrying us to the place where our response
to language is made, and where we can begin to see it and think about
it. For poetry often makes us conscious of the words it uses—as having
sound and shape, as objects in the world to be observed—almost as
though we were learning language again. Think how unnatural, odd,
physically real, and separate from us are the words written in a foreign
writing system like Chinese or Thai or even Greek, or the sounds of
people speaking in a language we do not understand. Whenever we
speak or read a foreign language, unless we are truly bilingual, we are
always aware of the language itself, as something external to the mind,
and of our necessarily incomplete grasp of it. As I hope to show in the
chapters on Greek, in reading such a language we are always on the
edge of something we do not wholly understand, and we know it. Our
own language was once like that, and poetry, or some kinds of poetry
at least, can bring part of it out from the recesses of the mind to a place
where it can be seen and heard as something different from us, different from the way the world is. This is clear enough with the poetry of
someone like Wallace Stevens, which constantly disrupts the reader's
desire for restateable meaning, for familiar and routine uses of language. But it is true I think of poetry more generally. Think of this well-
known short poem by Blake, a favorite of many and apparently so
simple:

> O Rose, thou art sick!
> The invisible worm
> That flies in the night,
> In the howling storm,

Has found out thy bed
Of crimson joy,
And his dark secret love
Does thy life destroy.

Images of disease, sexuality, and organic nature all emerge and interact, but not in a way that is reducible to a scheme of propositions or to a confident translation into ordinary speech. This is partly because the poem calls upon the visual imagination, almost as a painting does, which will not translate into words; but also because it calls upon the experience of the ear. The rhythms of the lines, mainly iambs and anapests, sweep us along till we get to the highly emphasized variation, "dárk sécrět lóve"; the emphasis lies not only in the "meaning" of the words but in the sounds they make together, in the significance of a pattern established and broken. Or listen to the sound of the vowels: all those Os and Is, until we get at last an O and I together in "joy," which feels like a culmination; this word is then united by rhyme with its mate, "destroy." It is in part the sound of the words that connects them in this way, telling us that "joy destroys." The poem makes both words mean something new and does so through their sound.

One could go on in this vein at length, but this is enough to suggest that in reading poetry, or poetry of this kind, the reader is brought to the edge of the language that is being used, to the edge of language itself perhaps, where he can begin to see it as made, as chosen, as the material with which the mind can work. Language loses the transparency it normally has and becomes opaque, or perhaps better, translucent.[1]

What is true of this kind of poetry can also be true of prose. Think of a sentence by Gibbon or Hooker, for example, with its complex construction over time, its cadences and emphases and transformations—all of which make us conscious of the reality of the words, as they work in new ways. Or take this sentence from Thoreau, early in *Walden,* to which we shall return more than once in what follows:

1. For an example of a different kind consider this stanza from Richard Wilbur, *The Disappearing Alphabet* (New York: Harcourt Brace & Company, 1998):

In the word DUMB, the letter B is mute,
But elsewhere its importance is acute.
If it were absent, say, from BAT and BALL,
There'd be no big or little leagues AT ALL.

> Moreover, I, on my side, require of every writer, first and last, a simple
> and sincere account of his own life, and not merely what he has heard
> of other men's lives; some such account as he would send to his kindred
> from a distant land; for if he has lived sincerely, it must have been in a
> distant land to me.

Of the many things that can be said about this sentence let me here
simply observe that Thoreau transforms the meaning of the word *sincere,* conceiving of it first as a quality of expression, then as a quality
of a life. In doing this he makes us conscious of the word in a new way,
giving it new meaning; and the connection he thus establishes between
writing and living will in fact prove to be his deepest theme.

One idea of this book, then, is that there is in each of us a place at
the edge of words, between language and no language, from which
language itself can begin to be seen, brought within the field of attention; not clearly and completely of course, but as it is given us to see
it—in parts, obscurely, with uncertainty, but seen nonetheless; and that
it is one of the functions of certain kinds of thought and art to bring us to
this point, to help us see what we normally cannot see about the way we
face and use language, about the way our minds work. This is most difficult, both because the language we wish to think about is the instrument by which we do much of our thinking and because this language
does much to shape our minds, giving us many of our expectations, our
ways of approaching and inhabiting the world.

At the place or moment to which art can in this way lead us, we
naturally find ourselves asking questions of many kinds, about the
world, about language, and about the self. The deepest question, I
think, the one at the center of it all, unites all three topics: it is whether
we can find, or make, a way of imagining the self and the world and
others within it that will fit with our experience—enable us to have
experience—in such a way as to make possible coherent and valuable
forms of speech and thought and action. The major aim of this book
will be to focus attention on this question, showing how certain writers
have addressed it and made it available to us, and in this way to make
it the object of thought.

To give some sense of what I mean by what I have called the "deepest question," let me ask you to imagine, or remember, the experience
of a small child learning to use language: learning to name things and
actions, to make appropriate gestures, to play games with her parents
(like peek-a-boo, say, or throw-it-on-the-floor-then-Mommy-picks-it-
up). What is the experience of learning language like for the person

doing it? For one thing, it is a source of enormous satisfaction, as she joins more fully the only human world she knows, learning its languages of word and gesture, of tone and quality of voice. And she is rewarded beyond measure for what she does: she pleases and is pleased, her capacities in the world and in relation to other people grow daily. But she is also frustrated, as she finds herself unable to find words and gestures to match her unspoken feelings and ideas, unable to make herself understood, unable sometimes to understand the expectations she is trying so energetically to meet. You may not remember this from your own experience, but you will have seen it in others, in the child who cannot say what she wants and shows her frustration in her face and gestures.

For most of us this process continues in both its aspects all our lives, giving us on the one hand an increasing sense of competence—of understanding and being understood—yet at the same time continuing as a source of frustration. Despite the claims of the institutions that make up much of our world, and perhaps the efforts of some of our teachers, we never become fully defined by our language, or by our languages; there is always something before, or beyond, the words, something they do not and cannot fit. We may hide this from ourselves, but I think it is true of everyone. Of course it is true in different degrees: some people seem to feel that almost everything they are and think can be expressed in the languages available to them; others are painfully conscious of the ways in which language not only enables and facilitates but frustrates, entangles, and misleads. What can I really say about the pain I feel in my knee when I walk, such a person might ask, or about the beauty of a sunset at sea, or about the fear that grips me on a dark night? We can use words to point or gesture, but compared to the intensity and vividness of the experience, what we say is pallid or obscure.

A person learning a language almost inevitably comes to ask another question, one that addresses not just the adequacy of a language as a means of expression but its own coherence. At first it is enough for the child that what he is learning works as part of the life of the family in which he is raised, and of the larger world into which he is being introduced. But at some time the question will begin to arise whether what he is learning really makes sense. Suppose, for example, he is learning a religion, a doctrine based upon a story: Can this doctrine, this story, be true? In what sense? Sometime or other he is sure to ask such questions. And the language of the family itself, his primary language, may be riddled with contradiction, distorted by sentimentality, or unconnected to the real in ways that make it incomprehensible to him, even as he uses it, and that also make him incomprehensible to it, or to those who speak that language.

Of course the depth and intensity of the questioning of coherence will vary from person to person, but I think that it is a part of every consciousness at some stage to ask questions of this kind. And the questions go beyond the family, for the language one learns is a version of the language of the larger world. Is it coherent? Good, or bad? Does it make sense? In what respects? What actions or feelings does it require, what permit, what render impossible? Think of the child learning a language of race, for example, or certain ways to talk about women—about herself as a woman—or being invited to talk as though human happiness is a matter of high consumption. How do I know that I am not being raised in some way to be the equivalent of a Nazi or a slave-owner, a moral and political monster? These are questions that are, or should be, at least sometimes present in every mind.

It is very difficult to pursue these questions, however, for in both cases, that of the family and of the larger world, the child is so rewarded for what he learns, what he becomes, that it is practically impossible to question one's language, even if it is truly evil: the language of Nazism or American racism, say, or the crazed jargon that adulates a leader, or a brutal ideology. For one thing, in what language can the person question the only language he has learned? It is all he has, and it has done much to make him who he is. He sees with its eyes, hears with its ears. For another, he is so invested in it emotionally, so connected to it, that it is hard to imagine criticizing it. We see this response in people learning professional or academic languages: the language is simply too valuable and important to permit its questioning. I have made my way in the world that is defined by the language of the law or English or anthropology, I say, or the marines or the police or the stock exchange: How can I imagine giving it up?

In using the image of the child learning a language, of his being introduced to a culture and a social world and to the practices that make it go, I may be thought to suggest that the process to which I point is in some way childish, something we give up as we grow older. But that is not what I think at all. I believe that the part of the self that meets language and withdraws from it, that tries to turn language to its purposes, that is ready to doubt its own impulses as these are derived from modes of thought and speech it learns to criticize, that seeks new formulations, new ways of imagining, is in fact the part that achieves, if any does, what we call maturity of mind. And, as I try to show with respect to the works discussed in the rest of this book, it is one of the great functions of art, including the art of law, to bring this part of the mind to life and consciousness, to make its questions real, and in this way to contribute to its continuing formation.

I think, then, that as a person works with the languages of her world, speaking this way or that, trying to figure out what another person expects by way of response, then trying to meet or frustrate those expectations, she faces questions of two sorts, both of real importance. The first is whether—and how—what she is learning actually works in her world, whether family or school or a larger community, to enable her to survive, to manage her social relations, to define and achieve certain goals. The second, a larger question, is whether— and how—any of these languages, or all of them together, offer her a way of imagining the world, and herself and others within it, that will make it possible for her to achieve coherent forms of thought and speech, effective and meaningful action. I think that this is as deep a need as a human being has: a need of the mind or soul, the need for what we call meaning in life. When it becomes clear that there is no way of meeting it, a person may die, either by simply withering away or by suicide.

I think here of Ajax, in Sophocles' play of that name. One of the very greatest of the Greek warriors, and totally committed to the dominant culture of honor, he is deprived, wrongfully he thinks, of the armor of the dead Achilles, which is given to Odysseus instead. This is an insult or degradation that, to his way of thinking, makes life unbearable unless he can find a way to retaliate. The solution he hits upon is characteristically blunt: he plans to kill Odysseus, Menelaus, and the others he holds responsible. When he goes forth to do so, however, Athena deludes him into thinking that a group of sheep are the enemies he seeks. He kills the sheep in triumph, then awakes, surrounded by their corpses, to the recognition of what he has done. He has made himself, as Athena planned, the humiliated laughingstock of his enemies.

One can imagine various responses to this situation that would enable Ajax to keep on, from retiring to fight another day to the abandonment of the heroic ethic itself. But none of these is possible for him; he goes to the beach and throws himself on his sword. He has no way of imagining himself in his world, no way of telling his story, that is tolerable to him. The only meaning he can see in the story of his life is unbearable, making death preferable to living.

Or think of Shakespeare's Coriolanus. Here is the man who fights for Rome, from which he receives honor and deference in return. But this arrangement works only so long as Rome functions as a unit; when the city divides into formal political factions through the establishment of tribunes representing the poor, Coriolanus himself becomes an item of political dispute. To have the honor of the office of consul he must do what he cannot do, which is to become a political actor within the world of Rome, to negotiate and compromise. Rome is divided and cannot speak with a single voice to give his conduct the meaning he demands that it have. He withdraws in fury to a "world elsewhere." But there is no world elsewhere in which he can function in the only way he knows. He joins forces with the Volscians and attacks Rome, but this simply leads him into the impossible position of being cursed and feared by those whose praise he needs, by "Rome." He cannot make a new Rome elsewhere; he cannot bring himself to destroy the only Rome there is. The result is a total collapse of his doomed effort to make meaning against the facts, his effort to do what Ajax does not even try to do. He dies not by his own hand, but by his own conduct, for he has put himself among those, the Volscians, who have no reason to let him live. In both cases—Ajax and Coriolanus—death follows upon the collapse of a system of meaning, a system that no longer works for the person in question but that he cannot replace.

Now consider the first three figures to be discussed in the chapters that follow. When Thoreau withdraws from Concord to Walden to spend two years living in a hut in the woods, what is he seeking? Not money, not fame in the usual sense, but a different kind of existence, more fully attuned to the natural world and to his own imaginative capacities. He has found the ways of thinking of the world and himself that are offered by what he calls "Concord" to be inadequate, dead, in a deep way intolerable; and he sets himself the task of fashioning another. Walden will be his world elsewhere. Or consider Huckleberry Finn, telling us the story of his life as a marginal figure, living half in the woods with Pap, half in town with the Widow, none of it making sense to him. When he escapes to the life on the raft with Jim, he finds an existence full of value and significance, for a crucial part of which—his friendship with Jim—he has almost no explicit language and with which the language he does have, of slavery and race, is totally incompatible. As Huck lives this life and tells us about it he desperately seeks to understand his natural and social worlds—to make sense of them and to define himself in relation to them—in a way that will reflect his own experience: the experience of his own mind and feelings, his experience of Jim. In this he never succeeds. Or take Odysseus: as he makes his way back from Troy to Ithaca, he finds that he needs new ways of imagining himself and the world, ways that will make possible coherent thought and action on the new conditions in which he finds himself, and to a large degree he succeeds in fashioning them.

It is this process of imagining the self and the world, including other people, and expressing that imagination in language, that is my subject—what it is that happens when the mind so engaged meets the languages of the world and seeks to turn them to its use, tests them against each other and the rest of experience, finds itself using the very thing it is trying to think about, and in all of this tries to come to a coherent way of imagining the self and the world. I approach this subject through the reading of a set of works, each of which seems to me to present the process I mean, and its difficulties, clearly and admirably; and I arrange these readings in a sequence that I intend to have a movement and a meaning of its own, as a kind of story in which both the writer and the reader of this book are characters.

In our reading there are four distinct levels at which we can see the mind meet language in the way I mean: (1) within the fictional world, where the actors, such as Huckleberry Finn and Odysseus, are presented as engaged in this process; (2) in the text that is composed by the actual human author—Homer or Mark Twain, say, or Frost or Herbert—of which we are readers; (3) in this book itself, for I am also necessarily engaged, as a reader and writer, in the process that is my subject; and (4) in the reader's act of reading it, for she too will be asking how to fit what she reads here with the rest of her world. For the most part I keep the focus on the first two levels, but from time to time make the workings of my own or the reader's mind the object of attention. For this reason I include an autobiographical element one might not expect in a book of criticism, particularly in the brief interchapters. This is a deviation from the conventions of critical writing, and as such perhaps slightly embarrassing; but this too has its point, for it is a moment at which the peculiar enablements and restraints, the expectations, of our common language may become partly visible.

The chapter that follows should be read as a continuation of this introduction, developing some of its themes in connection with the reading of a particular literary work.

PART ONE

ONE

Thoreau's *Walden:* Sporting with Proud Reliance in the Fields of Air

As a boy of thirteen, lonely and confused in my first year at boarding school, I heard, I don't remember how, of Henry David Thoreau, the man who had gone to live in a cabin beside a pond in the woods, alone for a year, and that he had written a book about his experience. I instantly knew I wanted that book and ordered it from the school bookstore, paying for it myself—$1.25—out of my fifty-cents-a-week allowance. I waited weeks for it to come, which it finally did, from Modern Library, in a wrapper marked with designs in golden brown and green. I can remember holding it in my hand, wondering at its reality, and the miracle by which it arrived. I remember its heft and smell.

I read it through, several times, not understanding long reaches of it, which seemed dull and talky, but feeling that at other places it spoke for me as nothing ever had, especially in the moments where Thoreau expressed a sense of unity with the world of nature. The woods he inhabited were, after all, continuous with the woods that surrounded my school, fifteen miles away, and I too escaped into them, as Thoreau did, though with feelings less articulate.

Walden

What can Thoreau's *Walden* have meant to the boy who pored over its pages? I can remember laboring through section after section, especially at the beginning, that seemed to me utterly dull. It was an act of faith to read it through. But the faith had a basis, not only in the idea of living alone in the woods that had originally captivated me, but in the freshness and directness of the opening sentences:

> When I wrote the following pages, or rather the bulk of them, I lived alone, in the woods, a mile from any neighbor, in a house which I had built myself, on the shore of Walden Pond, in Concord, Massachusetts,

and earned my living by the labor of my hands only. I lived there two
years and two months.

But Thoreau cannot maintain this tone. In the very next sentence he
lapses into a kind of self-conscious and portentous prose that will
characterize much of his work: "At present I am a sojourner in civilized life again." Next he is awkward and didactic: "I should not ob-
trude my affairs so much on the notice of my readers if very particular
inquiries had not been made by my townsmen concerning my mode of
life . . ."—as though he were writing this book to supplement answers
already given to particular questions asked by particular people, which
cannot be the case. Then, self-conscious again: "In most books the *I*,
or first person, is omitted; in this it will be retained; that, in respect
to egotism, is the main difference. We commonly do not remember
that it is, after all, always the first person that is speaking." Then he
tries humor, of the kind Twain could do well but in Thoreau sounds
lame: "I should not talk so much about myself if there were anyone
else whom I knew as well. Unfortunately, I am confined to this theme
by the narrowness of my experience." Then, however, he says something of a different kind, in a different voice, in a sentence we have
already seen:

> Moreover, I, on my side, require of every writer, first or last, a simple
> and sincere account of his own life, and not merely what he has heard
> of other men's lives; some such account as he would send to his kindred
> from a distant land; for if he has lived sincerely, it must have been in a
> distant land to me.

In this sentence there are seeds of much that is to come: Thoreau's
belief that all writing is autobiographical; his sense that writing is a
way in which one whole person speaks to another, speaking that can
be sincere or false; his insistent reliance on the teachings of his own
experience; his recognition that the experience of others, if real, will be
different from his, and in this way of potential value; and his identification of the activities of living and writing, here connecting them with
the word *sincere*.

From this point, however, he lapses into pages and pages of a kind
of preaching, directed mainly at his townspeople: they who lead lives
of self-inflicted penance, who think they are rich but are poor, "young
men . . . whose misfortune it is to have inherited farms, houses, barns,
cattle, and farming tools; for these are more easily acquired than got

rid of. . . . Who made them serfs of the soil?" (5) And later: "The better part of the man is soon ploughed into the soil for compost," he says. How, he asks, can we complain of southern slavery when we know so many forms of it ourselves? "Look at the teamster on the highway, wending to market by day or night; does any divinity stir within him? His highest duty to fodder and water his horses!" (7)

This is all a kind of jeremiad, an attack on the wasted lives of others; the tone is strident and didactic. It can be summed up in the famous sentence: "The mass of men lead lives of quiet desperation" (8). I am sure I did not notice it when I read this the first time, but it is now obvious to me that the real desperation here is Thoreau's, and that it is enacted in his tense and aggressive style, his declamations and pronouncements, his condemnation of others. In passages of this kind he seems to be aiming at a certain kind of philosophy, carried on in a language of moral generalization; I know other people have found it valuable, but to me it was, and is, somewhat tiresome.[1]

I can remember reading these pages through the first time, frustrated, as if waiting for something; I think I was waiting for the tone of the opening pages to return, and return it finally does, at page 36 of my edition.[2] Listen to the clarity of the sentence that opens the following paragraph:

> Near the end of March, 1845, I borrowed an axe and went down to the woods by Walden Pond, nearest to where I intended to build my house, and began to cut down some tall, arrowy white pines, still in their youth, for timber. It is difficult to begin without borrowing, but perhaps it is the most generous course thus to permit your fellow-men to have an interest in your enterprise. The owner of the axe, as he released his hold on it, said that it was the apple of his eye; but I returned it sharper than I received it. It was a pleasant hillside where I worked, covered with pine woods, through which I looked out on the pond, and a small open field in the woods where pines and hickories were springing up. The ice on the pond was not yet dissolved, though there were some open spaces, and it was all dark colored and saturated with water. There were some slight flurries of snow during the days that I worked there; but for the most part when I came out on to the railroad,

---

1. Of course this material has an important dramatic function in the book as a whole, in defining the world Thoreau seeks to leave. And his anger too has a positive role psychologically, for it was part of what enabled him to take the step represented in *Walden*.

2. Walden *and Other Writings of Henry David Thoreau*, ed. Brooks Atkinson (New York: Random House, 1950). All other references are to Henry D. Thoreau, *Walden*, ed. J. Lyndon Shanley (Princeton: Princeton University Press, 1989).

on my way home, its yellow sand heap stretched away gleaming in the hazy atmosphere, and the rails shone in the spring sun, and I heard the lark and pewee and other birds already come to commence another year with us. (40)

Imagine yourself as editor, going over this passage, with the object of striking out what seems false or contrived or clotted. What would you suggest he delete? I would propose the self-conscious and awkward declaration in the second two sentences, which are followed by the true tones of Thoreau's style—simple and plain, full of life and immediacy. Whether you agree with me or not, in performing such an experiment you would be doing, I think, just what Thoreau did, as he learned to write his own way, in his own voice, trying to transform the dead speech of Concord into his own living speech. For his account of his time at Walden does not provide simple and transparent access to the experience that lies behind it, but is written, composed, created; and in making his voice, Thoreau is making a self and a language that are distinctively his own.[3]

This moment of stylistic transformation comes, not accidentally, just as Thoreau speaks of his arrival at Walden, of his beginning to work and live there. The didactic and assertive style of the preceding pages, his podium style, is the style of Concord; what he will give us now will be the style of Walden. And, as I suggested earlier, the Concord that he leaves behind is not other people's but his own: it is not others who have been enslaved, who lead lives of imprisonment and penance and emptiness and desperation, but Thoreau himself. In going to Walden, and learning to write about it, he thus leaves behind a part of the self, a certain way of being, in order to make other things possible, both in his experience and in his writing. His *Journal* shows that he already knew this four years earlier: "I want to go soon and live away by the pond, where I shall hear only the wind whispering in the reeds. It will be success if I shall have left myself behind" (December 24, 1841). Or, in a famous passage in *Walden:* "I went to the woods because I wished to live deliberately, to front only the essential

---

3. Thoreau strikes this note of immediacy, naturalness, and ease for the first time I think in his *Journal* entry for January 30, 1841, where he describes a fox running across the snow, "as though there were not a bone in its back." *The Journal of Henry D. Thoreau,* ed. Bradford Torrey and Francis H. Allen (New York: Dover Publications, 1962), 1:186–87. The earlier pages are full of self-conscious declamations, quotes from Goethe, imitations of the style of Cooper, romantic generalizations; for me at least the fragment quoted above stands out against these as a model of what is to come.

facts of life, and see if I could not learn what it had to teach, and not, when I came to die, discover that I had not lived" (90).

His aim was to discover himself and his world, and to find a way to represent both in writing; in this sense the whole book is about the process of making the voice in which it speaks. To achieve this Thoreau retreats to what he calls "solitude," a place away from other people and their languages, a place from which he can begin to speak in new ways. And in the rest of _Walden_ he builds upon his new voice and style beautifully, making the music that is his to write. In chapters like "Sounds" and "Ponds," for example, and in the famous account of the melting sandbank described below, he is able to maintain this tone virtually without flaw or interruption, creating new visions of the possibilities of life.

Consider the opening paragraphs of "Sounds," where Thoreau makes explicit, what is plain in any event, that one point of the solitude he seeks is to enable him to reach a point beyond words, beyond language in the ordinary sense, from which he can make his voice—his language and himself—anew:

> But while we are confined to books, though the most select and classic, and read only particular written languages, which are themselves but dialects and provincial, we are in danger of forgetting the language which all things and events speak without metaphor, which alone is copious and standard. Much is published, but little printed. The rays which stream through the shutter will be no longer remembered when the shutter is wholly removed. No method nor discipline can supersede the necessity of being forever on the alert. What is a course of history or philosophy, or poetry, no matter how well selected, or the best society, or the most admirable routine of life, compared with the discipline of looking always at what is to be seen? Will you be a reader, a student merely, or a seer? Read your fate, see what is before you, and walk on into futurity.
>
> I did not read books the first summer; I hoed beans. Nay, I often did better than this. There were times when I could not afford to sacrifice the bloom of the present moment to any work, whether of the head or hands. I love a broad margin to my life. Sometimes, in a summer morning, having taken my accustomed bath, I sat in my sunny doorway from sunrise till noon, rapt in a revery, amidst the pines and hickories and sumachs, in undisturbed solitude and stillness, while the birds sang around or flitted noiseless through the house, until by the sun falling in at my west window, or the noise of some traveller's wagon on the distant highway, I was reminded of the lapse of time. I grew in those

seasons like corn in the night, and they were far better than any work
of the hands would have been. (111)

This is an image of life without language; yet it is presented in language, and it implies, what virtually every sentence shows, that for Thoreau language in the usual sense is full of metaphor, or more than that, is metaphor itself.[4] The springs of life lie outside the circles of our languages.

His achievement is of course partly a matter of imagining himself increasingly at home in the world of nature, but it is an activity of culture as well. He was well read in both Latin and Greek, and his mind was full of allusions to those literatures, as it was to the Vedic and other literatures of India he had recently discovered.[5] Not nature as opposed to culture, then, but nature as the place where culture can most fully have its place; the word itself tells us this, for "culture" and "cultivate" refer to organic as well as intellectual processes. When Thoreau says, "Morning brings back the heroic ages" (88), he is referring to his own reading of the *Iliad* and other such texts and bringing it to bear on his life by the pond. The promise is ultimately one of wholeness and integration, the inclusion in a single vision of the various parts of human existence.

This is made plain in the incredible completeness of the world Thoreau creates on his pages. Where you and I might see water and trees and birds and bugs, he sees a universe palpitating with the particular varieties of life: the fish beneath the ice, the blue color of the snow in a footprint, the loon which he tries without success to fool, the ants engaged in war (red against black), the pine tree hit by lightning across the pond with the sand at its foot turned to glass, the frogs (which he sees alternately as classical, urban, aldermanic, civilized, and crude), the prior human inhabitants who give the place a human history, the mysterious geology and hydrology of the pond, and so on and on, a world of perpetual interest and life. And he is aware, too,

4. "He is richest," he says in his *Journal*, "who has most use for nature as raw material of tropes and symbols with which to describe his life" (5:135).

5. For Thoreau's reading of Indian philosophy, see Robert Sattelmeyer, *Thoreau's Reading: A Study in Intellectual History* (Princeton: Princeton University Press, 1988), 67–68, and R. K. Dhawan, *Henry David Thoreau: A Study in Indian Influence* (New Delhi: Classical Publishing Company, 1985), especially 33, 68–69, 75. For his reading in the western classics, see Ethel Seybold, *Thoreau: The Quest and the Classics* (New Haven: Yale University Press, 1951), including, in appendices, a list of classical works used by Thoreau and an index of classical quotations and allusions.

that it is a world partly discovered, partly created, calling him in fact to the very activity of writing in which he makes it real and gives it meaning. The very same pond would have different significances in the mind of the Canadian wood chopper, the Irish family living in a shanty by the railroad, the ice cutters, and even the poet with whom he sometimes shared his evening. This world is in the first instance the creation of another, but in the second, a creation of his own.

Consider the structure of the book as a whole: in writing about them Thoreau transforms the two years that he lived by the pond into one, starting on Independence Day. The late summer and fall are thus presented, perhaps paradoxically, as a season of beginning, the winter as a season of normalcy; when spring comes, as the final chapter of the book, it works a grand conversion of what we have known into something else entirely, a vision of the whole world as a metaphor of transformation. This is not a cyclic return to summer, as we might have expected, but an elevation to another dimension of experience.

We have been prepared for this in many ways, most recently perhaps in Thoreau's account of the ice on the pond, seemingly so solid, which in fact undulates in the wind like water (292); seemingly so local, but in fact it is cut and packed in sawdust and sold around the world, to India and China. "The pure Walden water is mingled with the sacred water of the Ganges" (298). Ice is actually not a solid at all, but full of air, in bubbles that form patterns—"ice has its grain as well as wood" (300)—and it collapses into mush. It rings like a gong when struck with an axe on a cold morning, then softens and loses its resonance, then booms on its own as it refreezes at night. "Who would have suspected so large and cold and thick-skinned a thing to be so sensitive?" (302)

It is not only the ice that is organic. In a famous passage Thoreau describes the patterns made in the railway bank as the ice in the sand melts and runs down the steep incline, in forms that imitate those of vegetation:

> Few phenomena gave me more delight than to observe the forms which thawing sand and clay assume in flowing down the sides of a deep cut on the railroad through which I passed on my way to the village . . . . The material was sand of every degree of fineness and of various rich colors, commonly mixed with a little clay. When the frost comes out in the spring, and even in a thawing day in the winter, the sand begins to flow down the slopes like lava, sometimes bursting out

through the snow and overflowing it where no sand was to be seen before. Innumerable little streams overlap and interlace one with another, exhibiting a sort of hybrid product, which obeys half way the law of currents, and half way that of vegetation. As it flows it takes the forms of sappy leaves or vines, making heaps of pulpy sprays a foot or more in depth, and resembling, as you look down on them, the laciniated lobed and imbricated thalluses of some lichens; or you are reminded of coral, of leopards' paws or birds' feet, of brains or lungs or bowels, and excrements of all kinds. . . . When the flowing mass reaches the drain at the foot of the bank it spreads out flatter into *strands,* the separate streams losing their semi-cylindrical form and gradually becoming more flat and broad, running together as they are more moist, till they form an almost flat *sand,* still variously and beautifully shaded, but in which you can trace the original forms of vegetation; till at length, in the water itself, they are converted into *banks,* like those formed off the mouths of rivers, and the forms of vegetation are lost in the ripple marks on the bottom.

The whole bank, which is from twenty to forty feet high, is sometimes overlaid with a mass of this kind of foliage, or sandy rupture, for a quarter of a mile on one or both sides, the produce of one spring day. What makes this sand foliage remarkable is its springing into existence thus suddenly. When I see on the one side the inert bank,—for the sun acts on one side first,—and on the other this luxuriant foliage, the creation of an hour, I am affected as if in a peculiar sense I stood in the laboratory of the Artist who made the world and me,—had come to where he was still at work, sporting on this bank, and with excess of energy strewing his fresh designs about. I feel as if I were nearer to the vitals of the globe, for this sandy overflow is something such a foliaceous mass as the vitals of the animal body. You find thus in the very sands an anticipation of the vegetable leaf. . . . Even ice begins with delicate crystal leaves, as if it had flowed into moulds which the fronds of water plants have impressed on the watery mirror. The whole tree itself is but one leaf, and rivers are still vaster leaves whose pulp is intervening earth, and towns and cities are the ova of insects in their axils. . . .

Thus it seemed that this one hillside illustrated the principle of all the operations of Nature. (304–8)

In this book Thoreau both lives a life and writes about it; the life, and the writing, are transformative, carrying him from a kind of despairing conformity—expressed in the strident and judgmental tones of a man condemning his neighbors for *their* despair and conformity—

to what he sees as a whole and authentic life, expressed in a style that is immediate, particular, and alive. In the process his sense of the world changes; it becomes instinct with life and change. His writing is not only the record of this transformation, it is the agent of it. He writes himself from one condition to another. The meaning of his life and the meaning of his writing are one.

Thoreau not only observes the process of creation, he participates in it too. As he elsewhere says,

> It is something to be able to paint a particular picture, or to carve a statue, and so to make a few objects beautiful; but it is far more glorious to carve and paint the very atmosphere and medium through which we look, which morally we can do. To affect the quality of the day, that is the highest of arts. (90)

What starts as an effort to make a language and a voice with which to live thus becomes itself a way of life, a way that enables him simultaneously to focus with fresh attention upon the world around him and to create, in his own composition, a way of claiming meaning for that world and his own relation with it.

I once found myself reading this book, later in life, at a time of personal difficulty, and came upon the phrase, "Walden is melting apace" (311); I felt it to be true of me, and I think Thoreau felt it true of him as well: the frozen pond, the frozen feelings, the frozen language, all here melt, most beautifully in the passage quoted above, but not only there; throughout, as part of the deep rhythm of the text as a whole, and its movement towards meaning and metaphor: "The sun is but a morning star" (333).

His Voice and Its Limits

Of course I would not have been able to say this at the time, but you can perhaps see some of the qualities of this book that appealed to me as a boy, and still do: its insistence on authenticity as a criterion of life and speech; its assumption that writing is an act of the whole mind and person, directed to a whole mind and person; its way of using the materials of inherited culture not in rituals of deference, but to make one's own life richer and better; its sense that writing can be about what matters most to us, and can indeed transform it, giving meaning to life itself. For part of Thoreau's point is surely that the pond by which he lived was, until he lived there and made of it what he did, as ordinary and dull and prosaic a piece of real estate as one could readily find.[6] To read this piece of writing is to imagine oneself something of a writer too. To the boy reading this book, then, it promised not only an imagined escape to the woods, but the transformation of that escape into something else, a way of being with language and in the world—and the world not only of nature, but of other people—through writing.[7]

What Thoreau was seeking when he went to live by the pond was not money or power or fame, but a way of making sense of his life and his capacities. It is on this point that he begins in despair and moves to hope, and a kind of success, as he discovers his voice and puts it to work in a new way.

What are the elements of the success he seeks? Part of it is his desire to understand the conditions of his existence, including the natural and cultural contexts in which he feels embedded; he is a reader of his world. But what he seeks even more deeply is his own capacity to speak on these conditions, and success for him is largely a matter of voice: its naturalness, and ease, and spontaneity; its openness to the run of his imagination; its creativity, expressed in prose poetry, like the

6. People sometimes criticize Thoreau for pretending to live in the wilderness when in fact he was only a mile from town, which he frequently visited. This criticism I think depends on a misunderstanding both of Thoreau's circumstances and of his claims.

In his day the country around Concord was far less forested than it is today, consisting mainly of farms and fields. Only about 13 percent of Concord was wooded, and "one could see to the horizon from almost anywhere in Concord." Robert D. Richardson Jr., *Emerson: The Mind on Fire* (Berkeley: University of California Press, 1995), 209. The woods Thoreau used were in fact a wood lot—a source of firewood—belonging to Emerson. This means that no one in his local audience would have compared his woods with the great American wilderness, or even the woods of Maine. Rather, there is built into his performance a very different understanding and claim: that the utterly ordinary can be marvelous, the trivial and local of great importance. Even such "woods" as these, that is, can be full of wildness and beauty and originality.

7. Although as I say above Thoreau affected my mind long before I read anything by anyone else about him, some other books have naturally been of use to me in understanding him. The most important is Thoreau's own *Journal*, available in an inexpensive edition by Dover, especially his accounts of the two years by the pond that in *Walden* itself he collapsed into one. Theodore Baird, "Corn Grows in the Night," 4 *The Massachusetts Review* 93 (1962), was most valuable especially on Thoreau's later life. (It is from this article that I borrow the phrase that it is one function of *Walden* to "promise us happiness.")

I have also found valuable: Sharon Cameron, *Writing Nature: Henry Thoreau's Journal* (Chicago: University of Chicago Press, 1985); Stanley Cavell, *The Senses of Walden* (New York: Viking, 1972); H. Daniel Peck, *Thoreau's Morning Work: Memory and Perception in A Week on the Concord and Merrimack Rivers, the Journal, and Walden* (New Haven: Yale University Press, 1990); Robert D. Richardson Jr., *Henry Thoreau: A Life of the Mind* (Berkeley: University of California Press, 1986).

passage about the sandbank. It is to learn to speak sincerely, and in this sense naturally, that he retires into solitude, and, as he discovers, that means speaking with an artist's sense of language and its limits. What he achieves in the end is not merely authenticity of speech, though certainly that, but also the capacity to represent his life in such a way as to claim for it an essential harmony with the order of the world: he sees his own acts of creation as deeply connected to the other creation in which he is embedded. *Walden* promises us happiness, but this happiness is not simply a matter of pleasure or joy; rather it arises from his reiterated though momentary demonstrations of the possibility of internal and external coherence. Thoreau can imagine that he has a coherent self and that he inhabits a coherent universe; and these imaginings are reflected in his writing, in his voice, and in his representation of the world.[8]

In the epilogue he describes "a man from Kouroo" who decided to make a perfect walking staff. He became so utterly absorbed in the process of finding the wood, and cutting and shaping and polishing it, that for him all time stood still, though for others centuries passed; when he finished, all civilizations were at an end. "When the finishing stroke was put to his work, it suddenly expanded before the eyes of the astonished artist into the fairest of all the creation of Brahma." The entire world was remade anew. But he then saw, by the fresh shavings at his feet, that "the former lapse of time had been an illusion," for the whole thing had taken only a few minutes. But: "The material was pure, and his art was pure; how could the result be other than wonderful?" (327) This is an image of the absorption of the mind in an activity, an essential element of the writing life and the reading life too: an attachment to one part of the world so intense as to be a detachment from the rest of it. It becomes the experience of another world, in the mind and memory, one that transcends time and space.

This passage is crucial, for it tells us what it is like to devote yourself to the activity Thoreau has exemplified, the activity of thought and art: absorbed in the materials of one's work, and in the work itself, time disappears. In a passage like this he achieves a removal from one

8. Of course I know that several of the terms I am using—"self," "authenticity," "sincerity," "coherence"—can be used in rather simpleminded ways, as though the "self" were a single thing that is expressed either "sincerely" or not, in a universe perceived as "coherent" or not. But Thoreau is as far from simpleminded as one could imagine. He is wholly aware that he is constantly engaged in the process of making a self, imagining the world; that this works differently different times; and that the coherences he achieves or perceives are momentary—and that this is indeed part of their glory.

world, our world, and a translation to another, in the imagination; it is this that in fact enables him to represent the real world as richly and meaningfully as he does, for that act of representation is an act of the imagination too, an act of poetry. Who else would see what he saw in the sandbank? It is upon his capacity to see it and say it that his hope rests.

Thoreau offers his reader an analogous experience, for in reading this book we forget where we are, and what we ate, and where we are going later in the day, and how we pay our bills, and all those things; we inhabit a world of another kind, imagined, a world of meaning.[9] We do not stay there forever, of course, but return to ordinary life, to what we think of as the real world; and when we do, we face our own version of Thoreau's problem, how to connect the imagined and re-membered with our direct experience of material and social reality. We know what Thoreau can manage to say, for he gives it to us; but his writing makes us ask what *we* can say. The reading in this sense makes us writers.

Thoreau's withdrawal into solitude is after all not a withdrawal from all social relations, for in this text he speaks to us. Whether the world in which he does so, the world of imagination, is more real, or less so, than the one he and we otherwise inhabit is a matter still open, perhaps permanently open; but that human beings need some such space, some participation in the activity of imagining themselves and their world, and speaking to others about it, seems to me undeniable. The hope Thoreau holds out is a hope of meaning, here defined as a comprehensible relation to nature and humanity; it is expressed or en-acted in a voice that is for the moment coherent and sincere—sincere above all, as he tells us, for this is what he requires of others: and if "he has lived sincerely, it must have been in a distant land to me."

But it is plain that Thoreau represents his own transformation in *Walden* as far more secure and permanent that it was or could have been. He creates as it were a character, "Thoreau," who undergoes an epochal change in the course of a single year in the woods, writing himself from one condition to another. Yet in some ways the transfor-mation began earlier, and it certainly continued later, through the six major rewritings of *Walden* itself; and it was less complete than it may

9. Compare: "Any book of great authority and genius seems to our imagination to per-meate and pervade all space." *Journal* 1:268.

seem, for of course the real Henry Thoreau continued to struggle with
the voices of Concord within him, and other voices too, all his life,
including at the end of this book.[10] Indeed it is hard to imagine how
he, or anyone, could continue for a lifetime to make the claims, engage
in the performances, he began in *Walden*.

Yet *Walden* still stands as a text offering its reader the transformation of a voice and the articulation of a hope, exaggerated though it
is, of a perfectly expressive life, perfectly attuned to the world. As a
definition of such an ideal, in American literature anyway, it can hardly
be matched. Thoreau represents as intensely and purely as one could
conceive the impulse at the center of the self from which the activity
of imagination that is our subject springs, the desire for what we call
meaning in experience. And he sees that this desire cannot be satisfied
by observation or understanding alone, but by its nature requires an
act of expression. How this impulse can be checked and frustrated and
redirected when it meets the sometimes disastrous, sometimes rewarding, difficulties presented by other people, and by the culture with and
within which the mind must work, is our next subject.

But first to close with Thoreau. Near the end of *Walden* comes a
passage that for me captures beautifully Thoreau's hopes for himself,

---

10. As his *Journal* goes on, in fact, his claims to find happiness in his capacity to write
become less and less persuasive. The mode of life he invented, real and wonderful though it
was, seems not to have been a foundation for a whole life for him after all. The *Journal* at
the end became simply a series of observations, the observations of a naturalist, of which
Thoreau made nothing—when earlier each would have been the occasion for a performance
of his belief in the fecundity of the world and his own powers. As Theodore Baird noted it,
"[t]he sad truth is that within the short lifetime of forty-five years this vision of the world
and this use of language proved not to be durable." Baird, "Corn Grows in the Night," 100.

> As a story of a man's life or a writer's career, this does not come out right,
> and a reader who tries to express his mixed responses to Thoreau may well
> feel that his dominant emotion is sadness. Here is a man who promises us
> everything. Consciousness alone, unaided by armies or money or dynamos or
> political power or tradition, can shape the world to our own expectation. The
> force of a single mind—if only you can write a lecture or hire a hall and give
> a lecture—can do anything. Or in the simplest terms and in one of his best
> sentences, "To affect the quality of the day, that is the highest of arts." Why,
> then, should life end in counting and measuring and labeling according to
> Gray's *Anatomy*? It is hard to feel that there is not some kind of defeat here.
> (101–2)

Baird's is one account. For a much more positive view of Thoreau's last years and last
projects, see Richardson, *Henry Thoreau*, 373–89. For our purposes it is enough, and this is
surely true, that Thoreau never attained the perfection he so intensely sought.

and also suggests the limitations of the life he has made. He sees a hawk tumbling in the sky over the river:

> It did not simply flutter like a butterfly, nor soar like the larger hawks, but it sported with proud reliance in the fields of air; mounting again and again with its strange chuckle, it repeated its free and beautiful fall, turning over and over like a kite, and then recovering from its lofty tumbling, as if it had never set its foot on *terra firma*. It appeared to have no companion in the universe,—sporting there alone,—and to need none but the morning and the ether with which it played. It was not lonely, but made all the earth lonely beneath it. (317)

The double image of the hawk as artist, the artist as hawk, soaring and tumbling and catching itself just in time in a perpetual and creative act of play, seems just right for Thoreau. The world constantly creates itself anew, and so does he, in relation to it. Yet the loneliness that he here denies on behalf of the hawk is also an essential part of the life he represents, overcome only a little in the act of writing itself, perhaps more deeply in his way of imagining himself in relation to the natural world—the sandbank, the pines and firs, the ice on the pond, and the hawk above the river.

❧

Between the ages of four and six, from 1942 to 1944, I lived in a small village in Maryland, called Garrett Park. This is where consciousness, or at least continuous memory, began for me, and it was a kind of heaven. I remember these days, this world, mainly by thinking of particular places—in the woods or the village or the house—where certain events occurred, and by arranging those places in relation to each other. I put the world together as a map in my mind. Garrett Park is for me a world, not a story.

What kind of world? Most striking to me now is the sense that it was a whole world, entire, bounded, alive, a magnificent person in whose presence I continually lived. This presence, always there if only in the background, was Nature, and I felt it everywhere: in the overgrown grass of the field across the street, in the garden, in the fruit trees outside the window in the soft dark night, in the smell of wet earth, in the very air itself, but above all in the woods that completely encircled the village and my world.

Life was embedded in these woods: they began right behind the house, at the back of our Victory Garden, where a path wound into the wall of trees. From there they dropped down behind the widow's house next door, ran south along the side of the huge potato fields of Corby's farm across the street, behind Georgetown Prep School on the other side of the Rockville Pike, with its carillon and goldfish ponds, then circled north to the far edge of the village of Garrett Park itself, where the tracks of the Baltimore and Ohio railroad met the muddy stream of Rock Creek, and finally came back to form the green curtain behind our garden. The woods for me were towering, green, safe, and lovely. They bounded the known world.

Beyond the train track on the far edge of the village was a wilderness that we never entered alone. Through it a dirt track dropped down to the muddy banks of the brown and forbidden Rock Creek, where there were said to be water moccasins. Our neighbors the Bartrams swam there on hot summer afternoons, diving off the rocks into the murky water in their underpants; but my father, a young doctor, had the water tested for purity and discovered that it was badly polluted, with typhus or typhoid I forget which, so we could not swim there.

In those woods by Rock Creek lived Eugene Sparrow, a boy my age who dressed in rags and brought to school as his only writing instrument an inch of purple-colored lead taken from a pencil stub. He lived with a man, perhaps his father, in a shack we were not permitted to approach. I pitied and feared his poverty, which was extreme and obvious even to me—his face was pinched and pale, I thought from hunger—but I also envied his life in the woods, in a shanty at the margin of the world.

TWO

Huckleberry Finn: Doing Whichever
Come Handiest at the Time

Like *Walden, Huckleberry Finn* is a story about a person at the margins of his world, trying to establish a position from which, and a voice with which, he can speak. Huck is in fact on the edge of two worlds: the town, representing the tones and values of white American culture, and the woods and river, representing a set of deeply contrasting possibilities. For him the contradictions between these worlds are deeply confusing, and he tries desperately to make sense of them, to learn to act and speak on the conditions they afford. In one way his effort fails, for he can never make sense of the fact of "race" that dominates his culture and his own mind; in another way he succeeds, for he establishes—at least for a moment—a relation with Jim of a kind that Thoreau, for example, cannot begin to imagine. If Thoreau represents the core of the self setting out to find or create meaning in experience, Huck shows us what happens at the next stage, when the imagining mind meets realities it cannot manage, including the reality of other people. And he shows us too how the resulting frustrations can be turned to good account, defining new possibilities, even if these cannot be securely attained.

This book contains one of the high points of all literature, the moment at which Huck tries to turn Jim in to the slave hunters, finds he cannot do it, and reveals at the same time that he has no adequate language in which to describe or explain what he has chosen to do. This moment is the center of the book, and of this chapter, but I shall begin at the beginning, asking how Huck is imagined and presented as a person seeking to understand his world and himself.

Beginnings

Huck first appears of course not in the novel that bears his name but in *The Adventures of Tom Sawyer*, which is a rather straightforwardly humorous tale of boyish life in a town on the banks of the Mississippi, told by an omniscient narrator who stands outside and above his characters. The narrator is in a patronizing way constantly affirming his own superiority, and that of his reader, to the boys whose story he tells. In a sense the main point of the book is to affirm exactly that superiority in all its fullness. In *Huckleberry Finn*,[1] by contrast, Twain makes Huck himself the narrator—an ill-educated, semi-literate, and deeply naive boy who is trying to make sense of his world but failing to do so. I think Twain's original idea was to make fun both of the boy himself, as a kind of social idiot, and of the society he cannot comprehend, in both cases once more affirming the superiority of the his audience, who of course know so much better than Huck and Petersburg both. But this does not quite work: as the novel actually works we see things from Huck's point of view, we hear his voice, and in this light his struggles and failures have a kind of urgency and poignancy—a reality—they would otherwise have lacked. In a sense the story gets out of Twain's control to become much better than he originally intended, a moral drama of the first significance.

This is in part the effect of Huck's voice, almost certainly the single most important feature of the book, for it is this voice that leads the reader to take Huck seriously.[2] Listen to his very first words, alive and natural:

> You don't know about me, without you have read a book by the name of *The Adventures of Tom Sawyer,* but that ain't no matter. That book was made by Mr. Mark Twain, and he told the truth,

1. All references are to Mark Twain, *The Adventures of Huckleberry Finn,* ed John Seelye (New York; Penguin, 1985).

2. Twain introduces the topic of voice explicitly, even before the novel begins, in a note in which he explains his use of dialects:

> In this book a number of dialects are used, to wit: the Missouri Negro dialect; the extremest form of the backwoods South-Western dialect; the ordinary "Pike-County" dialect; and four modified varieties of this last. The shadings have not been done in a hap-hazard fashion, or by guess-work; but painstakingly, and with the trustworthy guidance and support of personal familiarity with these several forms of speech.
>
> I make this explanation for the reason that without it many readers would suppose that all these characters were trying to talk alike and not succeeding.

This passage expresses Twain's awareness, crucial to Huck's experience within the story and to ours as readers of it, that each of us is a center of necessarily different meanings, for our languages do not coincide—we do not "talk alike." We can talk across these differences, but they are always there. One of Twain's aims—reminiscent of what Thoreau said about "a simple and sincere account" of one's life, from a necessarily "distant land"—is to be faithful to these differences, particularly as they work to bewilder or mystify Huck.

> mainly. There was things which he stretched, but mainly he told the truth. That is nothing. I never seen anybody but lied, one time or another, without it was Aunt Polly, or the widow, or maybe Mary. Aunt Polly—Tom's Aunt Polly, she is—and Mary, and the Widow Douglas, is all told about in that book—which is mostly a true book; with some stretchers, as I said before. (1)

The book thus presents at the outset the topic of honesty and dishonesty, both in speech and life, which will be with us in ever more complicated ways to the end of the novel. To begin with the obvious, one of the deepest characteristics of the language of Petersburg is its unconscious dishonesty, which puzzles and upsets Huck. On the other hand, he himself will cheerfully lie whenever it suits him, sometimes brilliantly so. Yet he does not deceive himself or us. His overriding need is in fact to discover and state the truth, in a language authentic to him and his experience, against the often false formulations of his world. This is a deep source of the comedy of the book, for the truth as he sees it sometimes makes him, sometimes the rest of the world, look like a fool. But it will prove to have wider resonances and implications as well.

The Town and the Woods

The story begins where *Tom Sawyer* leaves off. After the disappearance of his father, Pap, Huck has been living in town with the Widow Douglas:

> The Widow Douglas, she took me for her son, and allowed she would sivilize me; but it was rough living in the house all the time, considering how dismal regular and decent the widow was in all her ways; and so when I couldn't stand it no longer, I lit out. I got into my old rags, and my sugar-hogshead again, and was free and satisfied. But Tom Sawyer, he hunted me up and said he was going to start a band of robbers, and I might join if I would go back to the widow and be respectable. So I went back. (1)

This passage establishes much that will follow, especially Huck's switching back and forth between his two worlds, the woods and the town, which seem to work on such utterly different principles. Here he responds to this split in his life by trying to transform the values of the town: "regular and decent" now means "dismal," and a life of rags, lived out of a barrel, makes him "free and satisfied." But this reversal is not confident or successful, and Huck's confusion is increased by

Tom's statement that a "robber" must be "respectable," a seeming impossibility. But this will prove not so impossible after all, for Tom's resistances to Petersburg turn out to be highly formulaic, really just different versions of the system of cultural authority he pretends to resist—in fact this very gesture seems consciously designed to lure Huck back into town. Huck is at the moment understandably confused, and in his confusion will challenge that culture at its heart.

He is of course fully conscious of his distance from the world of the town. When the widow prays before eating, for example, he sees it this way:

> When you got to the table you couldn't go right to eating, but you had to wait for the widow to tuck down her head and grumble a little over the victuals, though there warn't really anything the matter with them. That is, nothing only everything was cooked by itself. In a barrel of odds and ends it is different; things get mixed up, and the juice kind of swaps around, and the things go better. (2)

At this and similar moments Huck, almost as much an outsider as a Martian would be, sees with fresh and naive eyes the practices "we"— the people of the town, and the readers of the book—habitually engage in. As I said earlier, this is part of the humor of the book, making both him and "us" somewhat ridiculous: him because he knows so little about the world, us because his debunking perceptions have an element of truth.

This kind of gesture is repeated through the opening chapter, for example in his conversation with Miss Watson, who sets herself the task of educating Huck, including telling him about "the bad place." "I said I wished I was there. She got mad, then, but I didn't mean no harm. All I wanted was to go somewheres; all I wanted was a change, I warn't particular." When he is told that Tom Sawyer will certainly be in the "bad place," while Miss Watson would be in the "good place," his initial resolution is confirmed, now on a better, and highly revealing, basis: "I wanted him and me to be together" (3). In these brief passages one can already see that Huck's action on the values of Petersburg is not simply to reverse them—as, for example, Satan does in *Paradise Lost* with the values of "heaven"—but to substitute for them positives of his own: freedom from restraint; what food means when it is scarce and cooked by oneself; and companionship in an uncompanionable world.

When he goes to bed he thinks again about the world outside the house, the world of nature, where he just said he was so "free and satisfied." But now he sees it differently, as frightening:

> I felt so lonesome I most wished I was dead. The stars was shining, and the leaves rustled in the woods ever so mournful; and I heard an owl, away off, who-whooing about somebody that was dead, and a whip-powill and a dog crying about somebody that was going to die; and the wind was trying to whisper something to me and I couldn't make out what it was, and so it made the cold shivers run over me. Then away out in the woods I heard that kind of sound that a ghost makes when it wants to tell about something that's on its mind and can't make itself understood, and so can't rest easy in its grave and has to go about that way every night grieving. I got so down-hearted and scared, I did wish I had some company.(3)

The opposition between town and country, civilization and nature, is not after all an opposition between bad and good, or tainted and innocent. Neither the woods nor the widow offers Huck a place he belongs.

Tom and Pap

At the end of the chapter Tom comes to get him and they sneak out in the night. They find Jim asleep outside and decide to "play something" on him: they take his hat off and hang it on a tree. When Jim awakes he thinks this was done by spirits, and he tells the neighbors how he was taken by witches all the way to New Orleans and beyond. "Niggers would come miles to hear Jim tell about it, and he was more looked up to than any nigger in that country" (6–7), says Huck, in his choice of words, as in his conduct, unselfconsciously expressing the apparently universal attitude of the white man towards the black in his world. The ease with which he says this, like the ease with which he first used the term—"By-and-by they fetched the niggers in and had prayers, and then everybody was off to bed" (3)—expresses the sense that in this world, for this boy, this was the only way to talk.

Tom seems at first to offer a middle ground between the woods and the town, but Huck quickly discovers, or rediscovers, that Tom's mode of life is also profoundly unsatisfactory. Their robber band is no robber band at all, and it is run by principles, which Tom gets from his reading, that make no sense to Huck:

> "Must we always kill the people?"
> "Oh, certainly. It's best. Some authorities think different, but

mostly it's considered best to kill them. Except some that you bring to the cave here and keep them till they're ransomed." (9)

When Tom tells him about the genies that come from a lamp rubbed the right way, Huck tests this claim out in his own practical way: "I got an old tin lamp and an iron ring and went out in the woods and rubbed and rubbed till I sweat like an Injun, calculating to build a palace and sell it; but it warn't no use, none of the genies come. So then I judged that all that stuff was only just one of Tom Sawyer's lies" (16).

What Huck says about playing hookey is deeply puzzling: "At first I hated the school, but by-and-by I got so I could stand it. Whenever I got uncommon tired I played hookey, and the hiding I got the next day done me good and cheered me up" (17). What can he possibly mean by that last phrase, uttered without apparent consciousness of what he is saying?

We quickly learn something of the answer when Pap arrives and wins custody of Huck in an action brought before a judge who is new in town and, having no idea what he is doing, says that "courts mustn't interfere and separate families if they could help it" (23–24). Pap mocks and beats Huck for his educated superiority, and takes him out of school to live with him in a cabin across the river. What Huck's remark about the "hiding" doing him "good" in fact means is that this kind of abuse is so familiar to him that it seems natural—as natural as saying "nigger"—as though there could be no other way. For such a person there can indeed be a kind of comfort in the repetition of abuse, for it confirms his sense of the way things are and ought to be. All this tells us that Huck, despite his remarkable honesty, is not and cannot be in every way a narrator whose judgments we can trust.

In fact, hardly surprisingly, he is deeply confused both in his language and his sentiments. He says, for example, that he comes to like the mode of life he leads in the woods, "lazy and jolly, laying off comfortable all day, smoking and fishing, and no books nor study" (27), and in a sense of course he does. But he is beaten with a hickory stick over and over again, a fact with more significance to us than to him, until at last he comes to see it as threatening his life. We can see, even if he cannot, that he is not experiencing a life "free and satisfied," or "lazy and jolly," in a benign world of nature away from the corruption and hypocrisy of man, but a savage and brutal existence of which he is the repeated victim.

As the reader will remember, after his drunken father nearly kills him, Huck finally escapes, leaving behind him evidence that will make people think he was murdered and thus give up any pursuit of him. He goes to Jackson's island, across from town, where he meets Jim, who has run away from Miss Watson upon hearing that she planned to sell him down the river. When they learn that slave hunters are after them, they escape downriver on a raft, planning to go to the junction of the Ohio, then upstream along that river into free country where Jim will not be known.

Huck's Great Moment

It is after several days on the river that Huck faces his great and famous crisis. Prompted by his "conscience," he tries to turn Jim in to the slave hunters but finds that he cannot do it. Then:

> They went off, and I got aboard the raft, feeling bad and low, because I knowed very well I had done wrong, and I see it warn't no use for me to try to learn to do right; a body that don't get *started* right when he's little, ain't got no show—when the pinch comes there ain't nothing to back him up and keep him to his work, and so he gets beat. Then I thought a minute, and says to myself, hold on,—s'pose you'd a done right and give Jim up; would you felt better than what you do now? No, says I, I'd feel bad—I'd feel just the same way I do now. Well, then, says I, what's the use you learning to do right, when it's troublesome to do right and ain't no trouble to do wrong, and the wages is just the same? I was stuck. I couldn't answer that. So I reckoned I wouldn't bother no more about it, but after this always do whichever come handiest at the time. (101)

Huck is disgusted with himself for what he sees as his incurable immorality; of course the reader by contrast admires his capacity to see and act on the central fact of his experience—which his language and culture want to deny—namely, that Jim is both a human being and a friend.

This passage presents two almost opposite questions. The first, which I defer till nearly the end of this chapter, is why Huck is unable to say directly what he in some sense knows to be the truth about Jim and his friendship with him, and to ground his conduct confidently on that understanding. Why, that is, can he not see what we see and say what we say, namely, that Jim is his only true friend, that slavery is a hideous wrong, that racism kills the reality of love? The second question, considered immediately below, is equally remarkable, though it cuts in the other direction: How is it that Huck is able to resist or transcend his culture as successfully as he does? After all, he does manage to refuse to turn Jim over to the slave hunters. Somehow he finds a ground in his own experience from which to resist what seem in his world to be the universal truths of racism and slavery, even though he can find no words in which to say these things. How is it that he can possibly do this? One cannot believe that Tom Sawyer would have done anything like it, had he, not Huck, been on the raft with Jim, and we may well ask whether we ourselves would have done so.

Marginality

Part of the explanation of Huck's capacity to resist his culture lies no doubt in his lifelong experience of marginality: he is both of the town and its values, and not of it, living sometimes with the widow, sometimes with Pap in the woods. He is in this sense bicultural, and can use his experience of one world to criticize his experience of the other. Thus practices that are so familiar as to be beyond question to those in town—such as prayer, or asking a blessing before eating, or regular bathing—to Huck often seem odd, and thus to call for thought and explanation. As Achilles in the *Iliad* becomes a cultural critic almost against his will, by finding himself forced to the margins of his world, Huck begins in such a place, from which a kind of criticism is natural, not surprising.

But both of Huck's worlds are pronounced mixtures of good and bad, and neither can therefore be used in any complete or unreflective way as a standard with which to criticize the other. Life in the woods, for example, involves contact with nature and freedom from constraint, which Huck likes; but it also means subjection to the savage brutalities of his father, which he hates—although, as his casual remark about "hidings" that "done him good" reveals, he does not always know enough to do so. Likewise, there are good things about town life, including school and reading—reflected in the pride and pleasure with which Huck refers to the picture he was given "for learning my lessons good"—as well as aspects that are bad or incomprehensible.

Still worse, his two worlds, which are so opposed in everything else, agree wholeheartedly about what is most deeply at issue in Huck's life, namely, the essential propriety of slavery and of the racial ideology upon which it is based. To these principles the town is of course completely committed; and there is, to say the least, no challenge to them in Huck's life with Pap, for Pap is an even more openly vicious racist than the people of the town:

> "Call this a govment! why, just look at it and see what it's like. Here's the law a-standing ready to take a man's son away from him— a man's own son, which he has had all the trouble and all the anxiety and all the expense of raising. Yes, just as that man has got that son raised at last, and ready to go to work and begin to do suthin' for *him* and give him a rest, the law up and goes for him. . . . A man can't get his rights in a govment like this. . . .
>
> "Oh, yes, this is a wonderful govment, wonderful. Why, looky here. There was a free nigger there, from Ohio; a mulatter, most as white as a white man. He had the whitest shirt on you ever see, too, and the shiniest hat; and there ain't a man in that town that's got as fine clothes as what he had; and he had a gold watch and chain, and a silver-headed cane—the awfulest old gray-headed nabob in the State. And what do you think? they said he was a p'fessor in a college, and could talk all kinds of languages, and knowed everything. And that ain't the wust. They said he could *vote*, when he was at home. Well, that let me out. Thinks I, what is the country a-coming to? It was 'lection day, and I was just about to go and vote, myself, if I warn't too drunk to get there; but when they told me there was a State in this country where they'd let that nigger vote, I drawed out. I says I'll never vote agin. Them's the very words I said; they all heard me; and the country may rot for all me—I'll never vote agin as long as I live. And to see the cool way of that nigger—why, he wouldn't a give me the road if I hadn't shoved him out o' the way. I says to the people, why ain't this nigger put up at auction and sold?—that's what I want to know. And what do you reckon they said? Why, they said he couldn't be sold till he'd been in the State six months, and he hadn't been there that long yet." (30–31)

Small wonder that Huck later has difficulty seeing and expressing what in some ways he knows to be the truth about Jim and his relation with him. But all this simply intensifies the puzzle: How is it that Huck can possibly come to challenge race and slavery in his conduct, even while affirming it in his language and his "conscience"?

Reliance on Experience

As Huck comes to see that he cannot in any systematic way use one of his two worlds as "right" to test the other, he learns to test everything by his own immediate experience. He tries out prayer, for example, and gives up on it when it fails to bring him a fishhook; he takes the lamp to the woods, in the passage quoted earlier, to see if it will bring a genie, and learns that it will not; he sees that the "A-rabs" whom the boys pillage are only a Sunday school class on a picnic; and so on. The irresolvable inconsistencies between his two worlds thus lead him to develop the habit of turning to his own experience, confused and untutored though it is, as the only possible standard of judgment. This practice naturally generates a mixture of error, superstition, and accurate perception, and he, naturally enough, does not know which is which. But to do this at all he must be resolutely, sometimes devastatingly, honest with himself, both in his perceptions and in his accounts of them. Although his marginality does not give him a firm place to stand, then, it does teach him to focus on his own experience, however flawed it may be, as a mode of thought and reflection. And while the conflicts between his two worlds do not reach the issues of race and slavery, the habit of mind and attention they stimulate will ultimately do so.

His attention to his two worlds and how they work also teaches him how to manipulate with great skill the languages that define them. This is in fact one of Huck's greatest strengths. In escaping from the cabin, for example, he figures out how to create a scene in which people will think he has been drowned or killed. This requires what might be called a theatrical imagination, as well as attention to hard, practical detail. And in chapter 16 itself, Huck is able to carry out his decision not to betray Jim with extraordinary social and intellectual deftness:

> Well, I just felt sick. But I says, I *got* to do it—I can't get *out* of it. Right then, along comes a skiff with two men in it, with guns, and they stopped and I stopped. One of them says:
> "What's that, yonder?"
> "A piece of a raft," I says.
> "Do you belong on it?"
> "Yes, sir."
> "Any men on it?"
> "Only one, sir."
> "Well, there's five niggers run off tonight, up yonder above the head of the bend. Is your man white or black?"
> I didn't answer up prompt. I tried to, but the words wouldn't come. I tried, for a second or two, to brace up and out with it, but I warn't man enough—hadn't the spunk of a rabbit. I see I was weakening; so I just give up trying, and up and says—

"He's white."

"I reckon we'll go and see for ourselves."

"I wish you would," says I, "because it's pap that's there, and maybe you'd help me tow the raft ashore where the light is. He's sick— and so is mam and Mary Ann."

"Oh, the devil! we're in a hurry, boy. But I s'pose we've got to. Come—buckle to your paddle, and let's get along."

I buckled to my paddle and they laid to their oars. When we had made a stroke or two, I says:

"Pap'll be mightly much obleeged to you, I can tell you. Everybody goes away when I want them to help me tow the raft ashore, and I can't do it by myself."

"Well, that's infernal mean. Odd, too. Say, boy, what's the matter with your father?"

"It's the—a—the—well, it ain't anything, much."

They stopped pulling. It warn't but a mighty little ways to the raft, now. One says:

"Boy, that's a lie. What *is* the matter with your pap? Answer up square, now, and it'll be the better for you."

"I will, sir, I will, honest—but don't leave us, please. It's the— the—gentlemen, if you'll only pull ahead, and let me heave you the head-line, you won't have to come a-near the raft—please do."

"Set her back, John, set her back!" says one. They backed water. "Keep away, boy—keep to looard. Confound it, I just expect the wind has blowed it to us. Your pap's got the smallpox, and you know it precious well. Why didn't you come out and say so? Do you want to spread it all over?"

"Well," says I, a-blubbering, "I've told everybody before, and then they just went away and left us." (99–100)

Huck's skill derives in large part from his habit of attention to the features of his world. He knows who these men are, what they are likely to believe and suspect and fear, and therefore how to fool them. And his ability to lie with such ease and naturalness rests simultaneously on his habit of telling himself the truth and his deep rejection of "truth-telling" as a general social virtue, based as it is on his experience of falseness in the language of Petersburg.

Jim's Friendship

All this is to suggest that we can discover certain elements in Huck's psychology and situation that begin to explain his achievement in chapter 16, just described. But lots of people could be marginal, and turn to their own experience, and practice invention, without coming close to what Huck manages to do, both internally—as he struggles with his competing commitments—and externally, as he fools the slave hunters. Our mystery remains: How is it that Huck achieves what he does?

This question is made even more difficult by the fact that Huck's nature has a distinctly unappealing side. We see this, for example, in another "trick" he plays on Jim, after they have discovered each other on Jackson's island.

This is how the story goes. At Jim's urging, and over the objections of Huck, they set up their camp in a cave on a ridge, in order to keep out of the rain that Jim says is coming, as in fact it does, in a spectacular storm. Over the next few days they share their life, mainly in hiding but sometimes venturing out. On one occasion they find a dead man in a small house being swept down the river. We do not learn it until later, but the man is in fact Pap; Jim recognizes him, when he turns him over, but keeps the knowledge of this fact—at least the conscious knowledge—from Huck. The next day Huck, without any visible feeling whatever, puts a dead rattlesnake by Jim's blanket to scare him. This attracts another snake, Huck later tells us, which gives Jim a poisonous bite that nearly kills him. (Perhaps we are to understand that the first snake was not really dead.)

Why does Huck do this? In one way it makes psychological sense: Huck is here responding to the presence of human contact and protection as an abused and damaged boy might be expected to do, first with joy, then with repudiation—out of disbelief, out of anger at what he has missed in life, out of denial of his own deep need, or because he has internalized the instinct of his father to injure the vulnerable (or the instinct of his society to degrade the slave), or, of course, all of the above. But the existence of this deep reactive impulse makes his achievement in chapter 16 all the more remarkable, for Huck must work himself not only out of the racist language and attitudes of his culture, but out of his own mute instinct to accept abuse and to inflict it too, specifically on Jim, both as a slave and as an incipient friend—and the closer the friendship, the greater the abuse.

This abuse is in fact repeated after Huck and Jim have been separated in the foggy night, just before chapter 16. We know when it happens that the separation is a frightening experience for Huck: he can see nothing because of the fog; he repeatedly calls out for Jim but hears no response; and he is afraid that they are permanently separated. It is with enormous relief that at dawn he sees the raft in the gray distance. But after he has landed on the raft, while Jim is still asleep, he pretends to Jim, as he awakes, that they were not separated at all and that Jim must have dreamed it all. When Jim describes his own experience of the night, worried and alone and missing Huck, Huck insists it was all part of his dream; he then gets Jim to interpret that "dream," and thus to speak and act out of a superstitious side of himself for which Huck has contempt—and a superstitious side that is related, as we know from Jim's response to the "trick" played on him in chapter 1, to his race and his condition as a slave. Only after Jim has acquiesced, and offered a full and energetic reading of the "dream," does Huck point to the trash on the raft, made visible by the coming dawn, and ask Jim what that "stands for" in his dream interpretation. He thus taunts Jim for the very beliefs into which he has led him, taunts him in fact for the trust which he elicited in him.

This is extraordinarily cruel and humiliating. Huck does it without apparent feeling or affect, as a child sometimes will do terrible things. What we can see, and he cannot, is that this is done in response to his own feelings of dependence on Jim, to his own recent fears of separation and loss. It is in fact a repetition of the trick with the dead snake.

What does Jim do? One would expect him to withdraw, salvaging whatever remained of his pride in injured silence; but instead he exposes himself once more to Huck, telling him how and why he has been hurt by him:

> "What do dey stan' for? I's gwyne to tell you. When I got all wore out wid work, en wid de callin' for you, en went to sleep, my heart wuz mos' broke bekase you wuz los', en I didn' k'yer no mo' what become er me en de raf'. En when I wake up en fine you back agin', all safe en soun', de tears come en I could a got down on my knees en kiss' yo' foot I's so thankful. En all you wuz thinkin 'bout wuz how you could make a fool uv ole Jim wid a lie. Dat truck dah is *trash*, en trash is what people is dat puts dirt on de head er dey fren's en makes 'em ashamed." (94–95)

Jim in effect says: What you have done injured me terribly, all the more because I have trusted and cared for you as a friend; indeed I still do care for you, enough to admit the injury and the caring, even now, and to tell you what you have done; in saying this I expose myself to further injury at your hands if you reject or ridicule me; but I hope that you will respond as a friend should, by recognizing the wrong you have done and making our friendship possible again. This is a performance of courage and love, unlike anything Huck has known. He cannot turn his back on it now; it has become the central fact of his life.

> Then he got up slow, and walked to the wigwam, and went in there, without saying anything but that. But that was enough. It made me feel so mean I could almost kissed *his* foot to get him to take it back.
>
> It was fifteen minutes before I could work myself up to go and humble myself to a nigger—but I done it, and I warn't ever sorry for it afterwards, neither. I didn't do him no more mean tricks, and I wouldn't done that one if I'd a knowed it would make him feel that way. (95)

The success of this moment is cooperative. It depends in the first place on Jim's great gift of generosity and love, and his willingness to risk injury. But that would not have registered on everyone; the other contribution is Huck's own, his habit of seeking the truth of his experience and looking for a way to say it, coupled with his unwillingness to lose what Jim has offered him. It is this experience of Jim that enables him in the next scene—when he refuses to turn Jim in—to do what is not only unsayable but unthinkable, including by Huck himself at the moment he does it.

But as the reader will remember, chapter 16 begins with Huck's impulse to betray Jim, a by now predictable destructive reaction to trust and intimacy, all the stronger as its occasion is more powerful. It is not only Huck's "conscience" that urges him to turn Jim in, then, but his desire to injure Jim and himself, to destroy the very possibility of love. It is that impulse, as well as the ingrained habits of racial thinking and feeling, that Huck overcomes in his great moment. No wonder we applaud.

Though he sometimes misjudges it, Huck's experience is real to him, in a sense the only thing he has; it is made real through his habit of insisting on its value; it comes to include a friendship with Jim that Huck cannot deny, though in the only languages he has been given it cannot be imagined or described. In reading about his early experiments, for example in praying for a fishhook, the reader is likely to feel superior to this ignorant boy; but when Huck relies on his own experience and character in chapter 16, we see his extraordinary superiority of mind, both in his capacity for commitment to another and in his willingness to reject, where necessary, the only world he knows. And we are, or should be, humbled.

Huck's Voice

There remains this question, which goes back to Twain's initial decision to make Huck the narrator: Why does Huck, in this imagined world, speak to us at all, why does he "write"? Does this make psychological sense? I think Twain wants us to imagine Huck as writing to us as he speaks to himself; he speaks to us as a part of himself, as a way of thinking about his experience, making it his own, and building himself upon it. He writes to himself and us, for there is nobody else in his world to whom he can speak, no one who sees him or recognizes him. He writes to create the voice in which he does so, out of which he lives, and with which he creates the sense of a possible audience. The self he makes by speaking and thinking in this way, insisting upon the truth of his experience, becomes, in the end, a self capable of giving and receiving love.

Huck owes his success partly to the circumstances that forced him into isolation from his world, partly to the teaching of Jim, but partly to something else as well, deep in his nature, which I have barely mentioned. For from the beginning Huck speaks not only in the contradictory voices learned from the culture and from his father, but in another voice, a voice of his own. This is the voice of openness and honesty with which he speaks to the reader about the natural world, as he tells, for example, of the noises he hears in the woods outside his room at the widow's and the feelings of desolation they occasion; of the river and of the woods by the cabin where Pap keeps him prisoner; of his escape at night in the canoe; of the island where he hides out, and cooks fish, and discovers Jim; and of the life on the raft under the night sky.

Consider this passage, for example, about Huck's escape from Pap:

> I didn't lose no time. The next minute I was a-spinning downstream soft but quick in the shade of the bank. I made two mile and a half, and then struck out a quarter of a mile or more towards the middle of the river, because pretty soon I would be passing the ferry landing and people might see me and hail me. I got out amongst the drift-wood and then laid down in the bottom of the canoe and let her float. I laid there and had a good rest and a smoke out of my pipe, looking away into the sky, not a cloud in it. The sky looks ever so deep when you lay down on your back in the moonshine; I never knowed it before. And how far

a body can hear on the water such nights! I heard people talking at the ferry landing. I heard what they said, too, every word of it. (39)

This passage is striking for its ease and naturalness; for its colloquialism—which is related to its sincerity, for it says that this is how he really thinks; for its precise rendition of external detail; for its interest in generalization; and for its insistence upon the simultaneous importance of feeling and thought. All these contribute to give it an extraordinary whole-mindedness. This is a speaker whose powers of thought and imagination are available to him. This passage, uttered at his moment of escape, is analogous in its way to the passage in which Thoreau describes his arrival at Walden.

Once he had escaped from Pap, as the passage just quoted begins to show, Huck could live a life in nature that made a kind of basic sense; at first he had to do so alone, yet even so he felt competent and at home, in the woods and on the river, as elsewhere he never did. It is upon this central part of himself, speaking in this way, that Huck can rely as his ground for being, for judgment, and for self-transformation. As the novel progresses, and Huck and Jim become friends, this voice changes its tone, from the "mournful and lonesome" to the deeply belonging and responsive. What Huck says becomes instinct with the pleasure and significance of human connection, as in his account of the thunderstorm, which he watches safely from the cave to which Jim led him, having correctly predicted the coming rain. Left to his own devices, Huck would have been soaked to the skin. This passage combines exact description of his observed experience with strong feelings of connection with another; indeed these two aspects are connected, for it is the stability and affection supplied by Jim that make his imaginative powers flow:

> It would get so dark that it looked all blue-black outside, and lovely; and the rain would thrash along by so thick that the trees off a little ways looked dim and spider-webby; and here would come a blast of wind that would bend the trees down and turn up the pale underside of the leaves; and then a perfect ripper of a gust would follow along and set the branches to tossing their arms as if they was just wild; and next, when it was just about the bluest and blackest—*fst!* it was as bright as glory and you'd have a little glimpse of treetops a-plunging about, away off yonder in the storm, hundreds of yards further than you could see before; dark as sin again in a second, and now you'd hear the thunder let go with an awful crash and then go rumbling, grumbling, tumbling down the sky towards the under side of the world, like

rolling empty barrels downstairs, where it's long stairs and they
bounce a good deal, you know.

"Jim, this is nice," I says. "I wouldn't want to be nowhere else but
here." (54)

Or, in the famous passage about life on the river:

This second night we run between seven and eight hours, with a
current that was making over four mile an hour. We catched fish,
and talked, and we took a swim now and then to keep off sleepi-
ness. It was kind of solemn, drifting down the big still river, laying on
our backs looking up at the stars, and we didn't ever feel like talking
loud, and it warn't often that we laughed, only a little kind of low
chuckle. (71)

THIS, IN OUTLINE, is the way I read *Huckleberry Finn*. With all the
differences, the parallels with Thoreau are obvious: each of them withdraws from the false and unsatisfactory world of the town to a kind of
solitude in nature, to a place that permits each to attend to his own
experience in a new way, using it to repudiate and transform the language of the culture, hence as the basis of a truer speech, which can
in turn transform his experience itself. This is achieved by a habit of
mind, an insistence upon the value of one's experience and one's mind,
best achieved in solitude, where one's developing voice can be heard.
But experience alone is not enough for either of them until it has been
made the object of thought and exposition, in "writing," and become
thus an experience of another kind.[3]

But *Huckleberry Finn* gives us something that is missing in *Walden,*
the active and transforming presence of another person. For it is Jim
who is in fact the moral hero of this book; his capacity for love and
truthfulness is what ultimately reaches Huck, who acts as he does because he cannot turn his back on what Jim has given him. This is hard
for the modern reader to see, certainly the modern white reader, and
still harder for Huck himself or Twain to acknowledge; the reason
in all cases, including our own, is the continuing meaning of what we
call "race."

    3. Thus both *Walden* and *Huckleberry Finn* show their protagonists learning to attend
to their experience; exercising the memory; trying to make sense of what they see and hear;
responding to the tension between the authorities of the world and the authority of the self;
seeking always to discover the art forms into which life falls; and doing this not alone, but in
relation to another, both in the world, as Huck does with Jim, and in the text, as both writers
do with their readers.

The relation of self and culture is much more problematic here than in *Walden,* for as Twain presents it there is in the end no solution. From the great moment at the end of chapter 16, neither Huck, in the imagined world of the novel, nor Twain in creating it, has anywhere to go. Huck and Jim cannot maintain their identities and relations in the world of the American South. (For example, we are not told what Jim said when Huck returned to the raft, and for very good reason: What could he say?) The novelist can proceed beyond chapter 16 only by separating the two characters, by introducing new and somewhat far-cical figures, by bringing Tom Sawyer back into it, and so on. In the second part of the novel, Huck himself acts and speaks as though he no longer knew what he had learned, and—to the extent we see him at all—much the same is true of Jim as well. The reader is thus faced with his own experience of cognitive dissonance: if the second half of the book is to work as the rather broad and genial social satire it seems meant to be, we too must forget what we have known; if we remember it, the whole thing, including both the breakdown of Twain's imagi-nation and the social facts compelling it, becomes unbearable. In pre-senting us with this issue, the book brings to consciousness simul-taneously the unspeakable evil of racial thought and its status as an indelible fact of our cultural condition. I say brings to consciousness; but it proposes no way of dealing with this tension in American moral and imaginative life, for it can find none, either for the characters within the novel or for the novelist himself.

Twain in fact stopped writing the book for several years at this point,[4] I think because he could not imagine how it could continue— how these two people could live and act out of their new relation of respect and friendship in the only world available to them. Twain was in my view right to feel this impossibility; there was no way that these two, as they have discovered and find themselves, could live in that social context. Whether such a relation would be possible today, and subject to what constraints, is a question with which the novel leaves us.

This returns us to the question I asked earlier: Why is Huck not able simply to see and to say the truth about his relation with Jim, to say, that is, what we would say? One point of the book is to make this question, with appropriate modifications, a real one for Twain and the reader as well. You might say that both the main character and the novelist con-

---

4. See Hamlin Hill and Walter Blair, "The Composition of *Huckleberry Finn*," in *Huck Finn among the Critics: A Centennial Selection,* ed. M. Thomas Inge (Frederick, Md.: University Publications of America, 1985), 15–25, at 18.

front a problem neither can solve—and neither can we—namely, imagining a world in which the friendship between Huck and Jim is a possibility upon which one can build a future. While Thoreau presents us with a promise of infinite possibility, then, Twain and Huck both face an insuperable limitation imposed by a fallen world.

I would add only this. On my reading it is Jim who is the hero of this story, the center of value and understanding. We do not see him from the inside, however, and must construct his nature and learn to hear his voice from the material Huck gives us, which is of course shaped and shaded by his views of race. But not only by his views, by our own: it is ultimately the complicity of the white reader in the system of race, and perhaps that of the black reader too, against which the novel works. If there were no such complicity, Huck's view of the world and of Jim would be rejected at the outset as a total horror like that of Nazi Germany. That there is such complicity, and that Twain counts on it, is I think the heart of the claim that this book, for all its virtues, remains a racist one. But in my view this complicity is present to be corrected and humiliated; the book is in this sense the deep enemy of racial thought.[5]

For me the book I love ends with chapter 16, at this moment of im-

5. To say this about the opening sixteen chapters is to say nothing about the rest of the book, except that a standard has been established here by which it can be measured. As I make plain, I think it fails to meet that standard, but also that this failure itself has real value, as a performance in our experience of the force of racial thought. On this point see *Satire or Evasion? Black Perspectives on Huckleberry Finn,* ed. James S. Leonard et al. (Durham: Duke University Press, 1992).

Whether *Huckleberry Finn* can properly be read, as I do, to resist rather than confirm the racist attitudes it represents is of course a living question. The best consideration of this issue I have found is by Wayne Booth, who argues that the kind of view I am urging is untenable because the evils of racism are confirmed even at Huck's greatest moments of intense self-struggle. Wayne C. Booth, *The Company We Keep: An Ethics of Fiction* (Berkeley: University of California Press, 1988), especially 3–4, 457–78. My response is to say, "Of course they are." This is why the book is so powerful and true. I think it would be false to Twain's achievement, as well as a plain impossibility, to ask that he present a clear-eyed and coherent view of race, of a sort that would fit with late-twentieth-century understandings. For me it is one of the deepest points of the book, and one of its greatest virtues, to show how utterly embroiled both he and Huck are in the language and attitudes of race, and to teach us that we are too. (On this general point, see Lawrence A. Hirschfeld, *Race in the Making: Cognition, Culture, and the Child's Construction of Human Kinds* [Cambridge: MIT Press, 1996].) Thus in chapter 16 we see a perhaps unintended consequence of Twain's decision to make Huck the narrator: we can see and hear Jim, but always from Huck's point of view, never Jim's own. Jim is simultaneously present and erased, and as readers we participate in making him so.

What of the fact that Jim is represented, even in the first sixteen chapters, as gullible and superstitious? Huck is too, of course, but both are presumably in this respect different from

possibility, just as the *Iliad* ends with a similar moment of impossibility, the friendship between Achilles and Priam, which could likewise have no future in the world they inhabit. In both cases the friendship and the impossibility of a future for it stand as grounds of criticism of those cultures—indeed, of any culture in which the common humanity of any human being is denied, which means any culture at all.[6]

***

In front of the widow's house next door was a turnaround where the street ended; beyond that lay a path into the woods, our woods, which we took—I and my older brother Tom, our friend Donnie Bartram, and perhaps Fritzie, the German boy, as well—it now seems daily. The goal was always one of three caves we had discovered. One was simply a hollow place under the exposed roots of a large tree growing at the top of a sandy river bank, one I do not remember, but the third was a real cave, with an entrance and two cavities forming the shape of a Y, each branch of which was big enough to hold one or two boys. It smelled of black earth. At the end of one of the cavities a natural shelf created a place so small that the bigger boys could squeeze in only with discomfort.

This is where someone would be sent for "punishment," if he broke the rules, I suppose; but we had no rules, there were only three or four of us in any case, and I did not understand

and inferior to the implied reader. Is it permissible to say that superstition may have been one of the consequences of slavery? Would such a statement be an instance of racism, of deploring the consequences of racism, or of both at once? Superstition is seen, in both actors, as an occasion for humor at their expense. Is this racism? Or would it be racism to refuse to find comedy in this human weakness? Or both? It is not irrelevant that at the moral crisis of the book Huck exploits Jim's gullibility and superstition, and does so to injure him; in this, in my view, he is acting for us, out of the views that Twain has tried to stimulate in us, and his correction at the hands of Jim should therefore work as our correction as well.

6. Years after first reading *Huckleberry Finn*, when thinking about the nature of a legal education and its effect on the mind, I reproduced for my students the great passage from chapter 16 and asked them: Why can Huck not see what you see, that racism is an evil and slavery an abomination? Why can he not say these things? Has language such control over the mind? All this was a way of asking another question too: What of your legal education? What will it make you unable to see, or to say? How can you protect yourself against the force of the language you are learning, the culture you are entering, so that you may use it, and not it you? This is a question not only for a lawyer, but for any person speaking a language made by others, which is any person at all. The only answer is a writing answer, and it lies above all in one's voice.

what was meant by this word in this place. I felt it as a puzzling threat. I once saw Tom cramped into this shelf, and felt a kind of uncomprehending sympathy and fascination at the sight of his humiliation and discomfort, his body twisted in its white shirt and his face grimacing with a pained expression behind his wire-rimmed spectacles, suffering. Was he being punished, or pretending to be, or simply trying out the punishment place to see how adequate it was to the purpose? It was unclear.

Later I tried the place myself, to see what it was like, afraid both of the idea of punishment and of the dark, earth-smelling end of the cave. With great relief, and a sense of ironic and rare superiority, I discovered that I was small enough to fit there with ease—unpunishable, then, in this way at least. But it was not just fear that drew me into that recess: I wanted to crawl into that dark place, cramped and airless, and to emerge from the black earth into the light once more.

One day in the cave Donnie Bartram showed me how to make a radio out of a soap box. He pasted on dials, made an antenna out of a stick, and drew a scale and a pointer for the stations. As I watched, I was at first full of anticipation at this exercise of superior competence and power—I expected the parts to go through the promised transformation and start to broadcast noise—then of disappointment and wonder, when I realized that it was not a real radio that he was making, not a radio at all but a decorated blue soap box. A promise disappeared into emptiness.

In the spring our garden was ploughed by an old man, with a crumpled hat, driving a horse or mule. The first time he appeared he showed up under the maple tree without sound or warning, silent and ready to work. I was fascinated by him, a study in darks and shadows and highlights, in stolidity and silence; by the horse, gigantic, pulling at his heavy harness; and by the ploughing itself, the turning of the earth inside out into rows of dark clods, black and fertile.

But more than that, for I knew, as a child knows these things, that there was something mysteriously different about him. It had something to do with the brownness of his skin but it really existed, I could see, in the attitudes that others had towards him, and he towards others, in the social not the natural realm. I did not know enough people to be able to think in terms of race—for me he was unique—but I knew there was something distinctive in him, for I could see it in my parents' feelings, hear it in their tones of voice.

This garden, our Victory Garden, down the white steps behind the house, produced tomatoes, eaten nightly by turtles, or so I thought, and corn, eaten in season by us, fresh and often so young that I could eat the cob as well as the corn. The children helped with the husking, sitting on the steps, and joined the nightly talk about this being the best corn in the world, cooked the only proper way, plunged as soon as husked into water already boiling. A perfected moment: I knew what to do and what to say, and my words fit, for the moment at least, my feelings.

THREE

The *Odyssey:*
Living in a Land Transformed

It may seem an enormous jump from *Huckleberry Finn*—written in America, in English, in the nineteenth century—to the *Odyssey,* perhaps at first not written at all but composed orally, in Greek, maybe in Asia Minor, maybe in the eighth century B.C. And the central characters differ entirely in age and situation: Huck a boy on the verge of adulthood, defining himself as a moral actor for the first time; Odysseus a fully middle-aged man, his greatest exploits behind him, trying with dubious success to make his way home. But the two works share much as well, especially a structure based on the adventures of a figure who finds himself on the margins of his world, and who for this reason, whether he likes it or not, becomes a kind of critic of it. Both works in this way represent a mind engaging deeply with the culture that has done much to give it shape.

As Huck escapes first to the woods, then to the river, so Odysseus moves from the heroic world of Troy—where he had been as successful as a man could be, a hero of heroes—first to the world of his wanderings, where the values and premises of the kind of heroism he once embodied no longer work, then to Ithaca, which proves to be a yet different world, calling upon different resources of mind and imagination. His circumstances thus change not once but twice, and do so in respects that make his prior ways of imagining himself and his world—his motives, his successes and failures, his relations with others, his own identity—inadequate; more than inadequate, dangerous, to himself and to his family. He must find or make other ways of thinking if his story is to work itself to a satisfactory ending; and when he does so, he undergoes transformations of his own.

As *Huckleberry Finn* introduces us to the difficulty that the culture we inhabit, that shapes our minds, may be corrupt or poisoned, the *Odyssey* brings us to face a different but equally intractable difficulty, that our cultural circumstances change, presenting us not only with the question of criticism—which stage is better, and why?—but also with the question of adaptation: How, and with what significances, do we respond to such changes? This will prove to be the ultimate challenge to Odysseus' resourcefulness, his central characteristic.

Odysseus' Story of His Life

Homer's *Odyssey* is often, and understandably, read as a tale of pure experience and adventure, voracious and masculine, the story of what happened to Odysseus, and what he did, on his ten-year voyage home from Troy. It is the first story about that great figure of Western literature, the isolated hero pitted against the world, and perhaps the first to define what we think of as the individual ego, full of appetite and curiosity, and distinct from all others. But it is also about a different kind of subject, about storytelling itself; especially about the kind of story one tells about one's life and thus about the kind of meaning that a life can have.

Think of the central stories of Odysseus' adventures, the fabulous ones about the Cyclops and Circe and the Sirens and the rest: these are told not by an external narrator but by Odysseus himself. They are a kind of autobiography, which he tells to the Phaeacians when, after finally being released from the island of Calypso, he is washed up on their island, naked and alone.

When Odysseus begins to tell this story, the world of Troy, where his great and famous deeds were done, lies in the past, long past—ten years earlier—and for all the actors in the poem it is part of a heroic era that can never return. In that world, now the world of memory, Odysseus exists as a hero. His exploits there are told and retold by those who were present—by Nestor and Menelaus and Helen, who report what they saw and heard. And they are sung by the bards, who have already made the Trojan War the subject of the celebratory verse, creating a poetic memory that confers a kind of immortality on the people and the events it honors, Odysseus among the rest. This form of immortality is what was chosen by Achilles when he preferred the short and glorious life—that is, the life made the subject of song— over a long and obscure one. Odysseus too became a hero, almost immortal, in the great, almost immortal events at Troy, but so far are the real events of the war now sunk in the past that Alcinous, the Phaeacian king, can say that the reason the gods brought the war into being was so that poets could sing of it to others (viii, 580).

In a sense it was a mistake for Odysseus to have lived so long. If he had died meritoriously at Troy, his life would have had a proper shape and meaning, especially since he is the one who devised the stratagem of the Trojan Horse that won the war. As Achilles learned, the price of a poetic *kleos*—the hero's reward—is a short life, and the reason is a good one: only a short life will reliably fall into the art forms that a poem requires. While the hero still lives, who knows what shape his life will ultimately take?

At the beginning of this poem Odysseus has become a wanderer, engaged in an interminable and unhappy voyage home, a voyage that he seems unable to complete, almost as if he were caught in a dream of unattainable desire. Troy is behind him, behind everyone, ten years in the past. It is the subject of immortal verse, that is true, but it is nothing to build a present life upon. Odysseus is no longer a hero and no longer dominates his circumstances: all his men have been killed, and he sits captive on the island of Calypso, looking out over the sea with a heart yearning for home. Calypso offers him immortality, and eternal youth as well, a literalized version of what the heroic bard offers in the world of memory and imagination; but he has no use for these things. His past is glorious, the stuff of poetry, but his present is humiliated and powerless. At Troy he had a role, an identity, a context. But that is forever gone and what can it avail him now? What connection can there be between that past and this present, between that past self and this present one? When he hears the singer at the Phaeacian court tell of the old heroic days, of his own past actions, he falls into uncontrollable weeping (viii, 522).

But the practical effect of his telling his story to the Phaeacians, in this way and at this time, is to enable him after twenty years to return to Ithaca, where he will rejoin his wife Penelope on new and infinitely deeper terms; where he will meet and face his growing son, Telemachus, who will soon surpass him, and his aged father, Laertes, who will soon die; where he will drive off the usurpers from his palace and establish himself in his town, in his family, as a man ready to lead a life of actual, not sublimated, meaning, as husband, father, and son. The miraculous effect of his telling this story is beautifully expressed in the narrative itself: when Odysseus has finished talking and gone to sleep, the Phaeacians carry him, while he sleeps, in their magic ships across the seas and home, and leave him, still sleeping, on the shores of Ithaca. In ten years of constant struggle he cannot get home; but after telling his story, this heretofore impossible journey is accomplished in a single night and in his sleep.

Why has this story this effect? I think the reason it is so aesthetically and psychologically appropriate is that in telling it Odysseus provides an answer to the question of identity that he faces, torn as he is between his past role as hero in the Trojan War and his present one as a confused and isolated wanderer. For the story he tells defines him as a new kind of hero, and one who is now, in his own telling in Phaeacia and in Homer's poem too, celebrated in poetry of a new kind. (When he has finished, Alcinous says that he has told his story "like a bard" [xi, 368].) Odysseus' story of his travels becomes as he tells it a second heroic past, which his own telling makes the object of poetic fame and glory: not the heroics of the warrior, as before, but those of a man treading the edge of nature and its possibilities, experiencing the limits of the human in a way that sets him apart from all others. Odysseus here indeed proves to be "the man of many turns, much-wandering," as the opening lines of the poem put it.

The new heroic identity supersedes the first: Odysseus is no longer merely the Odysseus who by his stratagems won the Trojan War—an enormous feat, of course, but this was, after all, the war of another man, prosecuting his personal revenge, and in it Odysseus worked always in the interest of another. Now he is the Odysseus who has seen and experienced all in the human realm and beyond it too, the world of the monstrous and the dead, and has come out on the other side. As the *Iliad* made heroic the world of battle, and gave it glory —*kleos*— in verse, so here Odysseus, and the *Odyssey*, make heroic, and glorious in verse, the wanderings of a hero's return (his *nostos*).

There is a certain parallel between the poet and the hero: as Odysseus moves from the heroism of the Trojan War to that of the isolated wanderer, the poet moves from the poetry of the Trojan War —seen here in the bardic songs of Demodocus, describing the quarrel of Achilles and Odysseus or the stratagem of the Trojan Horse (viii, 72–78, 499–513)—to a new kind of poetry, an epic in which the older songs are embedded as a significant but minor element. The new heroism and the new poetry are alike characterized—as the reader is perhaps likely to think the whole poem is: consider the Ulysses of Dante, for example, or that of Tennyson—by curiosity, by fascination with the unknown, by a love of the world, and by boundless individual desire for experience.

But this is an odd kind of heroism, for it is, to say the least, not marked by supreme practical or moral success. Odysseus ultimately loses all of his men and all of his ships, and does so to a considerable degree through his own fault. When they arrive at the island of the Cyclops, for example, he insists upon finding out more about the people of this land, and in so doing exposes his men to destruction; then, on leaving the island, he cries out his name in triumph to the blinded giant, which makes it possible for Polyphemus to curse him and his men effectively, invoking against them the rage of his father, Poseidon (ix, 504–5). And he settles in so comfortably with Circe, for a year, that he needs to be spurred by his men to continue his voyage home. His own role as leader weakens, too: he begins as a real commander, but during the Circe episode he shares power with his men, and finally, at the Island of the Sun, he is overruled by them. This hero's story is in part a story of increasing limits on his power and capacity, until he ends up on the island of Calypso, a solitary and helpless captive.

There is another limit, too, of an even more intractable and important kind; for in telling this story Odysseus brings to the surface, where it cannot be ignored, the fact present in all such narratives—that the meaning of the story of a human life is uncertain until it ends. This is dramatized most explicitly, for him and for us alike, in his voyage to the Land of the Dead, where he meets those whose lives and stories are over, and learns how much of the meaning of a life depends upon what happens at the end. The most obvious case is that of Agamemnon, with whom Odysseus has been implicitly and explicitly compared from the beginning of the poem: having been the greatest leader in the Greek world, managing its greatest triumph—the successful war against Troy to redeem the honor of his brother—Agamemnon returns to Argos only to be slaughtered by his wife, Clytemnestra, and her lover Aegistheus. The effect of this humiliating ending is to destroy the achievements of his heroic past by giving them a different meaning: Agamemnon will now forever be the man foully struck down in his prosperity by his wife and her lover.

What this means for Odysseus is that the meaning of the story he has started to tell, of his life itself, depends upon what cannot yet be known, the future that awaits him in Ithaca. The new identity he has claimed for himself is inherently unstable until his story is over. It is true that when he visits the Land of the Dead Teiresias prophesies for him a long life and a gentle death, far from the sea (or, on another reading of the Greek, death "from the sea" itself); but only if he can avoid killing the Cattle of the Sun and only if, upon his return home, he walks inland with an oar on his shoulder until he meets a man who mistakes it for a winnowing fork and there makes a sacrifice to Poseidon (xi, 100–37). This is a promise of a satisfactory ending, but a conditional one, and the conditions themselves are of interest, for they

involve the submission of Odysseus' will to another person or another force, the restraint of appetite and acceptance of limits. And by
rejecting Calypso's offer of immortality and endless youth, Odysseus
has accepted the most basic limit, death. What other limits are there
for him to face? What will the acceptance of these limits mean, not
symbolically, as Teiresias describes it, but actually, in the life Odysseus
will lead?

For Odysseus, and for us, this is most uncertain. He has attained
supreme excellence in two forms of heroism, celebrated in two forms
of poetry, the bardic and—invented for the purpose—the Odyssean;
yet none of this suffices for what lies ahead, which is different in kind
from what has gone before, and not only because it is unknown: it will
take place with different actors, on a different scale, and for different
stakes. The question Odysseus has for the moment so successfully addressed, how to connect his past with his present, is one to which life
can offer no permanent solution until it ends.

In this the poem speaks for all of us, for everyone has the experience
of remembering a past and trying to understand it, of telling the story
of a life and trying to make sense of it. Even if we do not do so in
words, or record them in writing, we all compose our autobiographies
all the time. Each of us has a past, and has had as long as we can
remember—for nearly every remembered moment assumes as part of
its meaning something that came before—and each of us is perpetually
telling the story of that past, over and over, both to himself (or herself)
and to others, in an endless conversation in inner and outer speech. As
we live we write the successive chapters of a story the future lines of
which are necessarily unknown to us; but they will certainly, like Agamemnon's murder, give new meaning to what is past. The sense that
our present life is an extension or transformation of what happened
earlier, that history and character and fate are realizing themselves in
time, is in fact an essential part, perhaps the essential part, of what it
means to be a human being.[1]

1. One might say that each of us is the person we make ourselves, over time, as we
remember our past and put those memories to work. For at the center of each of us is the
part of the self that seeks to locate itself in the world, to learn the languages and gestures of
life, and thus to learn its own identity and the meaning of the story it is beginning to live out.
And as we do this, we work against two deep fears, perhaps unconscious ones: the fear that
the story we tell will have a meaning that is intolerable to us, and the fear that it will have no
meaning at all. As a friend of mine once said towards the end of his rich and complex life: "I
mainly live in what seems like confusion; but after the fact, when I look back on it, my life
always falls into art forms." This is the voice simultaneously of experience and of hope; the
hope is that a life will have meaning as a text has meaning, working against the fear that it

Ithaca

As readers of the *Odyssey* we know more than Odysseus does about the future he must face, for at the beginning of the poem we were shown the condition of the household in Ithaca for which he, imprisoned on Calypso's island, yearned so deeply, and to which he is now, after telling his story in Phaeacia, about to return. The house has been taken over by the suitors of Penelope, who devour its substance and repeatedly humiliate both Penelope herself and Telemachus. Through her stratagem of the loom—unraveling at night the garment she weaves by day—Penelope has for years maintained a standoff, but, with the emergence of Telemachus into manhood, things have come to a crisis. Telemachus is no longer an excuse for Penelope's delays—no longer a boy she must care for—and he is becoming something of a threat in his own right, for the perpetual humiliation is less and less endurable to him, and he is ever increasing in competence and power. What is to be done? Odysseus has been gone, after all, for twenty years, virtually all of Telemachus's life, and nothing has been heard of him for ages. Although Homer does not suggest it until Book 24, there is actually some merit in the suitors' insistent demand that Penelope choose a new husband: Odysseus is almost certainly dead and by Greek law and custom a woman cannot be without a male protector. There is a vacuum here that can be filled only by a man, here whatever man she chooses. But it looks as if she will succeed in stalling until that place is taken, not by one of the suitors, but by her son. Small wonder they are angry.

In a manly speech to the suitors, Telemachus tells them that he will go to seek news of his father; if he can find none within a year, he agrees that Penelope should marry one of them and go with him to his house. Telemachus then travels to Pylos and Sparta, where he is entertained with grace and warmth by Nestor and Menelaus, learning from the latter, who learned it from Proteus, that Odysseus is alive but a captive on the island of Calypso. This section of the poem ends like a movie western, with the suitors lying in ambush, waiting to kill Telemachus as he sails home. This is the situation to which Odysseus will in the end return, the situation that is calling out to him. How is he to address it?

---

will not. To discover shape and coherence and significance in a work of art presents us with an acute form of this problem, for it stimulates the desire for meaning of this kind and at the same time reminds us that our own experience, like that of Odysseus, is unfinished, in doubt. In this way art always challenges life.

When Odysseus awakes on Ithaca, after his magical voyage home, his gifts piled beside him, he finds himself in a world transformed. Athena has wrapped the landscape in a mist so distorting that Odysseus does not recognize it. He thinks he has been deceived by the Phaeacians, abandoned in a strange land, and that once again his return has been snatched away on the edge of success—as before, when his crew members, within sight of Ithaca, opened the bag that had been given them by Aeolus, which proved to contain not the gold they imagined Odysseus to be hoarding but all the winds of heaven, which blew them back across the sea into their endless wanderings. In fact Odysseus is home, but he does not know it—he has no idea where on earth he is—for nothing looks the same.

When Athena appears before him, in disguise, Odysseus—to make himself formidable to this stranger— tells her a lengthy and false tale, in which he describes himself as a Cretan who has fled his native land after killing a man. Athena of course knows the truth and quickly reveals herself to Odysseus, affectionately admiring his skill in duplicity. She warns him of the conditions at the palace—an essential warning, Odysseus realizes, for if he had gone straight there, as a hero returned from war, he would have been slaughtered in his own hall, just like Agamemnon. The old kind of heroism would have meant his death.

Instead, Athena transforms his appearance, making him look even older and more worn than he is. He goes in disguise, as a beggar, to the hut of the old swineherd Eumaeus, who receives him, as a stranger, with dignity and warmth and generosity. Still in disguise Odysseus goes to the palace, where he is reviled and abused by the suitors and their minions; where he is received with warmth by his old nurse Eurykleia and, at first with guarded distance, by Penelope; and where, with the help of Penelope, Telemachus, and the swineherd, he prepares his revenge. At the end, when he has drawn the bow and shot the arrow through the ax handles, he leaps to the threshold and reveals himself, all disguise gone: he slaughters the suitors, purifies the house, and reclaims his wife and household.

How are we to read this story, the third stage of Odysseus' life, especially his role as beggar and outcast? One common way to understand his bedraggled appearance is as a stratagem, a way in which a man insinuates himself among his enemies in order to kill them, and there is of course much in this view. But that does not explain the changed landscape of Ithaca, and in any event both transformations can be read not as simple stratagems, whether conceived by Odysseus or by Athena, nor as miraculous or strange events, but as natural expressions of psychological truth. Of course the land looks different to him after twenty years; of course it seems alien, for he has a different relation to it, and he must himself feel alien with respect to it. His "disguise" is a way of thinking and feeling about his natural appearance, so utterly different from that of the man who left in the flower of his youth twenty years ago as to seem to require an explanation in terms of divine agencies. When he returns, the landscape is clouded and he is misfigured, for everything and everyone have changed: he is not who he was, his house and its people, especially Penelope, are not what, or who, they were. This is how he looks now, worn and fully middle-aged. In the scene with Penelope and Eurykleia, this meaning of the disguise is in fact marked for us, as they gradually come to see how much "like Odysseus" he actually is: his height and form and features are the same, we are told, so what is different? He is older, so much older that they do not recognize him. On this reading the ultimate "removal of the disguise" is really just the recognition that this man is indeed Odysseus, a recognition that both Penelope and the suitors have reasons for resisting.

But the transformation is real in another sense, and a most important one too. When Odysseus becomes a beggar, he discovers and acknowledges his dependence on the swineherd, on his wife, and on his son. For such a sublime hero of the individual self this is a transformation indeed, a kind of positive humiliation. In a sense of course he is only pretending to be a beggar, but, as in all such stories, the pretense is real as well as false: he becomes his role, and we read him that way. His truest welcome is from the swineherd (nearly the lowest of men), from his flea-bitten dog dying on a dung heap, and ultimately from his wife. This is as far from the values of male power and display that characterize the heroic world of the Trojan War as one can well imagine.

It is the people upon whom Odysseus comes to depend—the swineherd, son, and wife—and the relations Odysseus establishes with them, that the poem ultimately brings us to see and value, and this means valuing Odysseus' transformation as well. The making of these relations, and of this transformation, is in fact the point towards which the *Odyssey* has been proceeding from the beginning, for throughout it has concerned itself with the central human moment when one person meets another, as friend or stranger. It tells, over and over, of the arrival of a stranger, a person who might be a friend or an enemy, to a country he does not know. In Thoreau's terms, such a one is a person from a "distant land."

In the culture represented in this poem, this moment of meeting is governed by a ruling ethic, that of hospitality, which has its own clear rules and practices (including, for example, the convention that one must not ask who the stranger is, from what family and what country, until he has been fed). Homeric Greek has a wonderful family of words to describe these relations, and their associated ethical values, based upon the root *xein-*: a *xeinos* is a "stranger," meaning someone of whom you know nothing, but also a "guest-friend," meaning a person from far away with whom you enjoy relations of reciprocal hospitality. These relations are established when one person opens his doors to another, and once established they are normally inherited. (My grandfather welcomed yours and supported him, when he was in my country; now I am in yours, and I can expect you to treat me likewise.) *Xeinia* is the term for the gifts of hospitality, exchanged by the partners, and for hospitality itself, which is the essential social virtue of the aristocratic world at peace, mirroring the martial virtues of the same world at war, which the *Iliad* at once celebrates and criticizes. The Trojan War in fact had its roots in a gross violation of hospitality, the seduction by Paris of the wife of his host, and the *Iliad* concludes with a form of *xeinia,* when Achilles admits Priam as a supplicant to his tent and extends to him his protection as a host.

In the *Odyssey* hospitality is defined both negatively and positively: the former most clearly by the Cyclops—whose people are without laws or manners, and thus define the barbaric edge of human possibility—and by the suitors in Ithaca. As the one-eyed giant is the uncivilized host, devouring his guests, the suitors are uncivilized guests, destroying the household of their host: together they define what is human but uncivilized. (The monsters, Scylla, Charybdis, and the Sirens, who would destroy human life for the sake of it, and the witches of sexuality, Calypso and Circe, who would destroy what is human in the man they desire, mark out the periphery of experience in another way.) Positive performances of hospitality include the virtue in its most aristocratic form, as when Nestor and Menelaus welcome the son of their illustrious comrade with great ceremony and decorum, and with great personal warmth too, lending him their substance and their power and giving him gifts; and when Alcinous, the Phaeacian king, gives Odysseus a magnificent reception, over the muted threat of a different possibility, voiced by Nausicaa, when she cautions Odysseus to address himself first to her softhearted mother, and by Athena, who guides him unseen through the town, which she says is unfriendly to strangers. But the most important performance of hospitality is not aristocratic in the least, but simply human: this is the reception that Eumaeus, poor as he is, gives to the unknown wanderer, even poorer, who appears at his hut in the night. The kindness and virtue of this man are strikingly marked for us by the poet, who speaks not *of* Eumaeus in the third person but *to* him in the second, addressing him directly: "Then you, Eumaeus . . . ." (xiv, 55)

The meeting of strangers is an image of our central social experience, for we all are, or can become, strangers to one another, even— perhaps especially—in our most intimate and familiar relations. The *Odyssey* establishes this truth especially in the scenes in which Odysseus first meets as a stranger, then moves by stages into another kind of relation with, the three people upon whom he depends: Eumaeus, Telemachus, and Penelope. For without their help he cannot succeed, a fact that is enacted with brilliance and clarity in the scene with the bow, where it takes the cooperation of all three—Telemachus to authorize Eumaeus to carry the bow, and Penelope to back them up with words of justification—to get the bow into the hands of the beggar.

In the passages in which Odysseus meets these people, the pace of the narrative, which at the end of Odysseus' wanderings had been breakneck, slows enormously: the leisurely and repetitive conversations with Eumaeus, for example, enact an understanding that hospitality, attention to the relation between host and stranger, really does come first. If the reader thought that meaning lay in action, these conversations would be boring; but when one sees that they are about people talking to each other, and the kind of community they create, they become fascinating, full of feeling and significance.

This scene begins when Odysseus emerges from the dark in disguise at the hut of Eumaeus, pretending a material poverty that is false, but demonstrating a poverty in another sense, a dependence on Eumaeus, that is real. When the dogs attack he tries the trick of sitting down, defenseless, in the hope that they will desist, a hope the narrator tells us is wholly vain. (So much for the wily and adaptable Odysseus: he almost dies at the hands of a swineherd's dogs!) Eumaeus calls them off, with courtly grace inviting Odysseus into his hut; he is concerned for the damage the dogs almost did, laments his absent master, and offers Odysseus such hospitality as he can.

In the night by the fire Eumaeus describes his present situation, and that of Telemachus and Penelope too. He assumes that Odysseus is dead and laments his loss, in his deep affection defining a kind of relation with another that is different from anything we have seen in this poem. The two men then exchange the stories of their lives. The story Odysseus tells is false in detail, to maintain his disguise, but emotionally true, for it is a tale of a frustrated return from the war, of wandering and adventure—of men killed through their own folly, of captivity, shipwreck, isolation. Then he asks Eumaeus to tell his life story, and he does so: how he was kidnapped by Phoenicians and sold as a serf to Laertes, all told with vividness and detail. These are both stories of vulnerability and survival, and their mutual telling creates a relation of trust based upon shared attitudes and experience. Eumaeus speaks for both when he says that even the pains of life give pleasure when retold by one who has wandered and suffered much.

Compare with this the wonderful interview of Odysseus with Penelope: it too begins with an account of her life, of her history and present circumstances, including the story of her ruse and its failure, and the kinds of pressure she is now under to accept one of the suitors. Odysseus once more tells his "false tale," but this time he includes an account of his encounter with "Odysseus," at which Penelope collapses with grief, unwittingly demonstrating to Odysseus her faithful love for him. She then in turn tests his story, asking questions about the dress worn by Odysseus that only one who had actually seen him would be able to answer, as of course the "stranger" can. In different ways they thus examine each other, and both pass the test. Odysseus now tells her with urgency that he knows that "Odysseus" is near (as he has heard from the kings of Thesprotis) and in connection with this he recounts the last part of his own actual experiences, with the Phaeacians. He thus comes to tell her the direct and literal truth.

Later, after the episode in which Eurykleia privately recognizes Odysseus by his scar and is silenced, Penelope once more describes her circumstances in full emotional detail, now telling the story of a dream: twenty geese, eating grain in her house, are destroyed by an eagle; first she laments their loss, but then the eagle speaks to her, saying that he is Odysseus and will soon come to kill the suitors, as he killed the geese. "What does it mean?" she asks. Odysseus tells her that she already knows, for "Odysseus" has told her what it means, in the dream; she announces that on the morrow she will hold the contest with the axes and marry the victor; she then asks Odysseus what he thinks of her plan. Odysseus approves of it, telling her not to delay, for "Odysseus" will be there before the bow is drawn.

By telling and retelling their stories, by question and suggestion, these two minds move into disclosure and harmony, working out a common plan, without either saying, what Penelope at some level has learned to be true, that this man is indeed Odysseus. The kind of understanding they share—of circumstance, of demonstrated sentiment, of character—is in fact a far more secure basis for common action than anything an immediate disclosure could have afforded: if Odysseus had simply announced his identity to her, Penelope would have wondered whether he was telling the truth, what his feelings and motives were, and he would have been uncertain as to whether he could trust her. As it is, Odysseus has a ground for trusting Penelope and her motives, in her conduct, and she a similar ground for trusting him. At the end, when the suitors have been killed and Odysseus has passed the ultimate test—his knowledge of the bed carved out of an olive tree, still rooted to the ground—he and Penelope move into the final stages of harmony; and this is represented by their telling their stories to each other once again.

The position of the poem is plain, celebrating the virtue of "hospitality." But in the course of the poem there is a transformation of what is meant by "hospitality," for it begins with formal grace and wealth among the aristocrats and ends with the swineherd's kindness to the beggar and with the relation between Penelope and the stranger with whom she gradually comes into harmony, as her husband. This poem thus celebrates hospitality but defines it in a new way: as a virtue that cuts across the lines that divide human beings from one another. Hospitality is no longer a matter of aristocratic largesse among men of certain class—a largesse defining power and creating reciprocal security; it is the recognition of and response to another person, enacted in one form by Nestor and Menelaus, in another far more important way by Eumaeus, and most fully and beautifully of all in the sequence of scenes in which Penelope and Odysseus move into harmonious understanding. It becomes a form of love.

THE *Iliad* is a poem of youth: for Achilles the question is how he is to respond to his heroic culture, to his own heroic excellence, to his desire for glory. The *Odyssey* is a poem of middle age: for Odysseus the question is how to connect the story of his past—with its successes and failures of every kind, its incomplete lines of meaning—to his present and to his future. As the *Iliad* ends with Priam and Achilles meeting across the lines of enmity and murder in a relation of momentary sympathy and equality, recognizing their common humanity, so the *Odyssey* ends with Odysseus meeting Eumaeus and Penelope across the lines of status and gender, recognizing their common humanity and doing so in the deepest form of friendship. This is where human excellence and fulfillment ultimately lie, not in the conquest of Troy or the exploration of the world: not in object relations, but in human relations.

This I think is the point of the scene in Odysseus' second voyage to the underworld, in which Achilles and Agamemnon compare their lives, lives that have ended so differently with such different meanings—Achilles with a noble death, Agamemnon with an ignoble one. Agamemnon wishes he had died in Troy, ending his story there in prosperity and glory. But this emphasis on the ending of life, the ending of the story, is qualified at the same time it is uttered: For what does even the greatest success, the greatest ending, give a person? Achilles would rather be the lowest of men, a slave or a serf, than a king in the land of the dead; what gives him joy is not his own honor but the successes of his still-living son, Neoptolemus. It is in the world of uncertainty, of human life blessed as it is cursed by mortality, that human satisfaction can exist, that the meaning of human life can be faced; and it resides not in accomplishment, in the linear story of success or failure, but in the relations we have, the communities we make, with others. Its virtues are those of Eumaeus and Penelope, swineherd and woman, with whom it is the greatest achievement of Odysseus to move into harmony and understanding.

To shift now from the story of Odysseus to the poem itself, it is striking that Homer can use the resources of epic in such a way. For this poem is entirely composed in a distinctive art-language the function of which is to celebrate heroic life of the kind represented in the *Iliad,* the world Odysseus find he must leave. Even more important, the poetic conventions of epic do not lend themselves to the representation of interior life, certainly not to inner transformations. At no point does Odysseus tell us that he is experiencing transitions and anxieties of the kind I describe above; yet if my reading is right, Homer finds a way to make us see these things, though his language cannot express them directly. He makes us see an inner life, and even more re-markably—in the relation between Penelope and Odysseus—a shared inner life.

For us to recognize this, we have to see Odysseus himself, like Thoreau and Huck, as something of what I have called a "writer," and this both in the story of his travels, which he tells to the Phaeacians, and in his conversation with Penelope. In both instances what he says enacts a re-imagining of the world, of the self, and of others. By the end of the poem his prior self, like the world that once gave his actions meaning, has no place. This is dramatized for us when, at the very end, the parents of the dead suitors threaten to attack Odysseus. Homer does not give us another battle, but cuts it short with the intervention of Athena. For by this time such a battle would have nothing of the heroic in it; the time for that is totally in the past, psychologically irrelevant.

At the end Odysseus is no longer a superman—indeed he has turned his back on that possibility in rejecting Calypso—but a man, and the story of the poem is his movement to, and acceptance of, that condition, with all that it means, including especially his relation with Penelope, a woman, who is his full psychological and intellectual equal. This gives new meaning to the opening words of the poem: "Speak to me of the man, who . . ." *(andra moi ennepe).*

č

Pelham School was a community marked by extraordinary self-love; it idealized itself, and did so successfully. There was no reason for anything or anyone to be defective in this beautiful place, a utopia set aside from the world. Here every facility, every attention, we could want was offered us, and we were introduced to our culture in the most high-minded way. We went to the Friday afternoon symphonies in Boston, and occasionally to the Fine Arts museum; we learned languages (Latin, French, and either German or Greek were required); we had plenty of books and a wonderful reading room in the library, with great casement windows, a huge fireplace, a balcony, and comfortable chairs in alcoves; and best of all, well-educated, kind-hearted, and well-mannered grown-ups with whom to be and to talk. The idea of the School was not that it forced its students through a set regimen, as a kind of competitive academic training ground, but that it made the widest range of opportunities available to them, so that when an impulse struck a particular boy there lay before him the art studio or the athletic facilities or the woods or the library, or the teacher ready to teach him about biology or poetry or drama, in a special class if necessary. The aim was not so much training as growth, and it was understood that slack periods, failures, and poor performances were a healthy part of that process.

For me perhaps the best single thing about Pelham was that I learned to regard reading, and intellectual life more generally, not as a duty but as a pleasure, and as a pleasure of a deep and natural kind, related in fact to the pleasures of the woods. Reading connected my emotional world, and my sense of nature, with a cultural world, and it did this not in the usual academic way—in which the mind becomes an instrument of competition—but by connecting the mind to the person as a whole, to the desire for friends and to the pleasure of imagining.

The same year I discovered Walden I bought a small book of Wordsworth's poems, which brought nature and literature together in a somewhat different way. They helped me to find in reading what I had theretofore found only in nature. I memorized many of the poems, which seemed to be about the kind of feelings I had when I walked down the dirt road to the river in the spring, through the woods just green, or crossed a November field, brown and gray beneath the marbled sky, or sailed in the sun in the summer. Culture could appropriate and transform nature, and make it available on the page.

At the top of Pelham's cultural scale was Greek. The School was founded on the English model, and naturally looked to England in the first instance as its cultural standard; but the English Victorian upper-middle class that Pelham admired itself looked to Greece, which was the fountain of all that was best in the world. Thus when I labored through twenty lines of Homer or a page of Plato I felt in touch with something immeasurably valuable. Latin was almost as good, and I remember with pleasure one June day studying Cicero, with two friends, in a great grassy field beside the woods, all of us in our neckties and jackets despite the heat, and feeling that this was an education.

Pelham offered a language that was said to be adequate to all the purposes of life, from religion to sports to intellectual life to a career to politics, a language that integrated everything. Its key term was "gentleman"; its basic ground was a combination of a certain kind of Christianity with a class, a style, a tone. For various reasons it was not a place where I felt that I naturally belonged, to say the least. But this expansive and generous world, this language for the whole of life, was something I needed, and I absorbed it, was absorbed by it; it was a first experience as an anthropologist and, except for the occasional rebellious marks of difference, I went completely native—as if Odysseus had stayed with the Phaeacians. Pelham seemed to offer a coherent world: one that I could largely understand, and in which I could, some of the time at least, be understood.

But it was in fact not so coherent after all. It excluded the larger social and economic and political world upon which it depended, and which it had no way of criticizing. The Nashua River, for example, on which I rowed so happily, was gray with industrial pollution; this fact Pelham could lament, but not condemn. And, most of all, it was a world I was to leave behind me, at eighteen, never to return, to make my way in another world for which the expectations so carefully shaped at Pelham were all wrong. It was like growing up in a century before my own.

PART TWO

FOUR

Reading Greek: *Autar ho ek limenos*

In the last three chapters we have been exposed to three different versions of the human mind trying to locate itself in a comprehensible
world. Thoreau performs wonderfully a crucial first stage, withdraw-
ing to the edge of the culture that he finds dead and meaningless in
order to establish a position from which he can make something new
and valuable, which he does, imagining afresh the whole world and
himself within it, a creator at work in the world of creation. In his
writing he circles and dives and dances like the hawk of which he
spoke, exuberantly performing possibilities of meaning. In doing this
he defines the central activity of his life as expressive; for him writing is literally a struggle for life. Huck Finn, though of course much
younger, represents in the world of the novel that bears his name a
later stage in the development of the imagination and the self: his culture and society, his very language, present him with obstacles to understanding that he can never overcome, or, rather, that he can miracu-
lously almost overcome, but only for a moment, and that moment
without a future. He starts and ends in fundamental confusion, unable to manage the reality of race (who can?), yet between these points
he achieves a relation with Jim in which he can both learn and grow,
moving to a moment of deep and responsive mutuality. Odysseus is the
great confronter of limits: those presented by the military might of
Troy itself, in the first stage of his heroic life; those presented by nature
and monsters and magic and the boundaries of the known world, in
the second; and those presented by time and human difference, working as obstacles to the establishment of relations of understanding and
trust, in the third. He is able to imagine himself and his world afresh
not once but twice, ending at last in a relation of extraordinary intimacy and depth with Penelope.

In all three cases the desire to understand, to make sense, to imagine
coherently includes, or better ripens into, a desire for what Thoreau

would call a sincere relation with another—for friendship, ultimately for love. In Thoreau's case this relation is with the reader, in Huck's with Jim, in Odysseus' with Penelope. This marks a line of thought that will emerge as a central theme of this book, especially in connection with the *Phaedrus*, which is about the nature of love.

But at the moment we shall move in a different direction, towards language, trying to give ourselves some of the experience of being at the edge of a world of understanding and meaning that we have seen in others. Our subject will be the Greek in which the *Odyssey* is composed, which is for none of us a first language, for all of us strange and foreign. As Thoreau and Huck and Odysseus all found themselves on the edges of a world of meaning, we shall deliberately place ourselves in an analogous position. The aim is to establish some sense of what it is like to move from incomprehension to comprehension, from outside to inside, and then to look back on the place from which we began.

The two succeeding chapters build directly on this one: the first looks at a form that is in some respects second nature to us all, the sentence, but in such a way as to make this element of our experience of language the object of self-conscious attention. The next chapter, the longest in the book, turns to Plato's *Phaedrus*, a work that is explicitly about competing ways of imagining the self and the world, both in intellectual life, for the rhetorician or philosopher, and in erotic life, for the lover. We shall read it with attention both to its Greek and to the shape and drama of certain of the sentences in which it is composed. Then, in the final section of the book, we return to English, looking at texts of both poetry and law, with the hope that we can engage with our own languages in a new and better way. In all of this one of my objects, to invoke once more Thoreau's great sentence, is to acquire a fuller sense of a particular distant land from which some of our kindred have written to us.

In asking here what meanings Homeric Greek offers, how they are established, and with what connections to the meanings of other languages, I do not mean to address these questions fully, for that would be a life's work, but to do so suggestively or in outline, as one might sketch out the major features of an island or valley one had visited, as a way of telling others something of what they might expect when they went there themselves. Even this will be a difficult process, asking a different kind of work from both writer and reader. In particular, to develop some shared sense of a foreign language will require us to move at a more deliberate pace.

Different readers will naturally wish to work through this chapter with different degrees of intensity. Some will want to puzzle through every question, every new piece of information; others will want to read more quickly, perhaps to come back to it later; but all, I hope, will acquire some idea of the reality and particularity of the language Homer spoke.

Alphabet and Writing

If you turned to a page of Greek with the aim of learning to read it, the first thing that would strike you is the alphabet. The writing would seem foreign, and it would make the language seem foreign too, as Latin for example is not; just as the street signs of Athens today may make the anglophone visitor feel that she is in a place more foreign than the perhaps equally unintelligible street signs in Rome or Amsterdam do. In another sense, of course, the Greek alphabet is not so very different from ours: it is close to the Roman, and both are based on the same Phoenician script. Yet in my experience, the sense of the alien does not ever wholly disappear; the very forms in which the language is written continue to mark its difference. This effect makes palpable and visible what would in any case be true, that two languages can never be written the same way, even if the alphabet is apparently the same, for the sounds are deeply different. Think how misleading it is to say that French is written in the same alphabet as English, for, although the letters are mostly identical, they invoke and stimulate very different sounds. To learn to read French you must unlearn as much as you learn.

A related point is that writing itself, and what we might call "publishing" too, were very different for the Greeks from anything we know. In teaching the *Iliad* or *Odyssey* to freshmen I like to ask what relation they think the book they have in their hand has with the poem as originally composed. The book, after all, is in English, not Greek; it is a book, not an oral performance, and it was published in the twentieth century. Upon what actual Greek texts can it be based, with what connection to whatever Homer said or wrote or sang? There are enormous spaces, only tentatively bridged, between what we have and what he did, spaces that the very form of the book, its claims to represent the original in English, necessarily obscure or deny.

No one knows the conditions of literacy that obtained when the *Odyssey* was composed, say in the middle of the eighth century. Perhaps that was a wholly oral world; perhaps writing had just come back to Greece—for it had existed, in another orthography, under the Minoans and Myceneans five hundred years before—and perhaps its first important use was to record the Homeric poems. We do not know. But we do know that in the world of fifth-century Athens, when writing had become common, it had a different quality and function from anything we would recognize in our world. Texts were written entirely in capitals, without word breaks or punctuation. They were made not for quick silent reading, but for slow reading aloud. A written text was really a kind of performance tool or memory aid, as remained largely the case until after the invention of printing.[1] One can think, for example, of the speech of Lysias that Phaedrus, in Plato's dialogue of that name (which is the subject of chapter 6), is trying to memorize for purposes of display; or of the fact that litigants in Athenian courts would themselves deliver speeches written by others, having committed them to memory; or of our texts of Aristotle, which seem to be lecture notes, either his or a student's, rather than composed texts. This was a world of speech, not writing: in conversation, in the theater, in the assembly, in the law courts, in the marketplace itself.

The composition of the Homeric poems was, as I say, an even more obviously oral process. It is true that the very early Greeks had writing, at least for purposes of trade and government, as the decipherment of some texts from thirteenth-century Crete has shown. But this was in a syllabary unrelated to the later Greek alphabet. At the first time for which we have substantial written records the control of the Aegean Sea had apparently shifted from the Minoans of Crete, of non-Indoeuropean culture—for whom the Greek fortresses on the mainland were apparently subject outposts, and to whom the Greek language and culture were of secondary importance—to the Myceneans, based of course on the mainland, who were speakers of early Greek. After the collapse of both the Minoan and the Mycenean worlds, and the Trojan War—say in the twelfth century—Greece fell for centuries into what is known as the dark ages, during which the art of writing was entirely lost. This is the same period in which the epic developed, the poetry that sang of the exploits of the heroes of the Trojan War, and it was necessarily oral in nature. By the time of Homer, maybe in the eighth century, the language in which his poems were written was a fully developed instrument of oral composition, designed for the description and celebration of the heroic world that

1. In the early history of English publishing, for example, there were no agreed conventions as to spelling; this was not a piece of primitivism, to be patronized by us, but represented the priority of the spoken over the written word. If the function of writing was to recall the spoken word to mind, why would it matter whether this was done with exactly the same letters every time?

was now far in the past.[2] It is this language and the culture it is designed to represent that the *Iliad* and the *Odyssey* transform, the *Iliad* by using it in such a way as to subject its basic value commitments to criticism, the *Odyssey* by extending it to include very different kinds of material, and with ultimately very different human values. The swineherd, for example, is in a sense a precursor of Huck's Jim: a person generally regarded as a complete inferior who turns out to have certain virtues in a higher degree than almost anyone else.

This history has many consequences for the meaning of the poem as we apprehend it. For one thing it helps explain the enormous clarity and precision with which the worlds of these poems are represented; this is I think partly the effect of the fact that the audience of this poetry gradually grew more and more remote from the world it described, and therefore required increasing fullness and specificity of representation. Perhaps in the earliest versions the poets were singing of what had happened only a generation or two earlier, and they could rely on their audience's sense of context; but five hundred years later the audience of the poems was almost as remote from the world they describe as we ourselves are. Thus, I imagine, the poets naturally included more and more of the context of the events they describe, where necessary using invention to do so. One effect of this kind of composition is a simple vividness, making accessible what might be obscure; another is a moral or attitudinal quality, Homer's famous acceptance of all things human, his extraordinary generosity of attitude. For him in writing the *Iliad,* and for us in reading it, the Trojan is just as real as the Greek; this perception of common humanity is in fact the fundamental ethic upon which its criticism of the heroic culture rests.[3]

---

2. One of the strongest arguments for orality of composition is the formulaic nature of the language itself, described briefly at page 98 below, which was evidently designed to facilitate oral composition by giving the poet sets of metrically appropriate phrases with which to build his verse. On the other hand, we know that writing came to Greece at roughly the time we believe the poems reached their final form. It is possible, then, that the last stages of the tradition before Homer involved writing, or that the Homeric poems themselves were written as they were composed. For a fresh view of Homer's language, see Egbert Bakker, *Poetry in Speech: Orality and Homeric Discourse* (Ithaca: Cornell University Press, 1997), discussed below at page 100.

3. For the classic statement, see Simone Weil, "*L'Iliade ou la poème de la force,*" Cahiers du Sud (Dec. 1940–Jan. 1941), reprinted as "The Iliad, Poem of Might," in *The Simone Weil Reader,* ed. George A. Panichas (Mt. Kisko, N.Y.: Moyer Bell, 1977), 153. I build upon this essay in my chapter on the *Iliad* "Poetry and the World of Two: Cultural Criticism and the Ideal of Friendship in the *Iliad,*" chap. 2 in *When Words Lose Their Meaning: Constitutions and Reconstitutions of Language, Character, and Community* (Chicago: University of Chicago Press, 1984).

Another feature of the poems that this history helps explain is a certain reversal of a modern reader's expectations that takes place as soon as one starts to read the Greek. We are usually trained to see these two poems as the beginning of something called Western civilization, the first stage of emergence from a primitive state; but in actually reading them one quickly sees that this is not how it looks from the point of view of the poems themselves, which are backward-looking, elegiac in tone. They come not at the beginning but at the end of a civilization, one that lies now in the remote past; what compensates for the loss of greatness, of the drama and importance and dignity of the heroic world, is the art of poetry itself; and this is as far from primitive as it is possible to be.

To return now to the question I ask my freshmen, it is plain that the relation between what we read and whatever Homer did is enormously problematic. Usually the science of textual criticism is meant to reproduce as closely as possible the original written text of the work in question. But here it is not clear that there was ever "a" written text, indeed that Homer ever wrote anything at all, or indeed that there was one poet who composed either poem out of the inherited materials I have described. Working back in time along the line of manuscripts and papyri, then, we aim at a very uncertain target; perhaps what was established as the canonical form of the poems in the fifth century, or even the third by the great scholars of Alexandria. Moving the other way, from the remote past to the point of composition, we realize that our target is equally obscure, and in important ways unattainable: we do not know how the poetic tradition was maintained, by what sorts of poets, performing on what sorts of occasions before what sorts of audience; we do not know whether the poems were said or sung, assuming that there is a large difference in as musical a language as Greek probably was; and, as my last remark suggests, we do not really know how ancient Greek was pronounced. In particular we do not know how far it was a tonal language, as the accent marks inherited from the Alexandrians (for whom they were presumably necessary) tend to indicate, or how the tone system worked. We do know that these poems are written in verse, and can reconstruct the basic elements of the prosody (which is dactylic hexameter based on the quantity or length of syllables); but the interaction of this music with that other music implied in the accentual system, let alone with the music of the lyre, which was apparently an accompaniment, is completely beyond us.

These are enormous losses: of sound, of accompaniment, of audience, of social occasion, and of the role, status, and training of the poet. Yet by the miracle of writing we have something, of which we can make some kinds of sense. The question is how we do this. In the preceding chapter I gave one possible reading of the *Odyssey* as a whole. Now I want to ask about what it means as it is read, in Greek, line by line, with a focus both on the way its special form of Greek works as a source of meaning and on the structure and significance of one of its sentences.

The Sentence and Some Translations

I shall carry out this investigation with reference to a single sentence from the *Odyssey,* chosen nearly at random. I once told a friend about the moment, referred to briefly in chapter 3, when the poet addresses Eumaeus directly, in the second person. My friend was fascinated by this, and interested in Greek, so we decided to work our way to the point of that gesture from the beginning of the book in which it can be found, which is Book 14. We began with the opening sentence of that book, and spent many weeks talking about it: he was teaching me how to think about a language, I was teaching him about Greek. We in fact never got beyond that simple sentence. So this can be taken as a sentence without special dramatic or literary qualities, a typical or average sentence, if there is such a thing, that can represent something of the experience of reading the *Odyssey.*

In approaching this sentence it is important to remember that Greek, like Latin, is a highly inflected language. By this I mean that individual words change their form to reflect their role in the sentence and in the thought, far more than in English. Thus every noun is placed in a "case," as grammarians say, that tells us whether it is the subject of the verb, or the object, or the indirect object, or the agent of a passive verb, and so on; this means that you know something about its role in the sentence wherever it may appear. Every adjective that modifies a noun is inflected to "agree" with that noun, and this means that the two words do not have to be placed next to each other to establish the connection between them. Every finite verb has endings that tell you whether the actor is one person or more, and whether the actor is the speaker, the person addressed, or a third person; whether the action takes place in past, present, or future time; whether it is continuative, punctual, or completed; whether it is a simple description of a fact (indicative) or expressive of hopes, fears, wishes, or commands (modal). And so on. None of these words can appear "bare," without any syntactic indicators, as "house" or "person," say, can in English. The effect of such a structure is that it makes possible a different kind of sentence, and a different kind of thought, from anything that we do in English.[4]

By the point at which our sentence occurs, at the beginning of Book 14, Odysseus has been brought by the Phaeacians to Ithaca, and met Athena, whom he has tried to trick. She of course saw through him, though with pleasure at his skill, and has given him her encouragement and advice. Now they part: she goes off to Sparta, to find Telemachus, he goes up a path to the hut of Eumaeus. Here is the first sentence of Book 14, in which his movement is described:

Αὐτὰρ ὁ ἐκ λιμένος προσέβη τρηχεῖαν ἀταρπὸν
χῶρον ἀν' ὑλήεντα δι' ἄκριας, ᾗ οἱ Ἀθήνη
πέφραδε δῖον ὑφορβόν, ὅ οἱ βιότοιο μάλιστα
κήδετο οἰκήων, οὓς κτήσατο δῖος Ὀδυσσεύς.

Here is how this might be transliterated into English letters:

autar ho ek limenos prosebē trēcheian atarpon
chōron an' hulēenta di' akrias hēi hoi Athēnē
pephrade dion uphorbon, ho hoi βiotoio malista
kēdeto oikēōn, hous ktēsato dios Odysseus.

4. This is a somewhat more complex matter than I suggest in the text. Here is what I first wrote at this point: "Instead of a sequence of items in order like beads on a string, their relation established by their sequence and by their place in a master paradigm—John hit the ball—such languages permit a thought to begin, to shift direction, to return, all subject to expectations established at the beginning of the sentence, which keep the whole structure open and alive until they are satisfied." But this won't quite work: the sentence I have just written does something very much like what it describes the sentence in an inflected language as doing. It is not that we cannot have our own versions of complexity and suspension in English, for of course we can, but that they work somewhat differently. And at a more particular level the effects achieved in the inflected languages are indeed different from what we can do.

Here is Milton directly imitating Latin forms at the beginning of *Paradise Lost:* "Of man's first disobedience, and the fruit of that forbidden tree, whose mortal taste . . . ." He can now go on forever talking about that tree, and other things too, and we shall know that the sentence has not closed until we get something that meets the expectations of the opening phrase, something like: "Sing, heavenly muse." This is the kind of effect that is second nature in Latin and Greek, and they are often complex and intricate beyond anything we can do in English. For a wonderful example of Latin style in English, see Richard Hooker's *Lawes of Ecclesiasticall Politie* (discussed in "Hooker's Preface to the *Lawes of Ecclestiacall Politie:* Constituting Authority in Argument," chap. 3 of my *Acts of Hope: The Creation of Authority in Law, Literature, and Politics* [Chicago: University of Chicago Press, 1994]).

Here are translations by Chapman, Pope, Rieu, Lawrence, Lattimore, and Fitzgerald:

Chapman:
But he the rough way tooke from forth the Port,
Through woods and hill tops, seeking the resort
Where Pallas said divine Eumaeus liv'd:
Who of the fortunes, that were first atchiev'd
By Godlike Ithacus in houshold rights,
Had more true care than all his Prosylites.

Pope:
But he, deep-musing, o'er the mountains stray'd
Through mazy thickets of the woodland shade,
And cavern'd ways, the shaggy coast along,
With cliffs and nodding forests overhung.
Eumaeus at his sylvan lodge he sought,
A faithful servant, and without a fault.

Rieu:
Meanwhile Odysseus turned his back on the harbour and followed a rough track leading up into the woods and through the hills towards the spot where Athene had told him he would meet the worthy swineherd, who of all the royal servants had shown himself to be his most faithful steward.

Lawrence:
Meanwhile Odysseus strode up the hill-path that climbed straight from the timbered plains into the highlands, the way Athene had pointed him to that devoted swineherd who cared more for his lord's substance than any of the other serfs Odysseus owned.

Lattimore:
But Odysseus himself left the harbor and ascended a rugged path, through wooded country along the heights, where Athene had indicated the noble swineherd, who beyond others cared for the house properties acquired by noble Odysseus.

Fitzgerald:
He went up from the cove through wooded ground,
taking a stony trail into the high hills, where
the swineherd lived, according to Athena.
Of all Odysseus' field hands in the old days
this forester cared most for the estate . . .[5]

5. *Chapman's Homer*, ed. Allardyce Nicoll, vol. 2, The Odyssey & the Lesser Homerica (New York: Pantheon Books, 1956), 241; *The Complete Poetical Works of Alexander Pope,*

When you read these passages you may well wonder what they have to do with each other, or with the Greek. As a way of exploring the second of these questions, I shall first work through the Greek, word by word, seeing it as a piece of a language that in some sense implies the whole. When we have done that, we shall be in a position to turn to the expression itself—the "sentence"—and to the question of its translation.

Reading the Sentence: Word by Word

Αὐτὰρ ὁ ἐκ λιμένος προσέβη τρηχεῖαν ἀταρπὸν
autar ho ek limenos prosebē trēcheian atarpon
Then he from the bay went up the rough path

AUTAR (αὐτάρ)—In Greek it is normal for each sentence to include at or near its beginning a particle that defines the relation of what is about to be said to what has just been said: thus *gar* means that what is about to be said explains what precedes it, *alla* (and many other terms) tell us we are about to hear a countering or adverse position, and so on. Especially common is the pair *men* and *de,* which are often translated as "on the one hand," "on the other hand," or something like that. (It is also true that particles are used in other ways, simply to add intensity, for example, or doubt to the assertion.)

Our question is: How to read *autar*? We are told by Denniston, the great authority on particles, that it is itself most probably a compound of *aute* and *ar,* the first denoting something like "again," evolving into "on the contrary," the second something like "Here is something new and interesting."[6] It is normally read as adversative, either very strongly so ("But . . ."), or gently, even to the point of being a pure progressive, marking the "successive stages of a narrative" (55). Its other form, *atar,* is used with similar meaning, in Homer and elsewhere; Denniston tells us that the choice of one form over another in the poems is dictated by considerations of "metrical convenience" (51)—as here, where the first syllable must be long, as *aut-* is and *at-* is not—and that there is "no distinction in sense" between the two (55).

ed. Henry W. Boynton (Boston: Houghton Mifflin, 1903), 585; Homer, *The Odyssey,* trans. E. V. Rieu (Baltimore: Penguin Books, 1965), 215; *The Odyssey of Homer,* trans. T. E. Lawrence (writing as T. E. Shaw) (New York: Oxford University Press, 1932), 194; *The Odyssey of Homer,* trans. Richard Lattimore (New York: Harper & Row, 1967), 210; *The Odyssey of Homer,* trans. Robert Fitzgerald (New York: Vintage Books, 1990), 247.

6. J. D. Denniston, *The Greek Particles,* 2d ed. (Oxford: Clarendon Press, 1954), 32–33, 55.

Both terms will frequently be found following the particle *men,* answering its assertion of one thing with an adverse movement that is stronger than *de.*

So the grammarians tell us. But what help does this give us in our reading? One possibility is to turn to the preceding sentence, at the end of Book 13, with which *autar* implies a relation, whether continuative or adverse. If we do, we find that it has an unanswered *men:*

... ἡ μὲν ἔπειτα
ἐς Λακεδαίμονα δῖαν ἔβη μετὰ παῖδ' Ὀδυσῆος.

... *hē men epeita*
es Lakedaimona dian ebē meta paid' Oduseos

Roughly translated this reads: "Then she, on the one hand, went to shining Lacedaimon, searching for the son of Odysseus." The next line, in the next book, begins with *autar,* which, like the more familiar *de,* here answers the *men.* The idea is that the two particles, *men* and *autar,* mark the separate ways that the two actors take, Athena in one direction, Odysseus in another.

This is simple enough but it raises large questions. For one thing, we may well wonder whether the break between the books actually belongs here, or in what sense it does, when the last sentence of one book is so closely tied to the first of another. On this point our current understanding is that the poem as originally composed had no books at all; rather it was one long text, carried in the mind, either as a whole or in episodes. It was the Alexandrian scholars of the third century B.C. who made the division; we may therefore remove it, if we wish, from our sense of the text. If we do, we see that in some sense these two sentences form a single unit, one part speaking of Athena, another of Odysseus. This sense is reinforced by the fact that the first sentence begins with the pronoun "she," while the second ends with Odysseus' name, giving the whole the kind of shape and closure associated with ring composition.

What, indeed, tells us that these lines contain two "sentences"? Not the punctuation, which was also a late addition; as originally written down, the text was almost certainly a string of capital letters without word breaks. When we think of the original form of the poem the problem becomes more acute—or more irrelevant—for, as I said earlier, we believe its composition was largely oral.

What then is a "sentence" here? One answer is nothing; "sentence" is our word, not theirs, and it speaks out of concerns that would have made no sense in the world in which this text was made. If we were to look for an analogue to our sentence, we would look not for punctuation or periodicity or perhaps even predication, but for a sense that one unit was marked off from others, itself having a kind of completeness. Here *autar* and *men* become crucial: not useless little words adding unrecapturable flavor, but terms that shape and structure the text, defining the essential units and establishing relations among them.

To turn back to the translations given above: how little of all this does a "but" or "meanwhile" capture!

> Αὐτὰρ ὁ ἐκ λιμένος προσέβη τρηχεῖαν ἀταρπὸν
> *autar ho ek limenos prosebē trēcheian atarpon*
> Then he from the bay went up the rough path

Ho (ὁ)—The next word (as we think of these things) in our unit of expression is an *omicron* with a rough breathing, pronounced something like "haugh," in a clipped fashion. It is used here as a "pronoun," a grammarian would tell us, meaning "he," and it refers to Odysseus. It is marked as masculine and here paired with the feminine form (*eta* with rough breathing: pronounced roughly "hay"), which was used in the preceding "sentence" to refer to Athena.[7]

At this stage of the language these words seem to be demonstrative, meaning something like "this one," "that one." They are in a sense unnecessary, for Greek, like Latin, can simply use the third person singular verb, which implies a singular actor other than the speaker or audience. We could therefore simply have the verb standing alone. Does this mean that the use of these pronouns always marks or emphasizes something? Here the male pronoun seems to work as a kind of complement to the female one in the prior phrase, the gender being the key differentiating feature that tells us that the one going to Sparta is the female, the one going over the hill the male, which the verb alone would not do. This is a use of the pronouns that would work only where the context included a gender difference (difference in number would normally show up in the verb and require no special marking). Elsewhere the pronoun must function differently. We can think of this use of the pronoun then as one item in a repertoire of moves, each possible in its own set of circumstances.[8]

7. The third form is *tau omicron,* pronounced "taugh," which is of course neuter.

8. What appears here as a demonstrative pronoun becomes in later Greek what we call the article, regularly used as in English with nouns, but far more powerfully and significantly as what might be called a nominalizing particle, which can apparently be used with any other part of speech whatever—an adverb, a verb, a clause, anything—to create a subject or object of action.

Think of this word then as a gesture, a kind of pointing out; it is gendered, as all nouns and pronouns are in Greek; here the writer is taking advantage of that fact, and using it to make clear which actor is going in which direction. In a sense the pronoun is not necessary: we could figure out who was going where on the grounds of probability. But here as elsewhere in language there is a lot that is in some sense unnecessary or redundant but helpful; the reader need not work to get it, and his attention can thus be focused elsewhere.

> Αὐτὰρ ὁ ἐκ λιμένος προσέβη τρηχεῖαν ἀταρπὸν
> *autar ho ek limenos prosebē trēcheian atarpon*
> Then he from the bay went up the rough path

Εκ (ἐκ)—"from, out of"; "LIMENOS" (λιμένος): "harbor, bay," genitive of LIMEN (λίμην) (pronounced: leemayn); PROSEBĒ (προσέβη): "went face-forward," aorist of *pros-baino* (*pros* means facing forward, *baino* means go).

It will be useful to treat these three words together because of the way in which they interact. To start with *"ek"*: this is what we call a preposition; it would in many school grammars be said to "govern" *limenos* by determining its case: *"ek* takes the genitive." In Homeric Greek, however, it is the case, not the preposition, that has the primary force. The accusative, for example, regularly marks the limitation of action as well as what we call its "object"; and the genitive, standing alone, can have not only the familiar senses of possessing or being part of but the sense of "out of" or "from" (the sense of the ablative as that case was retained in Latin: the so-called ablative genitive). In Homeric Greek the case of the noun, and its meaning, do the main work; the preposition is not necessary, as it is in English, but in a sense gratuitous or just helpful. If it were missing here, for example, the reader could easily read the genitive, standing alone, as implying motion from.

It is true that the preposition can reduce an ambiguity: without it one might think that *limenos* modified the actor rather than the action and be inclined to read it "he of the harbor." But one would not maintain that reading long where there is no contrast with another "he" (say, "of the mountain"). The *ek* is in this sense a way of making the reading easier, directing attention away from the mild problem of the genitive by resolving it. This may be generally true of what we call prepositions in Greek: we could often do without them and rely entirely on the force of the case, just as in English we rely entirely upon the prepositions and (almost) eliminate case. Greek is here combining both resources in a kind of dance, with a sense of slight superfluity or fecundity.

The dance is complicated by the presence of another preposition here, the *pros* in *pros-ebē,* which is attached not to a noun but to the verb. *Ek* could also have been attached to the same verb—it would then be *ekbaino*—for in Greek what we think of as prepositions (governing cases in the nouns they specify) were originally what we would call adverbs, modifying the verb itself, and they can still perform that function, especially in Homer. The writer can thus choose where to put his "preposition": sometimes he will make it part of the verb, sometimes he will tie it to a noun or pronoun, and with the shift is a change of emphasis or meaning. Thus *pros* could have been carried forward and found with *trēcheian atarpon:* "face-forward towards the rough path." Sometimes, indeed, two "prepositions" will be found together with the verb, piled up like this: *pros-ek* as in *prosekbaino.*[9] Here too we are in the realm of choice not necessity; to begin to see the possibilities of choice we must be prepared to give up our terms *preposition* and *adverb* and try to see how the terms are used, which is very fluidly indeed.

If we start from this point we can begin to see the noun phrase itself as a kind of adverb, for its function is to limit or qualify the action. "What kind of going is this?" we ask; and are told that it is a going "from the harbor," "towards the rough path." Instead of thinking of the noun as a name of a thing, then, as representing on the verbal plane an object in the real or intellectual world, one can see it here as part of phrase that has the character of a gesture. In Homeric Greek perhaps it is right to think of the verb as central, and everything else as qualifying and conditioning it: a world of life and action, not of objects, concepts, ideas. If so, this would be an enormous difference from the way we are taught to think of our own language.

There remains this question: What need do prepositions meet? Since, as I say, the case of the noun does the main work, they can be regarded as grace notes, the verbal equivalent of hand gestures, used to reduce the ambiguities the cases leave us with. They define the relation of a speaker or actor to his environment, locating us inside the action. *Ek* itself: a kind of gesture of the hands, pushing? And *pros,* a sort of facing?

9. These two are in fact never found with *baino,* but they are with other verbs, for example, *ballo* (to throw).

Αὐτὰρ ὁ ἐκ λιμένος προσέβη τρηχεῖαν ἀταρπὸν
autar ho ek limenos prosebē trēcheian atarpon
Then he from the bay went up the rough path

LIMENOS (λιμένος)—As I have said, this is the genitive of *limēn* (λί-μην) (leemayn), and I have discussed the force of that case here. What about the word itself, which we are told means "harbor" or "bay"?

This brings to the surface a question I have touched on above, the origin and nature of the meaning of words. I have suggested that *ho* (pronounced "haugh") is a demonstrative, a pointing out, and that *ek* may be a gesture of another kind, a sort of pushing away. *Autar* may be read similarly, as a kind of shift from one thing to another. These terms can all be traced back to the speech situation itself, as you imagine two people talking and gesturing; one can even imagine hand gestures to go with them.[10] They can be about the language act itself, or can give it more specific or intense meaning. Such terms may in some sense be the primary elements of meaning, contrary to our usual understanding that they are merely ornaments or additions to something else, the heart of the sentence, that uses words that refer not to the speech situation but to the world—words like *limēn* or *atarpon* (path). Our question is: How do these words, the "nouns," get their meaning? Can their meaning be traced back to the speech situation too? If not, to what can it be traced?

Here the first step is to see if we can identify a root in the word that will connect it with others. But about the roots of *limēn* we know rather little. The dictionaries associate it with *leibō*, which means to pour, particularly to pour in drops—compare our "libation"—and with *leimōn*, meaning damp meadow or swamp, and more obviously with *limnē*, meaning lake or pond. All this make a sensible pattern.[11] But in later Greek it means haven, receptacle, and even womb (in line 1208 of Sophocles' *Oedipus Tyrannos*!). These differences probably represent developments since Homer, but we cannot be certain without an adequate record of the early language, which we do not have. It is at least possible, then, that the associations represented in the later uses were also present for the audience of Homer, and if so the word becomes more interesting.

10. In Homeric verse Bakker believes that particles mark what he calls "intonation units," the elements of which the verse is made (*Poetry in Speech*, 49).

11. See, e.g., *A Homeric Dictionary for Schools and Colleges Based upon the German of Georg Autenrieth*, trans. Robert P. Keep and rev. Isaac Flagg (Norman: University of Oklahoma Press, 1958).

Like other terms *limēn* can be used in such a way as to bring to the surface its connections with other terms, its deepest roots—perhaps the gesture of oval enclosure—or it may be used far more routinely, in such a way as to glide over its associations with other words and its own metaphorical life. It is one of the functions of poetry and a certain kind of prose to do the former, and the characteristic of much modern prose—built on the sense of language as indexical, pointing to objects, whether physical or intellectual in character—to do the latter. Which is it here? Odysseus is leaving Athena, not his mother but mother-figure, and setting forth on an adventure of a wholly new kind, for which his prior experience has hardly prepared him. He has just received advice and comfort, like a six-year-old starting school. Perhaps there are indeed senses of wombness here in what he is leaving, or certainly of enclosed safety.

This is a way of thinking about the root of a term not so much as an indexical pointing to a certain class of items, but as a way of generalizing: perhaps the original and still living meaning is not "bay," plus a later "womb" but the more general sense of protective oval enclosure that unites both. (Perhaps the closest English word would be "haven.") We are habituated, as Whorf has told us, to think that the natural direction of language is from the physical to the spiritual or intellectual; first we have objects, then "ideas." But this is not necessarily so: perhaps sometimes in our language we first have ideas, and only gradually concretize them in various ways.[12] This does not mean that we don't live in a physical world, for of course we do; but that what occasions language, what calls for speech, may not be naming of things—we can point after all—but a sense of their meaning for us. The historically first meaning may thus be what we call metaphorical, not what we call literal; or, to put it the other way, the "literal" meaning may be general, attitudinal, spiritual, not material or indexical. "Enclosed safety": *limēn*.

I mean this line of thought as suggestive only, and I suppose that the probabilities run against it. But I want to include it here as an example of a kind of speculation that seems to me useful if only because it breaks down the sense we are otherwise all too likely to have that we can in an easy way understand the words of another language. They are always used in contexts from which they get much of their meaning and of which we have an imperfect grasp.

---

12. See Benjamin Lee Whorf, *Language, Thought, and Reality,* ed. John B. Carroll (Cambridge: MIT Press, 1956), 156–57.

Αὐτὰρ ὁ ἐκ λιμένος προσέβη τρηχεῖαν ἀταρπὸν
autar ho ek limenos prosebē trēcheian atarpon
Then he from the bay went up the rough path

PROS-EBĒ (προσέβη)—"went face-forwards." Here the verb is a compound of *pros* with *baino,* which has *ebē* (pronounced: ebay) in its most common past tense form, which grammarians call the second (or "strong") aorist.

The verb in Greek is especially rich, offering the writer or speaker a wide range of significant variations, along several axes. *Prosebē* is marked for past time, but not only that, for there are several different ways in Greek to locate an action in the past: the "imperfect" *(prosebaine),* which is progressive or continuative in meaning, and might thus be translated "was going"; the aorist, reproduced above, which expresses a sense of single action, at a point in time; and the perfect *(prosbebēke)**, which is perhaps better thought of as a form of the present than the past, for it would mean "has for some time been going, no longer is, and is now in the condition of having completed his action."[13] These differences in what is called "aspect"—continuative, punctual, perfective—are powerfully felt in Greek, especially the continuative and perfective.[14] It may thus be right to read the Greek verb as in general much more heavily marked for aspect than for time: it is the aspect that does the main work, or in which the speaker and hearer are most interested. This is of course a difference from English, as is the subordination of the force of the preposition to that of the case. For with us, time is almost everything; for the Greek, aspect.

The other major choice made by Homer in the form of the verb is to place it in the "indicative mood," which is the form used for describing actual events in the real world. There are two other main moods, subjunctive and optative, both of which add to the statement an ingredient of the speaker's feeling: hope or fear or wish or sense of possibility or probability. Here this choice is not heavily marked, for the use of one of the other moods would be improbable, given the role of the poet as storyteller.[15]

13. The perfect form does not exist in our texts but a past perfect does, *prosebebēkei,* which would locate this moment of completed action in the past.

14. The aspect system overlaps the tense system of past, present, and future in this way: the continuative and perfective aspect occur in all three tenses, the punctual only in the past, except for occasional uses in the future passive. (The mark of past time is the "augment," usually as here a simple epsilon at the beginning of the word, and it is used in all aspects.)

15. The modal system interacts with both the tense and aspect systems. Only the indicative has tense: thus the augment, marking pastness in each aspect type, is used only in the indicative. The subjunctive and the optative have aspect only, not tense (except in con-

What we have here is *ebē,* pronounced "ebay": past (not present or future), punctual (not continuative or perfective), indicative (not subjunctive or optative).[16]

Αὐτὰρ ὁ ἐκ λιμένος προσέβη τρηχεῖαν ἀταρπὸν
autar ho ek limenos prosebē trēcheian atarpon
Then he from the bay went up the rough path

TRĒCHEIAN (τρηχεῖαν)—a word meaning something like "rough," or "rugged," and like those English words, an adjective. This is the term regularly used to describe Ithaca itself; here it is used for a part of it, with some of the effect of a camera zoom: what is true of the whole is true of this small piece.

The Greek adjective, like the noun, has a standard set of cases—nominative, genitive, dative, accusative, and vocative—both in the singular and in the plural, and in the three genders. This one is in the feminine accusative singular form and thus raises an extremely specific expectation, of a noun that matches it exactly, for in Greek there must be concord in all these respects between noun and adjective. In the more highly elaborate syntax of Greek prose, or later poetry, the matching word might have already occurred in the sentence or might be substantially deferred. Here, however, it comes as the next word, *atarpon* or "path," in keeping with the more open Homeric style, paratactic rather than syntactic in nature, as is perhaps natural in a language made for oral composition.[17]

ATARPON (ἀταρπόν)—this is *a-tarpon,* perhaps from a *trb* root meaning tread or rub, as in our word "tribulation," added to which is an

---

ditions and indirect discourse, where the function of the future seems to be to establish relative temporality). One could put it this way: finite verbs can have mood or tense, not both, but verbs have aspect in all moods and tenses. This too seems to establish the priority of aspect over tense.

16. Our understanding of tense is further complicated by the suggestion, made by Chantraine and others, that the future was originally not really a tense in our sense, that is, a location of definite action in future time, but a mood, in Chantraine's view a desiderative. Pierre Chantraine, *Grammaire Homerique,* vol. 1, Phonétique et morphologie (Paris: Librairie C. Klincksieck, 1958), 440. It makes sense that the indicative not reach the future, if it is thought that the role of this mood—or lack of mood—is to indicate how things are, for the things in question do not exist yet. There is always an element of expectation and judgment, then, in what we call the future, and perhaps this should be reflected in the way we talk about it. See also Guy L. Cooper, after K. W. Krueger, *Attic Greek Prose Syntax* (Ann Arbor: University of Michigan Press, 1998), 1:650–51.

17. One other note: the Attic form of this word would be *tracheian,* with an *alpha* instead of an *eta;* the letter *eta* marks Homer's language as Ionic in origin, that is, as the Greek of the eastern islands and the coast of Asia Minor. Homer's language actually uses a mixture of dialectical forms, Ionic, Aeolic, Cycladic, and perhaps some simple neologisms. One effect of this is to give the poet a large repertoire of nearly equivalent words in slightly

initial *alpha,* which can be either privative (negating) or, here much more likely, intensive (repetitive).[18] On this reading the word means, "the often treaded thing," or what we call a path. (Notice that this noun has its origins in a verb.) Another possibility is that the *tarp* stem comes from *trepo,* meaning turn, and that the *alpha* is privative rather than intensive; in this case the word means, "the not turning thing," or straight way, though it is most unlikely that the path of which we are about to hear is straight. (Once again, the noun comes from a verb or gesture.) In any event, it is feminine accusative singular and thus meets the expectation raised by *trēcheian.*

We have now completed the first line of our passage and another source of meaning is now fully apparent, namely, the verse form into which these words are cast. This is, I said above, dactylic hexameter— that is, six metrical "feet," each either a dactyl (long, short, short) or a sponde (two longs). The items thus patterned by the meter are not stresses, as in English, but quantities. In English we are not much sensitive to quantity, let alone sufficiently so to make it the basis of a system of verse, but we have it, and we can recognize it—compare the way you pronounce the "a" in "bat" and "bag," for example—and good poets writing in English employ this resource too. Against this music of the dactylic hexameter runs another, that of the pitches or tones of Greek, but we can no more than guess at how they sounded.

Our sense of the meaning of this passage is thus deeply impaired, for one source of that meaning, the sound, is almost entirely missing, and with it the interaction between these two orders, the syntactic and the aural. Yet, once more through the miracle of writing, we can see something of the metrical order of the line, even if we cannot sound it as Homer would have done. What we can learn about this meter from data available tells us that it would "scan" this way:

AUTar ho EK limenOS proseBE TRECHEIan atARPon.

It is all dactyls except the fourth foot, which is, as often, a sponde, and the last, which is always two syllables, either a troche, as here, or a sponde (that is, either long–short or long–long). In every line there is

different forms, very useful for one composing poetry. We see something of the same thing in English, when a poet uses an archaic or poetic form—"ne'er"—or asks us to rhyme "wind" with "mind." Another effect may be the sense that this language is the property of no one dialect, no one people, but a panhellenic phenomenon, as befits a panhellenic poem— or perhaps it is expressive of the ambition to be such a poem in the first place.

18. The *alpha* "privative," with negating force, has its origins in the sound "n," and is thus cognate with "in-" or "un-."

a pause or caesura, here I think after *limenos;* the movement of the caesura from place to place in a sequence of lines is one of the means of variation within a form that this prosody allows, and it is often used, sometimes for emphasis or clarification, sometimes simply to change the music. Again we have this in English; our great master of the caesura is Milton, who uses it to make his highly regular decasyllabic line an instrument of variation, full of highlight, stress, uncertainty. In reading Homer, and Milton, one thus finds oneself perpetually asking, Where will the caesura fall this time, and why? The caesura is the kind of thing, like rhyme, that is sometimes enormously significant, sometimes simply the reiteration of a regularity against which the variation, when it comes, will have the force of surprise. Often the placement of the caesura is a matter of judgment or interpretation; it is thus one of the ways in which the reader participates in making meaning.

What is the effect of the caesura here? It separates *limenOS* and *proseBEH,* perhaps thus highlighting both, especially the verb. But I think it has another function too, to mark the interesting similarity between those two words, each of which is a freestanding anapest in a dactylic line; this is a point at which the rhythm of the meter and the rhythm of the words counteract each other, the same way in both words.[19] Here the anapests establish a speeding rhythm that runs into *trēcheian* like a rock, in some sense making us feel the roughness of that rough word more fully.

When the line comes to an end, with it also closes a complete syntactic and semantic unit, for we have subject, verb, and object. It could all stop here, except that we know that we are in the world of epic and that another line will follow. It is in keeping with the style of epic, however, and perhaps related to its oral roots, that the lines often function as complete units; having got to the end of one the poet can start afresh in the next, without syntactic commitments. This verse thus

---

19. This happens in English too, most frequently when a line nominally iambic has key words that are trochaic, setting up a counter-rhythm, as for example in Robert Frost's "Design":

> I found a dimpled spider, fat and white,
> On a white heal-all, holding up a moth
> Like a white piece of rigid satin cloth.

All of the two-syllable words are troches: "dimpled," "spider," "heal-all," "holding," "rigid," and "satin," establishing a pattern that (with two significant exceptions) runs through the poem, putting into question its own claims to an iambic "design."

tends to be paratactic rather than syntactic at the level of the line as well as of the sentence, proceeding, that is, by placing one thing beside another, rather than by defining relations of subordination and super-ordination, in the kind of complex musical tangle that is the stuff, say, of Plato's prose.

The first two lines of Book 14 have another kind of connection, however, for the next line begins by answering a question the reader will naturally have about the path and Odysseus' passage along it: What path, leading where, and how?

> χῶρον ἀν' ὑλήεντα δι' ἄκριας, ᾗ οἱ Ἀθήνη
> *chōron an' hulēenta di' akrias hēi hoi Athēnē*
> Up the wooded country through the heights, to which to him Athena

CHŌRON AN' HULĒENTA (χῶρον ἀν' ὑλήεντα)—this means something like "up the wooded country." The form of the phrase is of interest, for the preposition *ana* comes in the middle, between the word for "country" and the word for "wooded," so the experience of reading it is: (1) "the country," accusative masculine: to the Greek reader this makes perfect sense, for the radical force of the accusative is to mark the spatial limit of action, here indicating where Odysseus "goes"; but for us it is harsh, even incomprehensible. For Greek readers there is really no need of a preposition at all, especially since we have one— and it takes the accusative—as the first element of *prosebē;* (2) but we get one, *ana,* not so much to disambiguate the force of the case, as with *ek limenos,* nor even as a kind of helpful redundancy, but perhaps as a kind of emphasis: this path is indeed "up," as it necessarily would be from the beach of a Greek island to the high ground above it; (3) *hu-lēenta* is the masculine accusative form of an adjective formed from *hulē,* meaning woods, especially wild woods; it is from the same root as the Latin *sylva,* and Dante's *selva,* in "*selva selvaggio.*"

You may have noticed that the last syllables of the noun and adjective do not match, one being *-on,* the other *-enta,* (as was in fact also true, though less markedly, with *trēcheian* and *atarpon*). Is this a violation of the principle of concord between adjective and noun? The answer, at one level, is no: these two words belong to different systems of declension; they both indicate masculine accusative singular, but in different ways; therefore they are in concord. Nonetheless it is true that this is very different from terminations that are identical (both *-on,* for example) where the surface form of the words ties them together. Greek is full of words that have concord but do not seem to, and that seem to but do not, and part of the experience of reading it is living with those filaments of ambiguity, and learning to resolve them.

χῶρον ἀν' ὑλήεντα δι' ἄκριας, ᾗ οἱ Ἀθήνη
chōron an' hulēenta di' akrias hēi hoi Athēnē
Up the wooded country through the heights, to which to him Athena

Dι' akrias (δι' ἄκριας)—This means "through the heights (or peaks)." It is logically and syntactically superfluous, and hence emphasized, as it also is by its position just before the caesura. The sentence itself thus goes on a journey, paralleling that of Odysseus, from the rough path to the woody countryside to the heights, in Greece craggy, over which he will go. In so doing the poet gives us an array of prepositions: *ek, pros, ana, dia,* almost as though it is one of his purposes to show how these words work in relation to each other.

Here as often in reading Homer I have the sense that he is teaching his reader about the resources of his language; in this case about prepositions, elsewhere about the distinctions of meaning between similar sounding words, or about an array of related nouns, or about tense or aspect. Whether this element would have been perceived by a member of his original audience, or is just a feature of language use at its best that one would find, say, in Shakespeare or Swift or Johnson, is for me an open question.

χῶρον ἀν' ὑλήεντα δι' ἄκριας, ᾗ οἱ Ἀθήνη
chōron an' hulēenta di' akrias hēi hoi Athēnē
Up the wooded country through the heights, to which to him Athena

Hēi hoi Athēnē (ᾗ οἱ Ἀθήνη)—A complex moment: *hēi* is the dative of the feminine singular relative, meaning "to which or whom" or "at which or whom," or something like that, always with the recognition that it refers to a feminine person or noun. What is its antecedent? It must be a feminine singular noun, and the only one so far in the sentence is *atarpon,* or path. Thus: "to which path" or perhaps "along which path." But there is another possibility, for this word has also come to have a spatial meaning, "at which place" or "where." Both readings are possible, in a sense both present, and the text does not force a choice between them.

Hoi is the dative masculine singular of the personal pronoun, possibly referring here to the *chōron,* or country, or the *limēn* or bay, or to Odysseus himself. There is no way at the level of grammar to prefer one to the other, but by looking to the meaning of the words we can guess that it is far more likely Odysseus than either of the other candidates to whom—that is the force of the dative—Athena will say or do something. We can now see that the poet has given us another clue to this, at the surface of the language, at the point at which the existence of Odysseus was made explicit by the syntactically unnecessary *ho*. While *hoi* would perhaps be clear enough without it, the presence of the *ho* now has a kind of meaning that we could not have then foreseen, for it makes the reading of *hoi* easier.

What did Athena do or say to or for "him"? The line concludes without answering the question, thus carrying us over to the next by the force of syntax, as the first line, ending a complete syntactic unit, did not.

> πέφραδε δῖον ὑφορβόν, ὅ οἱ βιότοιο μάλιστα
> *pephrade dion uphorbon, ho hoi ßiotoio malista*
> pointed out the godlike swineherd, who for him the livelihood especially

PEPHRADE (πέφραδε)—This means something like "pointed out." It comes from *phrazo,* meaning declare, advise, pronounce; it is past aorist indicative, which means that it is punctual rather than progressive. It is active, meaning that it allows for the possibility of an object, here the indirect object, *hoi,* the person to whom she is speaking.

DION UPHORBON (δῖον ὑφορβόν)—Both are masculine singular accusatives. The first is an adjective meaning something like "bright" or "godlike," used as a term of general or unspecified admiration, most often of heroes. It was most recently used in the last line of the preceding book to characterize Sparta. The second word means "swineherd," coming from *hus* or *sus,* meaning pig (our "swine" and "sow"), and *phorbos,* from *phorbē,* meaning food or fodder. There is here, then, a startling conjunction of a term of heroic praise with a most unheroic object; this alerts us to the transformation of value that will soon give Eumaeus, and Odysseus' relation with him, such a prominent position in the poem.[20]

The use of *dion* is heavily marked in another way, not obvious to our ear but clear enough I think to those who lived with the *Iliad* and

---

20. What is the relation between this phrase and the verb "point out"? It looks like a direct object, marking as the accusative typically does the limit of the action (here verbal); the clause would thus translate, "along which Athena pointed out to him [the way to] the godlike swineherd."

the *Odyssey* as the basic texts of their culture. The word is normally used, with a proper name, as part of a phrase closing a line, as in *Nestora dion* (godlike Nestor) or *Mentora dion* (godlike Mentor). This final use is even more markedly pronounced with respect to the nominative *dios*, which has been used by now in the poem about fifty times, and will be used another fifty times, in every one of which, with a single exception, it is used as part of a phrase closing a line, most commonly *dios Odysseus*.[21] The nonfinal use in our passage, at the first introduction of Eumaeus, thus stands out as a highly significant variation from an established pattern. And the significance of this phrase is confirmed by the fact that several more times in the course of the poem the final formula, associated so strongly with Odysseus, will be used with Eumaeus himself: *dios uphorbos*. And it is only in the case of Eumaeus that this adjective is used not with a proper noun, but with the word for his status and activity, *huphorbos*. All this supports at the level of diction and placement the view taken in the last chapter, that despite his status Eumaeus is to be seen as one of the heroes of this poem, a center of value transforming the values of the earlier heroic world.[22]

Next we take two whole phrases together: HO HOI BIOTOIO MALISTA KĒDETO OIKĒŌN, HOUS KTĒSATO DIOS ODYSSEUS (ὅ οἱ βιότοιο μάλιστα κήδετο οἰκήων, οὓς κτήσατο δῖος Ὀδυσσεύς). "Who eminently cared for his source of livelihood, more than all the servants

21. For the instances of use see Henry Dunbar, *A Complete Concordance to the Odyssey of Homer,* rev. and enl. Benedetto Marzullo (Hildesheim: Georg Olms Verlag, 1971).

22. Others have read *dion* differently—as a way of mocking the low-class Eumaeus, for example—though this seems impossible not only as a matter of general tone and attitude, but because the later uses of the epithet tend to come at moments where he displays important and real virtues. Another possibility is that this reflects his noble birth, for as he says he was kidnapped into serfdom rather having been born in such a status, but this too seems a weak basis for such a pronounced honorific. Others have suggested that it is compelled by metrical requirements, or that the epithet has become stale, really meaning nothing more than that its object belongs to the epic world. (For references and helpful discussion, see Alfred Heubeck and Arie Hoekstra, *A Commentary on Homer's Odyssey* [Oxford: Clarendon Press, 1990], 2:192.) All these are possibilities, but I think this is a case where the epic language is used in a highly significant way, deeply related to the central theme of the poem, which redefines human excellence to include not only the hero but the swineherd, the child, and the woman.

The special status of Eumaeus is confirmed by the feature that brought my friend and me to these lines in the first place, the fact that the poet addresses him several times in the second person. This may be the remnant of an old formula, it may be partly dictated by metric considerations; but in my view it remains a highly salient gesture expressing the real worth and importance of this person of very low status indeed.

whom godlike Odysseus acquired." The initial *ho* is exactly the same word that referred to Odysseus in line one; but there it functions as a demonstrative, meaning "that one," here it is a relative. There we would translate it as "he," here as "who"; the operative difference between the two situations is that in the first we have a word, *autar,* that marks the beginning of one independent syntactic unit, or what we call a sentence, and the end of another, while here we do not. This fact led those who prepared the text to punctuate it accordingly, with a period before the *autar,* starting a new sentence, and with a comma before the present *ho,* which does not do so but instead begins what we would call a relative clause. It is worth stressing what this means: the poet can, at his option, either stop at *dion uphorbon* and commence a new sentence with *ho,* plus a particle—perhaps *de,* meaning "and" or "but"—or he can use the same word *ho* as a relative, in a clause that is identical to the new sentence we imagined above, except that it will have no sentence-marking particle.

To whom does the *ho* refer? It could be either Odysseus or the swineherd; since *uphorbon* directly precedes it, the latter is far more likely. This is not certain, however; the juxtaposition simply provides a strong presumption to be tested in what follows.

The *hoi* we have also met, in the preceding line, as the dative of the pronoun "to him," in this case almost certainly Odysseus. Why dative? We do not yet know. *Biotoio,* which has as its root *bios,* the word for "life," means something like "means of life" or "source of livelihood": whatever it takes to maintain existence, in this case a generalization of the swine for which it is the special task of Eumaeus to care. This word is in the genitive: Why? We do not yet know. *Malista:* an adverb meaning "especially" or "eminently." *Kēdeto:* third person singular aorist indicative of a verb meaning "care for"; it regularly takes a genitive object, hence, we can now see, the genitive *biotoio;* the dative can serve, as the genitive usually does, as the case of possession, hence *hoi,* meaning "his." Thus: "who cares for his means of livelihood . . . ."[23]

κήδετο οἰκήων, οὓς κτήσατο δῖος Ὀδυσσεύς.
kēdeto oikēōn, hous ktēsato dios Odysseus
cared for than the servants whom godlike Odysseus acquired

23. If *hoi* were genitive too, it would create an ambiguity as to which word was really the object of *kēdeto.* We could still work through the sentence relying on the context to clarify things; it is much more likely the "goods of him" that the swineherd cares for than "him of the goods." But Homer saves us that step; the dative is at least in part motivated by the desire to reduce ambiguity, to make connections more clear.

Oikēōn (οἰκήων)—This is the genitive plural of a word meaning "household servant." Why genitive plural? This requires reading back over the sentence; the best connection is with the *ho,* thus creating a phrase meaning "he of all the servants." By grammarians this is called the partitive genitive. But the genitive is also used in comparisons: in "she is more handsome than he," the "he" would typically be the genitive singular. Is there a comparison in our passage? There is no explicit word meaning "more than," and thus invoking the genitive, but *malista*—"especially" or "most"—suggests the idea of comparison, for there must be some others in relation to whom this observation is made. (If I say, "he ran very quickly," there is no explicit comparison, but there must be others who establish the standard I am implicitly invoking.) The *malista* thus provides a second justification for the genitive, slightly overdetermining it; this in turn makes up to some degree for the uncertainty that this genitive plural at the end of the phrase otherwise stimulates, for we have two hooks on which to hang it, different in syntax but expressing the same deep idea. "He of all the servants; he especially of all the servants; he more than any of the servants."

More than that, we can now see that the partitive genitive, in this case at least, has a comparative element, and that the distinction between these two forms may be too crude. Not competing constructions, each of which justifies the genitive, then, but a single construction, uniting what we separate into partitive and comparative. This is another moment at which Homer seems to be teaching us his language.

Hous ktēsato dios Odysseus (οὓς κτήσατο δῖος ᾿Οδυσσεύς)—*Hous* (pronounced: "hoos") is the masculine plural accusative of the relative, "which" or "whom"; in this case it plainly refers to the *oikēon,* which is the only available masculine plural and in addition immediately precedes the relative. *Ktēsato* is the third-person singular aorist indicative of a word meaning "acquire," directly paralleling its near-rhyme *kēdeto,* or "care for." The last two words tell us that it is Odysseus who acquired and owned or possessed, and that he—like Eumaeus— is *dios,* meaning "bright" or "godlike." The similarity in structure and sound between the two verbs establishes and emphasizes a parallelism and contrast between the two activities and between the actors: it is Odysseus who "acquired" the servants; of them, it was Eumaeus who "cared for" his livelihood. The use of "acquired" *(ktēsato)* is odd in Greek, as in English, for one would expect "owned" or "possessed" or maybe "had acquired." Perhaps this slight awkwardness, like the similarity of sound, is meant to mark the difference between the activities of "acquiring" and "caring for," perhaps even to suggest a moral preference for the latter. If so, a hierarchy of property and status is here contrasted with an implied hierarchy of merit, on which the *dios uphorbos* ranks in some sense higher than his owner; a fact that will soon be confirmed socially, when Odysseus comes to his hut as a suppliant, to be received with a hospitality that is in moral quality noble and generous, however simple in material form.

Learning Greek

You may feel that this series of comments on a single "sentence" does not give you much sense of Greek as a whole, and of course it does not. On the other hand, you may be surprised to discover how much Greek you now know, if, for example, you try to translate this sentence into English.

Take *autar,* for example: What possible word do we have that will catch the simultaneously adverse and fulfilling relation *autar* has with the *men* in the preceding sentence, distinguishing Odysseus from Athena but seeing their action as at the same time conjoint? "Meanwhile" or "and" are hopeless. And we lack what *autar* presumes, the sense that a sentence must normally have a particle in its first or second word, defining the relation of what is to come from what has already been said; we have, that is, no sense of a slot here into which *autar* or some other word will fit. Sometimes a Greek writer will not fill that slot either, but when he does his silence has a striking significance.

Ho: not exactly "he," since "he" is implied in the verb; not exactly "that singular male," for one function of *ho* is to contrast with the *hē* referring to Athena in the preceding lines. *Ek limenos:* we have no way to capture the function of the preposition as a disambiguator of case, since with us the preposition does all the work, the case virtually none. In Greek the preposition is a gracious aid to the reader, in English essential to the functioning of the sentence. In fact, except for personal pronouns, we have no explicit cases at all in English, and thus lack the expectation that *limenos* fulfills, namely, that it will have terminations added to its stem that will tell us what kind of relation it has to other words in its unit. And what word do we have that combines the senses of lap and lake and bay, as *limenos* does? *Prosebē:* we have no way to express the sense of the aorist—its punctuality, its service as the standard aspect and tense of narrative, its limitation in the indicative to past time, its wide use in the other moods—nor do we have these floating adverb-prepositions (here *pros*) that can sometimes be tacked on to the beginning of a verb, sometimes appear in connection with a noun, as *pros* does with the *trēcheian atarpon* or ("rough frequently treaded thing").

So what can we say?

> Meanwhile he went out of the bay along the rough path.

Maybe, but awfully thin; and the "meanwhile" invokes for us the genre of the western, and in English it sounds as though he is emerging from the water, not the low places near it.

Chōron an' hulēenta: "up the wooded country" misses the force of the *ana* and of course that of the accusative, which marks the phrase as delimiting the action of the verb. *Di' akrias:* perhaps "through the high places," but our phrase misses what does not have to be specified in Greek, where nature and common observation supply it, namely, that the high places are rough and rocky, distinctly different from the wooded water's edge. Likewise *hulēenta* implicitly conveys to the Greek audience something about the particular kind of trees likely to be found there, and whether woods are the norm or relatively rare (as now), which neither it nor "wooded" does for us. *Hei hoi Athēnē:* here we break down completely. Can we say, "along which (path) or at which (point) to him Athena"?

So our second line can read: "up the wooded country, through the high crags, along which path Athena to him . . . ." Does that do it?

Pephrade dion uphorbon: "pointed out the godlike (or: brilliant) swineherd." That will not do; she cannot see the swineherd, nor can Odysseus; we must insert "the way to." "Brilliant" captures the sense of light in *dios,* but would do better in English than American, for there it tends to mean excellent rather than clever; though in England it has a highly slangy quality that is entirely wrong here. In any event entirely missing is its reiterated formulaic use throughout the *Odyssey,* over and over, to speak of heroes and heroic things, the reiteration that makes this use in connection with the swineherd so significant. And even more completely absent from any possible translation is the surprising location of the term in the line, standing out against all other uses. For a comparable effect we would need to draw a term from a text like the King James Bible, and use it in a surprising way.

Ho hoi biotoio malista: again a breakdown, for we cannot use pronouns in this dense and suspended way. "Who, for (or of) him, of the livelihood, especially . . .": *kēdeto,* "cared for"; *oikēōn,* "of the servants/more than any of the servants," *hous ktēsato dios Odysseus,* "whom godlike Odysseus acquired."

Our translation of the last two lines can be added to the others, thus:

> Meanwhile he went out of the bay along the rough path, up the wooded country, through the high crags, along which path [or at which point] Athena pointed out to him the way to the godlike swineherd, who took care of the livelihood of Odysseus more than any of the other servants whom godlike Odysseus acquired.

But this is all wrong: the original is poetry of the highest order, this the dullest prose; every word of the original invokes uses in the *Iliad* and the *Odyssey,* and the whole worlds of meaning they create—including a sense of an ancient past being brought into the present, a moment of panhellenic unity, the heroic values of glory and reputation, the poetic tradition on which the poet works in transforming ways, and so on. Every word of the translation, by contrast, invokes prior uses in English and American, from Chaucer to Hemingway to the *New York Times,* and in ordinary speech as well.

One language cannot do what another can; the gap cannot be bridged, except by doing what we can to learn the languages of others and to teach others our own ways of thinking and talking, our ways of imagining the world and acting within it. To the extent that the reader can see this to be true in connection with this segment of the *Odyssey,* and can be frustrated by the inadequacies of the translation I offer, or by those presented at the beginning of this chapter, he or she has begun to learn Greek, its modes and ways of meaning. And beginning is all, for one never learns a language perfectly; one is always living at the edge of understanding, at best giving clearer definition to the ambiguities that remain.

One final suggestion might be to return to the translations reproduced above at page 77 and ask what happens when one reads them. Each should evoke in a somewhat different way one's sense of the meaning of the Greek, partly by capturing some of it, partly by failing to do so. The prose translations are in one sense "closer" to what we have done, but they all erase the crucial poetic dimension of meaning.[24]

24. The verse translations try to give some sense of the poetry, but in no case is it remotely like Homer's. In fact these translations are of interest in part for the ways in which they represent different stages in the evolution of English verse, creating a sense of the varying norm that a translation tries to approximate. If today we tried a verse translation into "En-

On the other hand, each of the versions, prose as well as verse, has excellences of its own. To find them wanting is not to say that they are "bad translations," for they are not that, but only to say that they are translations and therefore of necessity wanting. The aim of this chapter is not to produce a better translation, but some sense of the Greek against which all the translations should be read.

I HAVE SO FAR SAID rather little about an important quality of the language of the *Odyssey,* namely, its nature as an art language, especially made for the composition of poetry about the heroic world. No person ever spoke this language as his or her first tongue. As the work of German philologists in the nineteenth century demonstrated to nearly everyone's satisfaction, it is artificial, put together out of several natural dialects—a language fashioned for the purpose of making epic poetry. Milman Parry, early in the twentieth century, saw it as having been designed to facilitate oral composition.[25] One sign of this is its use of variant forms of the same word, permitting the poet to choose whichever term in the array best meets the metrical needs of the moment (as with *autar* and *atar*). Another is what is called the "formula," or phrase of two or more words, cast in metrical forms to permit its ready use. Often there are several different ways of saying virtually the same thing, such as "then he stood up and spoke," among which the poet can choose; sometimes formulae are simply repeated verbatim, without notable equivalents: "and then the desire for food departed from them." How the formulae work more precisely is a subject of contemporary scholarly debate, some of it intense, the intricacies of which we need not explore. But it is worth saying that the paradigmatic formula, the one that gave Parry the idea of the formula in the first place, is the epithet that accompanies a proper name. For each commonly appearing name there is an epithet that will enable the poet to fill out a portion of the line, in fact a different epithet for different locations of the name in the line. Parry's idea was that the poet worked a bit like the old press compositor, who would have at hand what were called stereotypes, putting together words in sequences that were so common that they could be repeated over and over—"balanced budget," "fiscal

glish" it too would be a translation into a particular conception of verse, appropriate to a particular time in our history.

25. Milman Parry, "Studies in the Epic Technique of Oral Verse-Making. I: Homer and Homeric Style," *Harvard Studies in Classical Philology* 41 (1930): 73; "II: The Homeric Language as a Language of Oral Poetry," *Harvard Studies in Classical Philology* 43 (1932): 1.

responsibility," "affirmative action," "family values," and the like—in this case with each name having one epithet and only one for each metrical position. This notion has been shown to be too simple, but the basic idea has force. In the passage before us, the most obvious formula of all is *dios Odysseus,* which occurs over and over again in the *Odyssey.* But to say that is not to imply that its use here is automatic or insignificant, or without art; far from it, since the same word is used of Sparta and of the swineherd, working an affirmation by surprise that captures the central transformation of the poem as a whole.

Finally, I wish to return to the idea of the sentence itself, which I pursue in other contexts in subsequent chapters of this book. It is evident that the segment we have been reading has its own shape, and that part of the meaning of the passage lies in that shape. It tells the story of the passage of Odysseus from the shore, where he is connected to Athena, to the hut, where he will be connected to Eumaeus. In doing so, as I suggested above, it goes on something of a journey itself: from *ho,* referring to Odysseus, to "Odysseus" himself; from one relation to another; across a sequence of prepositions, the relations among which it clarifies; across the significant parallelism between *kedeto* and *ktēsato;* across the contrastive and surprisingly uniting uses of the word *dios;* and so on. The *Odyssey* as a whole tells of a similar journey, on a larger scale; both in the imagined world of the poem, and in the text itself, we have here enacted in small many of the ingredients of the composition at its largest level, perhaps most of all in the powerful use of *dion.* This passage is not just a string of items of information, reducible to a binary system on an atemporal plat, but offers its reader a shaped experience; much of its meaning lies in that experience and shape, a quality that other sentences also share, as we shall see in the next chapter.

But there is a problem with speaking of this segment as a "sentence" at all. As I suggested at the beginning, the division of this "sentence" from its predecessor, like the division of the text into books at this point, may be wrong. We could look at the relevant unit as beginning with the "sentence" that ends the prior book, about Athena going off to Sparta, and there is much to recommend that course: the *men* in that sentence, answered by *autar* in this one; the *ho* (he) here, answering the *hē* (she) of the first sentence; the use of *dios* to refer to Sparta, which will have such resonance in the passage we have read; and so on. Perhaps what we have here is not a sentence marked off from sentence, but syntactic units partly separated, partly joined, in ways that shift significance as the reader proceeds: "Now I see them as two; now I see them as one; now I see them as connected to a third unit, or a fourth," the reader may say. The establishment and modification of such shifting relations, as one climbing a hill sees the valley from which one has come in perpetually shifting ways, may be an essential part of the experience of reading this literature, perhaps of any literature worthy of the name.

This sense of the way this segment works is confirmed by analysis of its syntactic structure. Our expectation of a normal written sentence, in English as in Greek, is that it will consist of a set of parts related to each other by the rules of syntax and grammar, creating a coherent whole. As Egbert Bakker has to my eye quite convincingly shown, in his book *Poetry in Speech,* the Homeric utterance works quite differently, much in the way our own oral speech works, by adding units to units in a running style. Here is one example he gives:

> but *(autar)* he sacrificed a bull
> ruler of men Agamemnon
> a fat one, five years old,
> to the allmighty son of Kronos.[26]

The first unit states the entire action; the next specifies the actor more fully, the third its object, the fourth its beneficiary. The cases of the various nouns and adjectives of course fit with these roles, but there are no syntactic connectors or markers, except for *autar* in the first line. These units are typical of the small units in which we normally talk, shifting attention from one to the other as we work through a narrative or argument; they are also metrical units, for each is a part of the hexameter line. They are not placed in a structure of subordination and superordination, nor are they marked as requiring each other, as often happens in Greek prose.

We can see something of the Homeric method in our sentence. "But this one from the bay went"—that is the basic gesture, and everything else is added on, in metrically appropriate phrases, none logically or syntactically necessary: "down the rough path" "up the wooded country" "through the heights." But there now comes a syntactic complication: "along which Athene pointed," a phrase serving as a new base upon which other units are added: "to the godlike swineherd," "who," "especially of all the servants" "cared for the possessions" "which

---

26. See Bakker, *Poetry in Speech,* 95.

godlike Odysseus had acquired." Analysis of the way this language works is a complex and controversial task; Bakker's analysis seems to work better for the first part of the sentence than the second; but this much I think is clear, that the units of this verse are put together in complex, interesting, and shifting ways that we will misunderstand if we think exactly of them as like those we use when we write English. Of course, in a sense this is a sentence, but it is a sentence composed in real time to be heard in real time, and at every step it is moving its audience's attention from one thing to another; and it does so in a remarkably artful and significant way.

THIS IS OF COURSE only a beginning of a reading of these lines; one could go on and on with respect to each of the grammatical categories, each of the syntactic expectations and connections, each of the lexical items, drawing upon parallel or contrasting instances elsewhere in the *Odyssey,* or the *Iliad,* or the other much shorter pieces of literature from the same tradition that we still have. Out of questions raised by this passage, indeed, one could construct a grammar of Homeric Greek, which obviously I have not tried to do. But what I have done may give some idea of what it is like to work through a passage in Homeric Greek, including some sense both of the language itself, as a system of meaning, and of what working one's way into it involves. The more one works with this language, the clearer it becomes, to me at least, that to speak of "it" as a source of meaning is too restrictive, at least if by "it" one means what can be found in a lexicon and a grammar book: the source of meaning is the language plus the way of reading it that it invites, the kind of life it makes possible, as this is manifested in particular performances. And this can be different, in good ways as well as bad, for different readers, who will bring different suppositions and expectations to the task.

In reading our goal can never be the elimination of all uncertainty of meaning, or the achievement of perfect understanding; the goal is rather the gradual reduction of ambiguity or uncertainty, stage by stage, including the clearer specification of what is uncertain. It is a matter of having questions, and pursuing them as far as one can. There is always a limit beyond which one cannot go, always a sense of the mysterious and unknowable. This is especially true of the Homeric poems, I think, for we lack access to so many sources of their meaning: the medium in which they were presented, as said or sung, with pitch accents and perhaps accompanied by a lyre, the music of which we likewise do not understand; the social and cultural circumstances of their presentation, with a particular speaker, particular audience, particular occasion, all unknown and unknowable (except as described in the *Odyssey* itself); and the prior poetry made in this language, against which each new poem was a performance (except as the *Odyssey* is such a performance against the *Iliad*). What is in the end perhaps most striking about the *Odyssey* is the degree to which it remains accessible to us, despite these omissions, a fact for which, as I suggest above, the *Odyssey* is itself partly responsible, in that it reproduces so much of its context.

What can be meant by excellence in such a domain has been made problematic in our era by the common doubt that such judgments of quality can fairly or intelligibly be made. Matthew Arnold is regularly ridiculed for speaking of "the best that has been thought or said." But for me that language is not far from the mark. One part of the excellence of Homer, and of many other great writers too, is that they can be seen to take as their subject not only a story, or some facts, or an idea, or a value, but the language in which they themselves think and write, which means their culture too. In doing so, they teach us to do likewise, and this is a very great gift. This is certainly true of Plato, who was profoundly alienated from the culture in which he wrote and from the language that expressed and enacted its values, and true of Homer too, who in the *Iliad* and the *Odyssey* alike found ways to subject to criticism the inherited art language in which he wrote, against its own force as an instrument for the description and celebration of a martial and heroic world.

ë

I first started to learn a foreign language the summer I was thirteen, before going to Pelham, when I was tutored in Latin by an old teacher from a private school in Cambridge. I would bicycle to his house through the Cape Cod morning, warm and bright and moist, and sit with him at a table, where I would work through sentences about piratae who were boni or mali, and had pueros and puellas, and sailed in naves. It was an odd puzzle I could never figure out, but an engaging one.

Then, once at school, I remember holding in my hand the ink-stained green Latin grammar book, which I still own, again incomprehensible; or trying to work through a paragraph of

Caesar at night, spending hours looking blankly at the Latin and not understanding any of it; and finally, in a couple of years, catching some of the feel of Cicero and Virgil. Then, starting again with Greek, once more working through the grammar and not quite getting it; reading twenty lines of Homer a night, feeling mystified by the alphabet, the story—what is the "fillet of a goddess," or a "chaplet" or a "wimple"?— and much the same once more with Plato. Then, in college, trying to catch up with those who were ahead of me, finally being able to read Euripides, slowly but as literature, and parts of the Odyssey with something like comfort. Then, starting again ten years later in Boulder, reading first through the *Iliad*, then the *Odyssey*, each taking two years; in Chicago, working both with a teacher and a reading group and reading the *Gorgias*, some Thucydides, some Aristotle, the *Oresteia*, some Lysias, and so on. Finally, starting one more time, with my friend and teacher in Ann Arbor, an hour a week for the last fifteen years.

Reading Greek connects all these times and places in my mind, for it is what I did there; in another sense, however, it erases them, for as I read I inhabit the world of imagination and memory. The page of Greek is no longer, as it once was, an opaque piece of paper with odd marks, over which I labor, but a piece of language, through which another speaks. It carries the mind to a place of the mind, in contact with others across the chasm of time and language. This is the miracle of writing.

FIVE

Making Meaning in the Sentence

The main idea of the last chapter was to involve the reader in the experience of learning a little of a foreign language. Not very much of
course, but enough to see, not just in theory but in practice, that Homeric Greek works very differently from English, and to get some idea
of the way in which it does so. For this language offers its own ways
of imagining the world and the self, its own things to say and do with
words, its own ways of conceiving of human action and motivation. It
creates a world with it own possibilities of meaning. Homer could not
have done what he did in any other language.

If you did not already know some Greek, I assume that at the beginning you felt that this language was opaque, external to your mind,
something incomprehensible, into which you had to work yourself;
but also, by the end, that you felt that this incomprehensibility had
been reduced, if only a little. If so, you have in fact taken the first steps
towards learning this language and understanding its world. Of course
you do not have it all, but then no one has all of a language, even one's
native language. What we mean by knowing a language is really just a
version of knowing how to learn it.

In reading through the passage from Homer, word by word, we
were working out a sense of what we call the meaning of the passage,
negotiating the uncertain terrain between the English into which we
constantly wanted to translate it and the Greek that we increasingly
came to see as not translatable. In this chapter I want to continue to
focus on the process of reading and thinking about language, this time
particularly with respect to passages, mainly in English, that take the
form of what we call the sentence. My interest will be in the way this
form can work as a source of meaning in our language; in the next
chapter we return to Greek, this time that of Plato in the *Phaedrus*,
seeing that much of the meaning of that dialogue can be located in the

life of its sentences, in the experience it offers the reader word by word and phrase by phrase.

This chapter is in part an effort to move from Greek to English without entirely losing the sense of strangeness that the foreign language brings with it. The hope is to make not only Greek, but English too—even language itself—seem at least a bit alien, external to our own minds, and thus to begin to make it the object of our thought. For when we were first learning it as children English was in fact outside our minds, just like the Greek of Homer, and we are still learning it, every day; in this sense the experience of starting to read Greek offered by the last chapter can stand as a kind of representation of language learning itself.

In turning to the form we call the sentence I am continuing in this chapter a movement begun in the last, from considering a whole work as a unit of meaning—the *Odyssey, Huckleberry Finn, Walden*—to the examination of a very small piece of it indeed. This runs counter to a common idea, present in all of us, that the small is simple and insignificant, the large complex and meaningful. But this may be wrong: it may be that when the microscope is brought to it, the small will reveal as great a complexity of structure, and perhaps as great an intensity of significance, as the large. Not that it will simply be a microcosm of the larger structure: many things happen at the level of the work that find no parallel in the sentence; but the reverse may also be true, as it is of the cell in relation to the body. It may be that a sentence will prove to have its own order of significance, with its own limitations and capacities for meaning.

Of course I do not mean to suggest that the sentence is a single form in all languages. Obviously what Homer is doing as he puts his phrases and metrical units together into a whole is both highly artful and very different from what we do in writing English. The sentence has different possibilities not only in different languages—English and Latin, say—but even within English, as we move across time or from writer to writer. One might think of the sentence as a genre, like the sonnet—or more loosely, like the lyric poem or the novel—which exists not as a set of particular instances of a single model but as a family of related but different manifestations, shaped by different languages and different writers.

It is also important that the term is in a real sense a grammarian's invention, not a natural fact. There are many occasions on which people can perfectly comfortably speak their language—any language in the world—without much worrying about whether or not their utterances qualify as "sentences." In the passage we examined in the last chapter Homer himself seems to have paid rather less attention to the sentence as a form than to two other forms that were highly salient for him, the clause and the line. It is not clear, for example, just where the "sentence" in the Odyssey begins or ends, or how one would determine when the expression was "complete." It may be that the sentence as we conceive of it is a function of writing, or of oral expression that is meant to imitate writing, like parliamentary debates. It is a real question, indeed, why we speak of a sentence at all.[1]

Nonetheless it is an interesting fact of Western culture that considerable energy has been given to thinking about this form, and its implications, as it works in several languages. The reasons for this, and some of the effects as well, including on our own minds, are important. There is no eternal law of nature that requires that we talk about the sentence, but we do so. And in our writing and talk we do not in fact produce a series of unconnected clauses but fashion them into what we call sentences, built up by a process of subordination and coordination. How and why do we do this? To many great writers, indeed to whole civilizations, this has at times been a question of crucial importance.[2]

1. One prominent linguist finds the idea of the sentence so ill defined that he employs what to him is the more secure unit, the clause:

> It is usually assumed that the SENTENCE is the highest-ranking unit of grammar, and hence that the purpose of a grammatical description of English is to define, by means of whatever descriptive apparatus may be necessary (rules, categories, etc.), what counts as a grammatical sentence in English. In this way, the terms "grammar" and "sentence" are mutually defining. In the past, grammarians have aimed to define "sentence" as a prerequisite to defining "grammar," or to define "grammar" as a means of defining "sentence." But both approaches will be avoided here: indeed, neither of these terms can be given a clear-cut definition. . . .
>
> The CLAUSE, particularly the independent clause . . . is in many ways a more clearly-defined unit than the sentence. It is for this reason that we shall concentrate, in this and the following nine chapters, on the SIMPLE SENTENCE (*ie*, the sentence consisting of a single independent clause) as the most central part of grammar.

Randolph Quirk et al., *A Comprehensive Grammar of the English Language* (London and New York: Longmans, 1985), 47.

2. In English literary history the moment of sharpest self-consciousness about the shape of the sentence occurred during the Reformation, when people began for the first time to write seriously in English prose on a large scale. There was then no standard sense of what

Our question could be put this way: What is involved in the making of what we call a sentence, and why does it matter? In pursuing it we shall be examining not only a form of our speech, of our language, but also a way in which we think and talk about language itself.

---

an English sentence should be, or even which words should count as English and which not. Two centuries earlier, for example, Chaucer had brought into English an enormous French vocabulary and writers as different as Milton and Hooker continued to add Latin terms to the English stock.

With respect to the form of the sentence itself the main tension was not with French but with Latin, which was both the international language of the day—Calvin's *Institutes* were written in Latin, as was Erasmus' *Praise of Folly* and More's *Utopia*—and the language of ancient learning as well, brought into the present by the Renaissance. If English were to be a civilized language, it had to be cast in civilized forms, and these were Latin. The difficulty of course was that Latin was an inflected language, like Greek, and thus not rigidly dependent upon word order; this meant that it was relatively easy to create sentences of enormous complexity, full of dependent and coordinate clauses, yet all organized and held in shape by the suspension of grammatical fulfillment. In such a language a sentence can be a work of art, an art of which Cicero was the acknowledged master. But in English?

Some people, like Richard Hooker in the *Lawes of Ecclesiasticall Politie*, managed to write English sentences that aspired to the Ciceronian ideal, and with great success. There is a sense, indeed, in which Hooker finds a style in which each of his sentences can have a different form, with a different meaning, in much the same way that the poets of the day experimented in different verse forms, trying to give each poem its own prosodic shape. Other writers endeavored to follow a simpler model, based on the Latin of Seneca, which was less periodic in form, more directly progressive; still others tried to keep alive what they believed to be the native structures of English. (See, e.g., Roger Ascham, *Toxophilus, The Schole of Shootinge Conteyned in Two Bookes* [1545]. In the preface addressed to King Henry VIII he says he has "written this Englishe matter in the Englishe tongue, for Englishe men.") I have written about this moment elsewhere, in connection with a study of Hooker's style, and will not repeat myself except to say that the ultimate resolution was the sentence established primarily by Dryden: fluid, open, easy to follow, yet complex enough to have a form of its own. See my "Hooker's Preface to the *Lawes of Eccliasticall Politie*: Constituting Authority in Argument," chap. 4 in *Acts of Hope: Creating Authority in Law, Literature, and Politics* (Chicago: University of Chicago Press, 1994).

For present purposes what matters is not so much the particular forms of the sentence over which people struggled, but the fact that they struggled so intensely over such a matter at all, and why they did so, when no one today seems to think that such a thing matters at all. These people felt that they were fighting for their culture, and their religion too. Would the kind of thought made possible by the long periodic sentences of Cicero—organizing vast complexity into a single structure, moving the reader through a series of progressions and reversals before reaching a conclusion, sometimes suspending judgment while suspending closure until all the data of the sentence were in—be available in English? Without such a sentence would English thought itself degenerate? On the other hand, would English never develop its own genius for rapid sequencing, for a style that imitated cause and effect in the material world and was thus appropriate to a new scientific or empirical era?

There were both religious and political overtones: to the Protestant reformer an essential article of faith was that the word of God, in the Scriptures, directly conveyed to the reader all that was necessary to salvation, and that this essential content was intellectually simple. So simple that the Scriptures could be translated into many languages without real loss; so

The Sentence as a Structured Experience

One way to approach our question might be to imagine, if we can, a language with no sentences at all: perhaps a computer language that transmits information without regard to sentence or clause breaks, in a kind of undifferentiated stream of symbols. One could presumably find a way to cast much of the meaning of a series of natural sentences into such a form, but I think not all of it, both because language is not reducible to bits of "information" in such an easy way and because an important part of the meaning of the forms of natural language, including the sentence, lies in the way they shape the experience of the reader. You might say, in fact, that our interest here will be in everything a sentence does that cannot be reduced to that kind of information: in the sentence as a kind of action, on language and on other people; in the sentence as representing or enacting a way of thinking and being; in the sentence as taking place in time, and working by the creation and disappointment of expectations, by confirmation and surprise; and so forth.

If we were to translate a particular real-language sentence into the bits of information that it conveys, in the manner outlined above, we could still ask: What is achieved by the speaker of this sentence that is not reflected in that translation? Why, for example, does this sentence start where it does, instead of half-a-sentence earlier, and why does it end where it does, instead of half-a-sentence later? Why are its clauses and phrases arranged this way, rather than that, and how does

---

simple that their essentials could be understood directly by any literate reader, or any linguistically competent hearer, without explanation by members of a priestly caste. The difficulty of right comprehension was not intellectual but spiritual, a matter of faith and disposition, and these qualities were not the result of merely intellectual training or ability. One destination of such tendencies was the prose of Tom Paine, speaking simple—and utterly revolutionary—truths to ordinary people. This was to become the prose of radical democracy, and it is for the most part the language of public thought and debate in our world today.

On the other side were those, like Hooker, who valued complexity and tradition in the social and institutional order, in their modes of thought, and in a prose style that would simultaneously make that kind of thought manifest and give clearer definition to the ideal of social and institutional complexity. Roman Catholics of course affirmed the value of tradition in an even more intense and wholehearted way, and insisted on the special role of Latin as the language of the Church.

At issue in the struggle over the form of the sentence, then, was a question not of "mere" aesthetics, but an aesthetic question that involved choices about the centrally disputed questions of the day: the nature of God, of Scripture, of the human being, of reason, of the proper ends of human life, of salvation, of proper and just government, of civilization itself.

it move? What are its shape and tone, and what do they mean? For me language is not a code into which messages are translated so much as an activity, a set of gestures, like dance, say, or music, and its most important meanings lie in the particulars of performance.

I want to think, then, of the sentence as a structured experience for the reader, as an experience given shape and meaning by its form. To this way of thinking, time is crucial, for the sentence is seen as a temporal performance: as beginning somewhere, ending somewhere, and moving between those two points. Its first word establishes or confirms a set of expectations, some of them specific, some very general, upon which it builds. Recall the sentence from the *Odyssey*, for example: *autar* confirms the *men* of the preceding sentence and points forward, towards an action as yet unknown (but we do know that it is to be distinguished from what we have just read); the *ho* then tells us something about this action, namely, the probable identity of the actor, but not much more; and so on. As a grammatical matter each word we read has a set of possible or likely connections: a nominative connects with a verb, which will have one of the tenses, moods, voices, and so on, of the language in question; an accusative connects with a verb in another way, probably but not necessarily as an object; and so on. As the sentence moves from whatever expectations precede it— established by the last line of the preceding book of the poem, or by the signs announcing the lecture, or by what we already know is likely to happen when a bard picks up his lyre and looks out at his audience—it creates expectations of its own, which it confirms or upsets, until it reaches a kind of closure. And it works the other way too, for as we read we constantly look back as well as forward, running our minds over what we have read, recasting it in light of what has come after, all in an effort to give the whole as complete a coherence as it can bear. As the nature of the process suggests, the closure reached by any sentence will never be perfect and final. There are always uncertainties and incompletenesses in what is said, if only because every sentence must assume the existence of certain understandings—about the language used, the context in which it is uttered, the identity of the speaker and audience and the relation between them—which are the conditions of its utterance, and these in the nature of things can never be rendered entirely explicit. Every effort to do so would be another act of language, with all the uncertainties inherent in that fact.

A particular sentence in this way always has a form, enacting a kind of career, from one point to another; it moves from silence to ambiguity to reduced ambiguity, but never to completeness and certainty of expression. It creates tensions and uncertainty in the reader, and lives by them; it focuses attention, and transfers it from point to point, in a sequence of its own. In all of this, the maker of the sentence not only uses his language but acts upon it, often to transform it. Still more: the sentence is always a form of human interaction, for it always has a speaker and an audience. This means that it is a species of ethical action as well, involving the deepest question of social life, namely, who we are to each other. The sentence is not just an information exchange, but a form of life, an activity with language and with other people.

Such are the views this chapter will elaborate.

The Dimensions of Meaning

If we are to think of the sentence in the way I suggest, as working through time, as establishing and modifying expectations in a gesture of a certain shape, it would help to identify the elements with which it is working, or what might be called its dimensions of meaning. In this section I try to do this briefly, building upon what I said in the paragraph just above, and then turn to three specific sentences in which we can see the writer work in several of these dimensions at once.

Words

I want first to complicate the idea, common in ordinary talk about these matters, that a sentence is made of units of preexisting meaning, called words, which are assembled, like bricks or timbers, into the structures we call sentences. On this view, one word has meaning "A" and is connected with those that have meanings "B" and "C" to make the utterance "ABC." Sometimes a word may have more than one meaning, in which case the sentence will be ambiguous—"S = ABC or ABD?"—but it is assumed that the set of possible meanings can be identified and expressed ahead of time.

The trouble with this is that it fails to account for what happens to the words themselves when they are put together in these ways. For words in fact do not have stable and consistent prior meanings, to be employed as units in the construction of the sentence, but change their meanings as they are used. Indeed, it can be one of the most important functions of a sentence to act upon and redefine the words with which it is made. As the Spanish linguist and sociologist Ortega y Gasset says, a dictionary does not actually define the meanings of words, but rather marks out some of their potential for meaning;[3] it falls to the writer to complete the task, and if he does it well his words will have new meanings, as they act on one another in the structures he creates.

The power of the writer to change meanings is perhaps most obvious in the case of irony: Marc Antony makes the phrase "Brutus is an honorable man" ring in ways that directly reverse our expectations, changing the meaning not so much of "honor," which remains a term of high value, but of "Brutus," removing his right to the term and giving it to the "ambitious" Caesar. For another version of the same kind of thing, a surprising use of a word that changes its meaning, one can think of the use of *dios/dion* in the sentence from the *Odyssey* we read in chapter 4, where it is made an epithet not only of Odysseus and Sparta, but, most surprisingly, the swineherd. At a more general level, one can conceive of the achievement of a great poet as the fashioning of a language of his own, with its own terms and procedures. In the case of George Herbert, for example, whose work we take up in chapter 7, this is a language of religious experience; in it words like "heart," and "stone," and "joy," and "affliction" are given meanings distinct from, and deeper than, those in ordinary discourse, as their uses in one poem echo and reinforce and contrast with their uses in others. Or think of the distinctive poetic languages of Alexander Pope, or Wallace Stevens, or William Blake. Or, to consider not poetry but political oratory, consider Webster's once-famous *Second Reply to Hayne*: in a world that saw the increasing power of the federal "union" as a threat to "liberty," "liberty" as a threat to "union," Webster makes a speech in which he connects the two, establishing their mutual dependence, so that he can conclude in the famous ringing phrase, "Liberty *and* Union, now and forever, one and inseparable!"[4] Finally, to take an example from a text we have read, think of the richness of Huck's phrase, "whichever come handiest at the time," where "handiest" is given content by the kind of moral reflection and action in which Huck is engaging: it means not, as it seems to, "whatever is easiest" or "the least moral or practical trouble," but the course of conduct that conforms to one's deepest moral and emotional intuitions. When we are working at our best we do not just use words with preexisting mean-

3. José Ortega y Gasset, *Man and People,* trans. Willard R. Trask (New York: Norton, 1957), 235.

4. Daniel Webster, *Reply to Hayne [Pulpit and Rostrum]* (New York: H. H. Lloyd & Co., 1861), 184.

ings, but create relations among them that will give them meanings of
a new kind.

Sound

Another dimension or ingredient of meaning with which the sentence
maker works is its sound. Robert Frost, for whom this topic was crucial, had this to say about what he called "the sound of sense," in a
letter to John Bartlett, July 4, 1913:

> Now it is possible to have sense without the sound of sense (as in much
> prose that is supposed to pass muster but makes very dull reading) and
> the sound of sense without sense (as in *Alice in Wonderland* which
> makes anything but dull reading). The best place to get the abstract
> sound of sense is from voices behind a door that cuts off the words. Ask
> yourself how these sentences would sound without the words in which
> they are embodied:
>
>> You mean to tell me you can't read?
>> I said no such thing.
>> Well read then.
>> You're not my teacher.
>
>> He says it's too late.
>> Oh, say!
>> Damn an Ingersoll watch anyway.
>
>> One-two-three—go!
>> No good! Come back—come back.
>> Haslam go down there and make those kids get out of the track.
>
> Those sounds are summoned by the audile (audial) imagination
> and they must be positive, strong, and definitely and unmistakably in-
> dicated by the context. The reader must be at no loss to give his voice
> the posture proper to the sentence. The simple declarative sentence
> used in making a plain statement is one sound. But Lord love
> ye it mustn't be worked to death. It is against the law of nature that
> whole poems should be written in it. If they are written they won't be
> read. The sound of sense, then. You get that. It is the abstract vitality of
> our speech. It is pure sound—pure form. One who concerns himself
> with it more than the subject is an artist. But remember we are still
> talking merely of the raw material of poetry. An ear and an appetite for
> these sounds of sense is the first qualification of a writer, be it of prose
> or verse. But if one is to be a poet he must learn to get cadences by
> skillfully breaking the sounds of sense with all their irregularity of ac-
> cent across the regular beat of the metre. Verse in which there is nothing
> but the beat of the metre furnished by the accents of the polysyllabic

words we call doggerel. Verse is not that. Neither is it the sound of sense alone. It is a resultant from those two.[5]

By the "sound of sense," Frost means I think the sound or cadence appropriate to a certain verbal gesture in a certain social relation. Though somewhat different renditions of any one of the sentences he gives as examples are possible, they each have a distinctive sound, expressing a specific social relation, a clear tone and feeling. If you try reading them aloud you find, I think, that each has a distinct cadence. (You could certainly read them with emphases and stresses that were simply impossible in American English.) They are parts of what Wittgenstein would call "language games," and we all recognize them. It is this, the sense that they are drawn from a repertoire of vital speech, that gives them their force, against which the order of the meter and the rhyme will run.

For an example of the way this works, think of the opening lines of Frost's poem "Design": "I found a dimpled spider, fat and white." Try reading it to yourself two ways: first as a line of iambic pentameter, wholly regular; second as a line from a speech in a play, say, with no attention to its meter, but only to its "sentence sound." The two readings will I imagine be very different, the first rather sing-songey, almost chanting—each stress equal to each stress, each unstress equal to each unstress—the second rushing, with rising intonation, till you get to "spider," then a huge pause before "fat" and "white," each of which is heavily stressed by the silences that surround it. In the line read as a poem the two systems of sound will both be present, working against each other in a tension that functions as a source of life.

Much of the effect of the first line of "Design" lies in the contrast between the ordinariness of the rhythm of the line and the bizarreness of the image of a spider that is at once cute ("dimpled") and ugly ("fat and white"). And part of the poem's sense of the ordinary derives from the fact that its iambic forms are also those of relaxed English and American speech: "I found a broken bottle, by the wall . . ."; "I went to town to get a thing or two"; "I saw your aunt and uncle at the beach." The sounds of sentences like these, uttered and heard thousands of times in our lives, lie behind the line of poetry, both justifying its formal rhythm and making that rhythm seem the stuff of ordinary life. It is thus against the iambic pattern both of ordinary and of poetic

5. *Selected Letters of Robert Frost,* ed. Lawrance Thompson (New York: Holt, Rinehart and Winston, 1964), 79–80.

speech that the sentence sound of the first line runs, creating by the tension between them a music of its own. And this happens in a poem that will put into question the whole matter of design, design in the universe, design in our speech.

To return for a moment to our earlier topic, notice how this sentence works on its key words—"fat" and "dimpled" and "white" and "spider"—by putting them together in ways that surprise and trouble the reader, as they surprise and trouble the poet. Together they question the possibility of a coherent design, a coherent way of organizing these terms and their implications; yet at the same time they threaten us with the possibility of a malevolent version of just such coherence. As its ending shows, in a sense the whole poem is spun out of the implications of its opening line:

> What had that flower to do with being white,
> The wayside blue and innocent heal-all?
> What brought the kindred spider to that height,
> Then steered the white moth thither in the night?
> What but design of darkness to appall?—
> If design govern in a thing so small.

What Frost speaks of, and practices, can be seen as a special instance of a larger phenomenon, namely, the way in which the meaning of a sentence, or other text, is dependent upon the prior texts and utterances that live in the mind of its speaker and audience, against which it resonates.[6] It is this element above all that is missing in what might be called "translated language," that is the language spoken by someone who knows the grammar of a language, and possesses a good vocabulary, but has only a restricted range of uses, and hence of memory—the language of the tour guide, for example. It is what makes us miss jokes, or understand them only at a surface level, in a language we "know" but do not know; and it makes us dead to nuances of irony and distance, to shifts of voice. It is a miracle that we can read the *Odyssey* as well as we can.

Ethics

Verbal action is action, with or upon other people, with or upon language, and a part of its meaning is necessarily ethical in nature. One

6. For the phrase "prior texts," and my sense of its power, I am indebted to A. L. Becker. See his book, *Beyond Translation: Toward a Modern Philology* (Ann Arbor: University of Michigan Press, 1995), especially 188–93, 286–90, 413–16.

might think indeed of every utterance as having two axes, the linguistic and the social, along both of which it could be seen to engage in ethical action. On the social axis it does at least three things: first, it defines a character, or persona, for its speaker, who is present before us in the text, defined by his tone of voice, quality of mind, attitude towards others, and so forth. We know right away, for example, if someone sounds like a bully, or a salesman, and we can respond directly to that quality in his speech. (This relates to the original meaning of the word *ethics,* which derives from a Greek word meaning "character.") Each utterance also defines its audience in the way it addresses them—in the qualities of mind and character and knowledge it assumes they have—and thus defines a character for them too. Once again we immediately know, and respond, if we perceive someone addressing us as bigoted or ignorant, or—at the opposite extreme—as wise and good. Finally, in doing these things the utterance constitutes a community between speaker and audience, a relationship defined by the practices it engages in and invites in others.[7]

The other axis, linguistic and cultural in nature, is perhaps less obvious but nontheless real. For every sentence or other utterance can be seen to act upon the language its speaker has been given to use, replicating some of its forms, modifying others, and so on, and this too can be regarded as a kind of ethical action. Whether he knows it or not, then, in making his sentence the speaker is not merely communicating a message, expressing a feeling, or trying to achieve a material or social objective, but affecting, or tending to affect, the materials for meaning in our world—perhaps to change them, perhaps to affirm that they need not, or should not, be changed.

As one obvious example think of the effect of a bad political speech, or a good one, on the quality of the political process: the bad one trivializes or degrades, the good one elevates or ennobles. Much the same can be said of less prominent forms of speech too, good and bad, in a set of remarks made by a dean to her faculty, say, or a teacher to his students or parents to their children. Such utterances become a part of a community's common experience and help shape the way conversation or thought in that world will proceed. They are a set of prior texts that may be worked and reworked as allusions are made to them. Whenever one speaks, in fact, one reconstitutes one's language and

7. I am here describing a way of reading that is worked out in my book *When Words Lose Their Meaning: Constitutions and Reconstitutions of Language, Character, and Community* (Chicago: University of Chicago Press, 1984).

culture, in great ways or small; and, for good or ill, one of our deepest obligations is to the language we use and to the culture it defines.

All speech or writing is ethical action, for it always involves the reconstitution both of language and of the social world. The linguistic element is central: we are as ethically responsible for what we do with and to our languages as for what we do with and to each other.

Performance

There are occasions on which an utterance can be seen to enact its meanings as well as to state them. This is most obviously true where its explicit content is social or ethical: when a person talks about what it means to treat another with respect, for example, she is at that very moment treating someone, namely us, with something, and we can judge whether it is indeed respect, or whether we are by contrast being patronized or bullied or deceived; and if it is with respect, we can see how her performance gives increased meaning to the term she uses.

Other forms of enacted meaning are possible too. Consider for example this sentence from Frost's essay, "The Figure a Poem Makes," about the shape of a poem:

> It begins in delight, it inclines to the impulse, it assumes direction with the first line laid down, it runs a course of lucky events, and ends in a clarification of life—not necessarily a great clarification, such as sects and cults are founded on, but in a momentary stay against confusion.[8]

This sentence enacts the movement it describes.

Classic cases of enacted meaning also appear in the Platonic dialogues, where Socrates is constantly comparing something called "philosophy" or "dialectic" with other forms of activity, such as "rhetoric," recommending the first and not the second. These terms represent not merely modes of thought but ways of life, which are directly represented in what the characters say—what they do with language and each other—as well as described by them. Often there is a tension between what Socrates claims for philosophy and what he himself does, for sometimes he seems to perform his meaning rather well, at other times to act inconsistently with his own claims. On such occasions we are likely to accuse him of hypocrisy, or of a failure to understand, sometimes with feelings of triumph; but the situation is rendered more

---

8. Robert Frost, "The Figure a Poem Makes," in Robert Frost, *Collected Poems, Prose, & Plays* (New York: Library of America, 1995), 777.

complex when we realize that the dialogue is written not by Socrates but by Plato, and that it is possible that the very critical and refutational activities that it has stimulated in us are themselves versions of the philosophy it means to recommend and exemplify.

Syntax

What is unique to the sentence as a form is that it always has a syntactic structure or order. This may be simple or complex; it may be highlighted or taken for granted; it may be threatened, as the sentence changes direction, and it may even collapse. This dimension of meaning interacts with the others with particular force where the explicit subject of the sentence is related to a question of form—coherence, for example, or complexity, or elegance, or balance—for in all such cases the form of the particular sentence may be in harmony or disharmony with its explicit position, and in that way add meaning at the level of performance. This happens in the passage quoted earlier from "Design," for example, where a syntactically complete sentence, in the form of a question ("What had that flower to do with being white . . . ?") is followed by two fragments ("What but . . . ?" and "If design govern . . ."), which work as shifts that slightly but significantly threaten the order of the poem at the level of syntax. It is the political and religious significance of this dimension of meaning that exercised those writers who battled about the proper form of the English sentence in Elizabethan and Jacobean England.

The very fact of grammatical expectation establishes a hope of orderliness, indeed of complex and constituted order. In actual performances this hope will be confirmed, or disappointed, or given greater specification. In Greek, for example, there is a figure of speech, called *anakolouthon*, which consists of the deliberate breaking of the syntactical order: the sentence starts out one way, creating one set of expectations, and part way through the writer just abandons that form and starts off on another. This is "ungrammatical" writing, or perhaps "unsyntactical," and it would seem like a grievous fault in English; but in Greek it is felt to be highly expressive, when correctly used, of the mind at the moment of full inspiration when its thoughts cannot be tied and bound by the usual rules of syntax.

The expectations we call syntactic thus do much to give shape to a sentence, differently in different languages. But how do these in fact work? As a set of rules telling the writer what must or may go with or after what? This is often how they are taught, but we have seen enough, especially in our look in chapter 4 at the sentence from the *Odyssey,* to complicate that picture a great deal. It is more adequate to our experience of that particular sentence to see the grammar and syntax as establishing a range of capacities or options, sets of choices the writer may wish to make. Thus the first pronoun, *ho,* which is in a sense unnecessary, given the fact that the verb is in the third person singular, can be seen to have another function in relation to the earlier pronoun, *hē,* referring to Athena, namely, to distinguish the two actors. The second *ho,* as we saw, could be either a relative or a demonstrative; what determines that matter is the choice of the writer to include, or not include, a sentence-marking particle. On this view the rules of grammar and syntax are not so much directions to behavior as expressions of generally shared expectations; as such they give the writer or speaker material with which to work. Of course they restrain, for some locutions simply will not make sense, but at the same time they enable.

Here is a simple example from English. In America, though not I think England or Canada, the "rule" is that when one has a sequence of three or more elements a comma comes after each, including the one before the "and": "A, B, and C." This is true whether the elements are words, phrases, or clauses. In England and Canada the comma before the "and" is omitted.[9] Now consider the following line by Robert Frost in his famous poem, "Stopping by Woods on a Snowy Evening": "the woods are lovely, dark and deep." This was punctuated by his posthumous editor to read, "the woods are lovely, dark, and deep." The editor was insisting on the presence of the comma, apparently in compliance with the American rule given above; but in doing so he necessarily asserted that the three adjectives were in sequence, "A, B, and C." What Frost wrote, however, created an apposition: "lovely, [by which I mean] dark and deep," which is entirely different in meaning and feeling. Now for the main point: Frost could do that—and his editor could be wrong—only because of the existence of the American rule, which he seemed to violate; it is the rule that gave significance to the omitted comma. Had there been no such rule, creating such expectations, Frost's omission would have meant nothing. The rule thus not only restrains, it enables.

To return to a topic raised earlier, this helps explain one reason why translation from one language to another is in a full sense impossible.

9. For an explanation of the English rule, see H. W. Fowler, *A Dictionary of Modern English Usage,* 2d ed., rev. Ernest Gowers (Oxford: Oxford University Press, 1965), 588.

It is not just that each language has its own rules of grammar and syntax, but that these rules function by offering the speaker or writer a set of choices that will be different in different languages; and different also must be the character and meaning of the writer's response to them. One cannot replicate in English a choice made available only by the syntax of Hindi or Navajo.[10]

Three Sentences

So far I have presented a series of questions relating to the meaning of the sentence. In what follows I examine three particular sentences, as a way of testing out the value of those questions.

Caesar

As an example of a sentence working by complex syntactic expectations that are related to its larger purposes, consider the following famous sentence, familiar to all who studied Latin in school or college:

> *Gallia est omnis divisa in partes tres, quarum unam incolunt Belgae, aliam Aquitani, tertiam qui ipsorum lingua Celtae, nostra Galli, appellantur.*

10. The modes of meaning I describe are of course not the only possibilities. The linguist A. L. Becker has worked out a more comprehensive view of contextual meaning that identifies six such dimensions: "structure" (by which he means what is normally meant by language, that is, the pattern of syntactic expectations by which it works); "prior texts" (by which he means the whole world of remembered language—sentences, phrases, sounds, gestures—against which, and with which, the present utterance resonates); "medium" (by which he means the mode of representation, for example whether written—and if so in what alphabet and in what form of writing—or oral or sung or danced); "relations" (by which he means the social aspect of all communication, the definition of self and other, the form of action that the sentence constitutes, and so on); "nature" (by which he means the world out there, of rocks and stones and trees, in which language must work); and "silence" (by which he means the significance of what is unsaid, or not done, in language). Becker, *Beyond Translation*, 29, 186, 381.

My own list of dimensions is influenced by his, and some are rather close: his "structure" and my "syntax"; his "prior texts" and my discussion, using Frost, of the sound of the sentences we carry in our heads; his "relations" and my sense of the social and ethical dimension of meaning; his "medium" and my earlier discussion of orality and the alphabet in reading Homer; and so on. Neither list is offered as complete, but as an indication that the gesture we call the sentence may have meaning in several registers or dimensions at once, and that it is important to attend to as many of these as we can; and, in addition, that a part of its meaning lies in the way these dimensions interact with one another, in harmony or disharmony, for good or ill. The reality and significance of these dimensions of meaning is made especially apparent if one tries to translate a sentence from one language into another, or even simply to rewrite it in the same language but in different words: every change of form is a change of meaning, in the sense that something different—both more, and less—is now being said, and in several dimensions at once.

> All Gaul is divided into three parts, of which the Belgians inhabit one,
> the Aquitanians another, and the third those who are in their own lan-
> guage called "Celts," but in ours "Gauls."

As one would expect in a highly inflected language, this sentence creates and works by a set of complex interactions among the words: *Gallia* is a nominative singular feminine noun, calling for a verb, which it
gets in *divisa est,* the *divisa* tying itself by gender and number to *Gallia*
as tightly as it is possible to imagine. *Omnis* can be either masculine or
feminine, but in this case there is little doubt as to its connections. The
rest of the sentence is a dependent clause—hanging on *quarum,* "of
which"—that tells us about the three parts into which Gaul is divided.
The first two subclauses, dealing with the Belgians and the Aquitanians, present little difficulty, once you know that *incolunt* is the verb
(meaning "inhabit"), *Belgae* and *Aquitani* its subjects. The last is its
own minor work of art: *tertiam,* "the third," is accusative singular, in
sequence with *unam* and *aliam,* hence almost certainly an object; the
verb is carried over or understood from the first of the three subclauses,
incolunt, or "inhabit"; what we need is a subject, parallel to "Belgians" and "Aquitanians," and it is found in the relative, *qui,* "who,"
followed by "of themselves in the language Celts" (i.e., "in their own
language Celts"), "in our ['language,' understood] Gauls, are called."

One could go on at great length about the structures at work here,
but for present purposes this sketch is enough, for it enables us to
frame the question: What relation is there between the form and shape
and life of this sentence, and the explicit subject, or substantive concerns, of the text from which it is drawn? This is the first sentence
of a book written by Julius Caesar for the purpose of describing his
conquest of Gaul, including Britain. But why does he describe these
things? The object is to create a sense of him as author and mind and
leader, and of his capacities, a sense of his character, that will lead
others to support him politically, and perhaps militarily, as a leader of
Rome. Among the qualifications of a national leader is the ability to
present a vision of the world, and of one's country within it, out of
which one can imagine functioning. In this sentence, as of course even
more in the rest of the book, Caesar shows that he can do this; that he
can see a whole and divide it into parts, and then reassemble them, not
only with precision but with elegance. The first is an intellectual activity known to the Greeks, and hence the Romans, as *diairesis,* "division," an essential stage in the analysis of anything. Here we see that
the parts are analogous, but not identical; they call for slightly different

treatment; they fit together to form a complex whole. This brings us to a second great intellectual activity, that of composition, or putting together to form a whole, called *sunagōgē,* and in this sentence Caesar almost gratuitously shows that he has it. This is a mind that recommends itself to its reader as one that can see large objects, divide them appropriately, and then combine them in his mind in complex ways. As he divides Gaul in his sentence, and in this way rules it, he will divide and rule Gaul itself, as a commander.[11] The shape of this sentence thus affords access to his mind, not only as writer but as leader.

The qualifications Caesar establishes here are not the only ones for the position he will claim, of course, but they are not irrelevant either. There is a sense, as Shelley said, in which poets are the unacknowledged legislators of the world; or, to put it differently, that many of the greatest legislators and governors have much of the poet in them. Think how different this sentence is, and its political implications are, from the political slogans that characterize so much of our world. For a similar effort, not in fact wholly unconnected to this sentence of Caesar, one might look to Franklin Roosevelt's first "fireside chat," delivered to the nation on March 12, 1933, in circumstances of stark economic and political threat, in which he seeks to demonstrate his capacity to govern the country by his ability to create and work through with his audience an intellectually and ethically complex text.[12]

---

11. With this sentence one might compare the following by Gibbon, speaking of Augustus, the adopted son of Julius, who built the Roman Empire out of the institutions, practices, and material resources he inherited:

> When Augustus gave laws to the conquests of his father, he introduced a division of Gaul equally adapted to the progress of the legions, to the course of the rivers, and to the principal national distinctions which had comprehended above an hundred independent states.

Edward Gibbon, *The History of the Decline and Fall of the Roman Empire,* ed. J. B. Bury (London: Methuen & Co., 1909), 1:21.

12. Here is how he begins:

> My friends, I want to talk for a few minutes with the people of the United States about banking—to talk with the comparatively few who understand the mechanics of banking, but more particularly with the overwhelming majority of you who use banks for the making of deposits and the drawing of checks. I want to tell you what has been done in the last few days, why it was done, and what the next steps are going to be. I recognize that the many proclamations from State capitals and from Washington, the legislation, the Treasury regulations, and so forth, couched for the most part in banking and legal terms, ought to be explained for the benefit of the average citizen. I owe this in particular because of the fortitude and good temper with which everybody has accepted the inconvenience and hardships of the banking holiday. And I know

Thoreau

Let us now turn to a familiar and important sentence by Thoreau and ask how it works.

> Moreover, I, on my side, require of every writer, first or last, a simple and sincere account of his own life, and not merely what he has heard of other men's lives; some such account as he would send to his kindred from a distant land; for if he has lived sincerely, it must have been in a distant land to me.

This, you will remember, is from the opening page of *Walden,* where Thoreau is shifting from voice to voice in a somewhat awkward and unsettled way. He has just told us that he writes about himself because there is no one else he knows as well, saying that he is compelled to this course by the narrowness of his experience.

---

that when you understand what we in Washington have been about I shall continue to have your cooperation as fully as I have had your sympathy and help during the past week.

First of all, let me state the simple fact that when you deposit money in a bank the bank does not put the money into a safe deposit vault. It invests your money in many different forms of credit—in bonds, in commercial paper, in mortgages, and in many other kinds of loans. In other words, the bank puts your money to work to keep the wheels of industry and of agriculture turning round. A comparatively small part of the money you put into the bank is kept in currency—an amount which in normal times is wholly sufficient to cover the cash needs of the average citizen. In other words, the total amount of all the currency in the country is only a small fraction of the total deposits in all of the banks.

What, then, happened during the last few days of February and the first few days of March? Because of undermined confidence on the part of the public, there was a general rush by a large portion of our population to turn bank deposits into currency or gold—a rush so great that the soundest banks couldn't get enough currency to meet the demand. The reason for this was that on the spur of the moment it was, of course, impossible to sell perfectly sound assets of a bank and convert them into cash except at panic prices far below their real value.

By the afternoon of March 3rd, a week ago last Friday, scarcely a bank in the country was open to do business. Proclamations temporarily closing them in whole or in part had been issued by the governors in almost all the states.

It was then that I issued the proclamation providing for the national bank holiday, and this was the first step in the government's reconstruction of our financial and economic fabric.

FDR's Fireside Chats, ed. Russel D. Buhite and David W. Levy (Norman: University of Oklahoma Press, 1992), 12–13. Of course, this talk like the others FDR gave was not solely his own work, but he was deeply involved at every stage of its composition. Ibid., xv–xvii. The version quoted above is drawn from a recording of what he said, not from the originally printed text. Ibid., xix.

Let us first think of this sentence as a set of expectations created and modified in time, asking as we proceed how it functions in each of the dimensions mentioned: as it works on its words, as it creates a shape with a sound of its own, as it establishes and manages relations with other people and with its culture, as it performs or enacts its meanings rather than simply stating them, and as it does all these things within the life created by the confirmation or disconfirmation of the syntactic expectations its stimulates.

The first word, *Moreover,* like the *autar* in the *Odyssey,* marks the connection of this sentence with another and tells us that it is adding something. *I:* this of course does mark a nominative (for there exists an accusative of the first person pronoun) and hence suggests the likelihood of a verb of which it will be the subject, or one of the subjects. *On my side:* what does this mean? To test that, imagine the sentence without it: "Moreover, I require . . . ." The phrase here is a little like a cough, drawing attention to the claims the writer is making to speak for himself, and justifying them, or at least asking your indulgence while he does so. What is more, he here acknowledges the possibility of another side, another point of view. There is in this tiny phrase, that is, an important social element, an element of manners. *Require:* this explains something of his hesitancy, for this is a strong word indeed, and the reader may well ask, "Who are you to require anything of anyone, let alone every writer?" In this sense, the *on my side* can be said to "go with" the *require,* by softening it, just as much as it goes with the *I.* And with the *every writer,* too, which is another display of his ambitious claims to judgment.

What of the *of?* *Require* has told us that in all likelihood a direct object will be coming—the *account*—and what *of* does is mark the person of whom the requirement is made. Without it, the *every writer* would be the object, as in "require every writer to . . . ."

First or last: this is another gesture, meaning something like, "at some time or other but in any event before he is done, and what I am speaking of is really the only thing I do require." An extremely complex meaning, again mainly a matter of manner or tone, at once impossible to capture in other terms and itself extremely precise.

A simple and sincere account: here the two adjectives imply a noun forthcoming, which we get; the relation between them is reinforced by their sounds—both two syllables, both beginning with *s,* both with a short *i* as the main vowel and an *e,* in one case long, in the other reduced almost to a schwa—and by their meaning, for both are rather simple and sincere words. Why the *a*? In English it is normal for a common noun to have an article, definite or indefinite. Here the force of the indefinite is that of generalization, to say in effect "one of the many possible things that might be included in the phrase I am about to utter," and opposed to *the,* which would particularize, as in "the truth about their lives."

Why can't the sentence stop here, with *account*? It could, perfectly easily, if it were speaking of bookkeepers, for example, rather than writers; but in this context *account* is felt as incomplete, requiring something more to finish it off. This is not a matter of syntax, but of prior texts; it is our ears that tell us that something more is called for. And we get it: *of his own life.*

Here the sentence could indeed stop, but it does not, itself a significant fact: for what has been said is simple indeed—the thesis of the sentence—and what comes after will complicate or modify it. First by distinction: *and not merely what he has heard of other men's lives,* thus giving content to *sincere* by creating a difference. But notice that what is opposed to sincerity here is not false statement in the usual sense of affectation or hypocrisy or pretense, but something very different: simply not attending to one's own experience in the first place, and instead assuming that it must be the same as everyone else's, or, in a more malign version, that it must be what it ought to be.

What happens next throws the idea of the sentence itself into doubt, for Thoreau still does not stop, but adds an explanatory phrase, *some such account as he would send to his kindred from a distant land,* separated from—or joined to—what precedes it by a semicolon. He could have used a comma, in which case the new phrase would have been in apposition to the word *account.* (He could not use a period, for the new phrase will not stand alone as a sentence.)[13] Why then the semicolon? Partly as a mark of rhythm—of the sentence sound—to make the reader pause, and thus to emphasize the new material; partly to prepare the reader, I think, for what comes next, which is another semicolon, before the final unit of the sentence, *for if he has lived sincerely, it must have been in a distant land to me.* Could this clause have been preceded by a comma? Yes. By a period? Yes, for at least in American English one can begin a sentence with such a *for,* which can mark either a new and independent sentence or a dependent clause.

13. "Could not," that is, in the sense I have suggested, that if he were to do so he would disrupt expectations of syntactic completeness. Of course that might be his very object, in which case the rule would be enabling as well as restraining.

One effect of separating the three segments of the sentence by sem-
icolons is to claim a kind of equality among the three parts; another is
to capture the mind in the process of revising its own thoughts. A *sincere account,* of his own life, not of other men's lives. But what kind of
account? *Such as he would send to his kindred from a distant land.*
Good, but what of the tension between *kindred* and *distant,* and also
between *kindred* and the *every writer*? That will be explained too: *for
if he has lived sincerely*—(what is the surprise there? *lived* instead of
written)—it *must have been in a distant land to me,* thus at once acknowledging and valuing distance in human experience, and claiming,
paradoxically, that he is most *kindred* to the one who is most *distant.*
All this works in another way, of course, as an introduction to his own
writing, where he is telling us that this is the kind of sentence he hopes
to write: the sentence that he describes, and the sentence that he performs here, in the description.

This sentence does not simply use its words, but acts upon them,
especially upon "sincere." This is the kind of account Thoreau requires
from others, as opposed to something else, evidently an "insincere"
one. This distinction is given specificity in the idea that some writers
simply repeat what they have heard of the lives of others, as one reit-
erates cliches or platitudes, in the hope that they will be acceptable.
This turn invokes the deepest theme of this chapter and his whole
book, the sense that some lives are authentic and real, others false and
imprisoning, and that what is needed above all is attention to the demands and questions and needs of one's own being. And at this point
"sincere" shifts its meaning, in a surprising way, modifying not the
account but the living of the life.

The other major transformation involves the word *distant,* first
used in the extended simile, as one might write "to his kindred from a
distant land," then, in connection with the revised use of *sincere,* to the
effect that if one does live sincerely it will necessarily be in a distant
land. This converts "distant" from a bad thing into a good one, and at
the same time paradoxically brings it home, up close, to the relations
between any two people, however near they are in usual ways. This
transformation proposes—as Frost's remark about his poems, that he
was trying to make them "sound as different as possible from each
other,"[14] does too—a sense that human differentiation is to be welcomed, especially by comparison with the dull sameness of lives and

14. Robert Frost, "The Figure a Poem Makes," in Frost, *Collected Poems, Prose, &
Plays,* 776.

writings that are merely imitative, written in the same words, the same voices, as though there were nothing new or alive or distinctive in the mind producing them. What of the one who lives in a "distant" land? By the implication of the simile he is "kindred," deeply like us in his sincerity, though different in what that sincerity produces. This sentence thus gives new, specific, and somewhat paradoxical meaning to its two central terms, meaning of a kind that cannot be picked up and carried away but must be created or recreated in the way the words are used. The significance of the sentence lies in its movement and life, not in any otherwise reproducible propositional content.

One could go on at greater length, but I hope the main point is clear, that this sentence has a shape of its own that could not be confused with any other, and that the dimensions in which the shaping occurs are many: in the way the sentence works on its words; in its creation and modification of social relations, with the reader and with those it talks about; in its use of expectations governing syntax, punctuation, and the meaning of words to create a new experience, partly of surprise; in the sound or shape of the experience so created; and so on. This will be brought home with particular clarity if you try to translate this into another language, and ask what is lost, what added; or if you try to write a sentence of your own, on another subject, that imitates the form of this one; or, more simply, if you simply rewrite it in English, with a different shape and sound, and ask how its meaning changes:

> I insist that a writer report on his own experience, sincerely and simply, and not tell us about the experience of other people. All writing should be like a letter home from a faraway country. In fact, if the writer has had experience worthy of the name, it will be remote from my own, and all the more worth hearing.

Plato

Finally, to return to Greek and to anticipate our work in the next chapter, I turn to a sentence from Plato's *Phaedrus*. Plato's subject in this dialogue is complex in the extreme, including the nature of rhetoric, of love, and of the soul, the value of writing, and many other topics, among which he sometimes seems to shift oddly. At the point where we find the sentence that I wish to examine, Socrates and Phaedrus have been discussing the question—important for the modern lawyer too—whether the rhetorician, in order to persuade successfully about a particular subject, needs to know the truth of that subject, or only what his audience believes to be the truth. Socrates has just argued that one must know the truth, even to mislead, because one who moves away from the truth must do so on the basis of similarities to it, and by careful stages, which will otherwise be impossible. (This is an argument that persuades Phaedrus, or seems to do so, but it is a distinctly open question whether it should persuade us.)

What this means, he says, is that a manual of rhetoric—of the kind they have been discussing—prepared by one who does not know the nature of the things he is speaking of will be laughable, not at all entitled to the status of art or science. Here is the sentence in which Socrates says this:

> Λόγων ἄρα τέχνην, ὦ ἑταῖρε, ὁ τὴν ἀλήθειαν μὴ εἰδώς, δόξας δὲ τε-
> θηρευκώς, γελοίαν τινά, ὡς ἔοικε, καὶ ἄτςχνον παρέξεται. (262-c-1)
> *Logōn ara technēn, O hetaire, ho tēn alētheian mē eidōs, doxas de
> tethēreukōs, geloian tina, hōs eoike, kai atechnon parexetai.*

This means something like:

> A manual for speaking provided by someone who does not know the truth, but hunts only opinion, will then be, it seems, oh my friend, somewhat ridiculous and without art.

But the structure of the Greek sentence is altogether different, roughly like this:

> Of speeches, then, a manual, oh my friend, the person the truth not knowing, but opinions hunting, laughable somewhat, so it seems, and without art will provide.

To begin to see how this works, first remove for the moment *O hetaire,* which means something like, "friend," in the vocative, and *hōs eoike,* which means "it seems"—and seems to cast all the rest of the sentence into faint doubt. The second word, *ara,* like *autar* in the sentence from the *Odyssey,* is a particle defining the relation of this sentence to what preceded. Here it means something like, "it follows naturally." The main verb of the sentence is *parexetai,* which means "will provide," its ending implying a singular subject in the third person; that it comes only at the end means that the sentence is not complete until that point, thus suspending closure. The subject is a person defined in a double participial phrase, beginning with our by now familiar *ho: ho tēn alētheian mē eidōs,* "the one not knowing the truth," *doxas de tethēreukōs,* "but hunting for [mere] opinions *(doxas).*" Thus far, then: "The person who does not know the truth, but seeks only to discover what people think, will provide"—what? A *logōn technēn*—"of speeches a manual," or rhetorical handbook, emphasized by its location at the beginning of the sentence. But the larger meaning of *technē* is an "art" or "science" of the kind Socrates wishes to say rhetoric is not, so there is a kind of pun built into the phrase: an "art of rhetoric" is a handbook to rhetoric that claims by implication that rhetoric is indeed an art; and in purporting to teach it, the handbook further claims that it is reducible to a kind of scientific knowledge.— And what kind of *logōn technēn* do we have here? The answer is *geloian tina*, "somewhat ridiculous," *kai atechnon*, "and without claim to art or science." (A *technē atechnon*, where the *a* has a negating force: an artless art, a scienceless science, a worthless book.)

Now go back to the sentence and consider its shape, as an event taking place in time. (I will mark with S the subject of the verb, with V the verb, with O its object, and OM the modifiers of that object.)

> Of speeches (it follows) an art [O], Oh my friend, the person [S] who knows nothing, but searches after mere opinions, rather ridiculous [OM] it seems, and [OM] without art, will provide [V].

The separation of the adjectives "ridiculous" and "without art" from the noun "art" simply could not be done in English; here the effect is a strong and highly comic emphasis resulting from suspended expectations, an effect doubled by postponing the "without art" until after the interjected "it seems"—itself at least partly ironic, meaning not so much "it seems" as "it is painfully apparent."

I hope it is becoming clear how one might say of such a sentence that it has a shape and life of its own; and that much of the art of the writer lies in the way the sentence structures the experience of the reader, focusing and holding and moving his attention through time.

THE WRITING OF A SENTENCE, with some awareness of what one is doing, involves one in everything that matters, or so it sometimes seems; we could define it as a goal of a life to learn to utter the right sentences on the right occasions. For the occasion is always different, the moment different, and the sentence must be shaped anew to its circumstances. This is one way to think about the fact that we live in time and in change: that each moment is the opportunity for a new sentence, remaking one's language and culture, remaking one's relations with others, redefining one's own mind and character. This is the essence of moral life; its irreducibility to rules or principles of imitation. This is a point at which we engage in creation.

The sentence can be seen not as an array of information, but as a form of action, with language and with other people. It does not simply employ the words it uses, as if they carried all their meaning with them, but in using changes or defines them, as we saw Thoreau do with "sincere." The sentence acts on the language that it uses. Since it is a social activity, the sentence is also a form of ethical and political action, and can be judged as such: sometimes, as with other action, this significance is not great, but often it is, when, for example, a person manages to treat another with real respect, or the opposite. Since the sentence is a form of action, it enacts as well as states its meanings, in what it does with and to its language, with and to those to whom (and about whom) it talks; this enacted meaning may be consistent or inconsistent with its stated claims, in the former case adding an important dimension of significance, in the latter opening its author to charges of inconsistency or worse.

The meaning of a sentence thus lies in the experience it offers its reader, as the expectations aroused by particular words, and their forms, are confirmed, upset, clarified. The sentence is not a rigid paradigm with a constant meaning to which the writer rigidly adheres; rather, in writing a sentence well he or she builds upon a set of expectations in such a way as to create a new form, with new meaning. Here is how Emerson puts it, in a marvelous sentence of his own:

> The maker of a sentence, like the other artist, launches out into the infinite and builds a road into chaos and old Night, and is followed by those who hear him with something of wild, creative delight.
> Emerson, *Journals,* December 19, 1834

~
℮

Every freshman at Hadley College had to take a course in composition called English 1-2. This was the most powerful intellectual experience of my life, changing not only my sense of writing but of the possibilities of life itself. At school I had labored over assigned papers mainly as performances that were meant to meet the expectations of others. I would never have dreamed that I was asked in a paper to think or speak for myself, to reflect the processes of my own mind or the nature of my experience. I think I had the idea that there was a right way to write, just as there was a right way to dress and talk and behave, and that I was supposed to learn it.

Imagine the effect on such a boy of showing up in a required class in freshman writing and being asked as your first assignment to write a paper, due the next class, in response to such questions as these:

English 1   *Thurs.–Fri., Sept. 20–21:*
During the last few days you have been asked a great many questions by a lot of people. Try to recall exactly what some of these questions were by making a list of those you can remember. Look the questions over and ask yourself what all this questioning has been about.

a) Select 5 questions from your list, ranging from foolish to interesting, marking the most foolish with a # and the most interesting with a *.

b) Why do you apply the adjectives "foolish" and "interesting" to these particular questions?

c) What has all this questioning been about? How do you explain this social manifestation? After all you can go to lots of places, to a hotel, to a country club, and not be subjected to such persistent questioning. What's going on here?

These questions astounded me. They were unlike anything I had ever seen. To begin with, they asked me to speak out of my own experience, which I don't think anyone else had ever done; and they assumed that this experience included making judgments of my own, and judgments about such things as "foolish" and "interesting." I was thought to have my own scale of values; to be able to set my own speech and conduct, and that of others, on that scale; and to have something to say about how I did this—about what my scale was, where it came from, how and why I applied such labels as "foolish" and "interesting" to my experience; and so on.

Notice the opposition to "foolish": it is not "wise"—you can imagine what my eighteen-year-old self would have to say about wisdom!—but "interesting." (This was in fact a way of defining "wisdom" for me, and for the others in the class, in terms of our experience of finding things interesting.) This in turn assumed that we did find things interesting and that we were motivated by our interests, rather than, say, by the demands or expectations of others or by our own careerism or ambition. Such a person as the one we were assumed to be would naturally be interested in his own interests, interested in saying something about them, interested in speaking in his own voice about his experience of life and language and himself. The questions thus assumed, and in making this assumption created a demand, that each of us had a self, had experience, had something to say of his own—that each of us was a center of meaning and value and language. They created a vacuum each one of us had to fill.

Yet more: this course invited us to see our world as made up of languages, of different ways of talking; to see our college, for example, not as a thing or a structure, but as a set of more or less shared expectations as to how to talk and live, and much the same could be said of other institutions, from country clubs to the law. Each of these languages consisted of patterns of response and action, which could be learned, and learned well or badly. If one learned them by rote, unreflectively, one might become too much shaped by these patterns, by social and moral cliches, and perhaps never be capable of independent thought and action. The task of life was therefore a writing task, to learn to use our various languages reflectively, in such a way that we controlled them rather than they us; to use them to express our own experience, or to attain our ends; and this meant learning to have both experience and ends worthy of the name in the first place.

SIX

The *Phaedrus:*
Philosophy, Rhetoric, and Love

It has been a premise of this book that a person trying to make sense of his experience must do so in some language or other, whether in what we normally think of as a "language," like French or Chinese, or in some other medium of meaning, like painting or sculpture or dance. In any case, the language he uses is a social and cultural arte-fact, made largely by others, and the expectations by which it works must be taken as facts of the world with which he must deal. One cannot simply make up a new language, for example, even if such a thing were imaginable.

From the point of view of its user each language is a source of mean-ing in the world, each different from every other, offering different ways of imagining the world and the self, different materials of mean-ing and motive. As we saw in chapter 4, for example, English and Greek really are different, working in different ways to different ends, and the same is true of Japanese and German and every other lan-guage. Indeed this is true of every dialect or sublanguage: think, for example, of the language of baseball or that of the stock market or the law.

Since it is also true that each person speaks a somewhat different version of a shared language, or what is called by linguists an idiolect, our systems or sources of meaning do not perfectly overlap. Every ex-pression, every response, is an exercise in translation, speaking across barriers of difference. This is part of what Thoreau means when he says that sentences from a life lived sincerely will be like letters to one's kindred from a distant land. For each of us is a distant land to others—the more deeply we live, the more distant—and every conversation has to take account of this fact. The closest relations in-volve elements of distance; the most distant relations have elements of shared significance and concern. The art of talking and writing is in part a navigation in tension and uncertainty through this very problem, namely, the degree to which we are understood or understand. Yet perhaps the most remarkable thing about language is that despite its imperfections it can sometimes work to achieve a communication of internal experience, however incomplete, and even a mutual shaping of internal experience. It is a field of tension all right, but one where people can in fact meet one another, from a distant land yet also as kindred.

The form we call the sentence can be taken as a paradigmatic instance of the use of language. But the word *use* is not quite right, for one who uses language does not merely employ it, as an unchanging instrument: for in one direction it affects the way he thinks; and in the other he has the opportunity to act upon it, changing its meanings, sometimes in powerful ways. The dynamics of the sentence provide an important occasion and a purchase for such transformations, as the words work upon each other, sometimes in strong ways. As we saw in chapter 5, the meaning of the sentence is multidimensional, and the writer or speaker must choose which dimensions to emphasize, and in what ways. No sentence can be pure sound, not even Rimbaud's "Voyelles," nor pure image, not even William Carlos Williams's "Red Wheel Barrow," nor pure logic, nor pure ethics, nor pure linguistic structure. In framing the sentence the writer has to work in several modes at once, like a musical composer writing for several instruments at once, and in both cases the art is one of balance and relation across time. The sentence is an occasion for the creation of new meaning out of old.

In this chapter I build on the work of the last two, reading Plato's *Phaedrus* with particular attention both to Plato's use of the Greek language and to the shaping of certain of his sentences. In this I will be trying to catch something of what the experience of reading the *Phaedrus* is like; for it is here, in the experience of reading, not in any conceptual or narrative summary, that I think its meaning lies—here that one meets, so far as one ever can, the mind of Plato.

This dialogue carries us, as I try to show, to the edge of language and brings us back into it again. In so doing it explicitly offers us a way of imagining the world and the self within it, including one's relations with others, both intellectual, enacted in speech, and physical, performed in one's erotic life. It is thus self-consciously about the nature of meaning, and in many ways simultaneously: about the meaning of

Lysias' speech, which provides its occasion; about the meaning of Socrates' first speech in response to it, which he quickly repudiates; about the meaning of his second speech, in which he reverses his position; about the meaning of the complex conversation he has with Phaedrus about these texts. In each case meaning is sought not simply interpretively or analytically, but socially and ethically: What does it mean to live a life on the terms offered by Lysias, by Socrates in his first speech, by Socrates in his second speech, by Phaedrus or Socrates at various points in their conversation, and so on? The *Phaedrus* is also about its own meaning as well: What does this text mean, including as an exemplification of a way of life? At the center of the whole thing, raising questions of meaning of all these kinds, is the great myth of the soul, which offers a comprehensive way of imagining the world as a whole and human life within it.

In contrast to the texts read earlier, in the *Phaedrus* there is rather little by way of narrative of the past, for which a meaning is claimed or resisted; rather, Plato and Socrates both concentrate on certain activities of mind and feeling, as they are exemplified and contrasted in the dialogue, and to the kind of futures to which they respectively point. The focus is thus on the meaning of present and future experience, not on the past. As often in Plato's Socratic dialogues, the real question is how—by what activities of mind, and in what relations with others—one should lead one's life, and why.

In keeping with Plato's usual practice, Socrates represents one mode of life, that of "philosophy" or "dialectic," while an explicit or implied antagonist—in this case the orator Lysias—represents another. Between these two Phaedrus is in a position of choosing, with real consequences for his character and future. But there is another crucial presence here, that of Plato himself, who engages us not in "philosophy" exactly as Socrates does it, nor in "rhetoric" as Lysias practices it, but in a different set of activities, defined in the experience of the text itself; and still another presence, that of the reader, who faces choices and responsibilities directly analogous to those faced by Phaedrus.

It used to be rather common to think that the form of the Platonic dialogue is really only a surface and that the real meaning of the text lies in the propositions, ideas, and arguments that it asserts, or in the world of eternal forms and ideas to which it is meant to point. More recently, however, readers have come to see the form of the Platonic dialogue as essential to its meaning, and in what follows I try to show how that is so in the case of the *Phaedrus*.[1] For I think that Plato defines philosophy not as a set of propositions but as an experience and activity of mind, which it is the object of his own writing both to manifest and to stimulate.

Every text creates its reader's experience sentence by sentence, phrase by phrase, and that is true of Plato too. In what follows I accordingly attend with particular care to the shape and life of certain of Plato's sentences. Not that every Platonic sentence is the same; quite the reverse, for Plato seems to write on the assumption that every sentence should have its own shape, as it has its own meaning.

As I say above, I focus also on the fact that the *Phaedrus* is written in Greek. In the *Phaedrus* Greek functions as any language naturally does, both as a resource—a set of enablements and capacitations—and as a limit, a set of problems and obstructions. For Plato both aspects of the language are especially salient: he is one of the world's great artists, and can make his words do wonderful things; yet he was

---

1. I have developed this point with respect to two other dialogues, the *Gorgias* and the *Crito*. In the *Gorgias* the topic of the dialogue is rhetoric, against which Socrates poses "dialectic," the Platonic term for philosophic thought; I try to show how dialectic receives its most important definition not in any descriptions or explicit accounts, though these exist, but in the very activity the text demands of the reader as he reads it. "Dialectic" is thus most securely defined as the mode of thought this text teaches you as you respond to it. See "The Reconstitution of Language and Self in a Community of Two: Plato's *Gorgias*," chap. 4 in *When Words Lose Their Meaning: Constitutions and Reconstitutions of Language, Character, and Community* (Chicago: University of Chicago Press, 1984). With respect to the *Crito* my argument is analogous. Here the explicit topic is the authority of law, or of the jury's verdict given in accordance with law; what I try to show is that the true authority defined and appealed to in this dialogue is not that verdict, or the law, but once more, the activity in which the text engages its reader. It is not rules of law, or institutions, to which we should accord authority, but certain practices of mind and language, as they are exemplified here, or so I read the dialogue as arguing. See "Plato's *Crito*: The Authority of Law and Philosophy," chap. 1 in *Acts of Hope: Creating Authority in Literature, Law, and Politics* (Chicago: University of Chicago Press, 1994). For recent and more sustained arguments on the functions of the dialogic form, see Charles H. Kahn, *Plato and the Socratic Dialogue: The Philosophic Use of a Literary Form* (Cambridge: Cambridge University Press, 1996), and Hayden W. Ausland, "Reading Plato Mimetically," *American Journal of Philology* 18 (1997): 371–416. For views similar to my own, that Plato's dialogues are intellectual and social dramas, see Danielle S. Allen, "Plato's Paradigm Shifts," chap. 10 in *The World of Prometheus: The Politics of Punishing in Democratic Athens* (Princeton: Princeton University Press, 2000), and Berel Lang, *The Anatomy of Philosophical Style: Literary Philosophy and the Philosophy of Literature* (Oxford: Basil Blackwell, 1990), 12–15, 32–33, and 78–79.

deeply alienated from many of the central commitments of his culture,
and these commitments of course are manifested and concretized in
the language.[2] His Greek was thus a constant problem for him, as well
as a resource, and I hope to be able to show some ways in which that
is true. This work will also require us to think about the kind of English into which Plato is normally translated, and in which very little
of the experience I mean is or can be present.

When I speak of the experience of reading Plato I want to include
what might be thought somewhat simple or even naive elements, for I
think they can be of great significance. One is its humor: as a friend
and I read through the *Phaedrus* a couple of times, meeting once a
week for the purpose, we found ourselves laughing out loud, over and
over again; not at the stark and heavy-handed and somewhat unpleasant "Socratic irony" that comes across in translation, but at something else, built into the experience of the text at its most immediate level; something not only humorous, but good-humored. Another
similar point: in reading the *Phaedrus* one slides from passages that
are clear and accessible, written in pellucid Greek, to others that are
difficult, contorted, hard to read and hard to understand; and much of
the meaning of the text lies, I think, in this very shift.

The experience of reading the *Phaedrus* is, of course, far too rich
and full to be represented schematically, or even in full translation,
for it is created by each word and phrase and sentence working together in time as the text proceeds. My aim here is to show some of the
ways in which it works, both focusing on particular passages and suggesting some connections between the meaning of these experiences
and the meaning of the dialogue as a whole. To use the images of travel
and exploration that are so congenial to me, it is as though I am trying
to give some sense of life on a distant island by focusing with some
care on three or four events, against a lightly-sketched background,
rather than attempting a full description of everything that happens. In
either case you must go there if you really want to see it; my hope is to

2. The Greek words for "good" and "excellent" and "just," and their opposites, have
meanings in the language with which Plato profoundly disagrees. Yet that is the only language he has. Much of the work of his philosophy therefore consists of a struggle to redefine the central terms of value in his culture. For a brief account, see my "Reconstitution of
Language and Self in a Community of Two: Plato's *Gorgias*." The most dramatic performance of his alienation is no doubt the *Apology of Socrates*, the speech Socrates gives to the
jury that convicts him, and sentences him to death, for what Socrates calls his philosophy.

give you a sense of what it would be like, and why it is really worth doing.[3]

The Shape of the Text

The *Phaedrus* is a difficult and problematic dialogue, not least because it seems to shift its subject matter and its style throughout. I therefore start with an outline of its basic structure.

It begins as Socrates meets Phaedrus on a walk outside the city walls. Phaedrus has just been to hear Lysias read a speech at a small gathering, and is full of excitement about it; in fact, as Socrates makes him reveal, he has a copy of the speech with him, which he is trying to get by heart. At Socrates' insistence—for he would rather hear the actual words of Lysias than Phaedrus' remembered version—Phaedrus reads the speech to him.

It is on a subject close to the heart of Socrates, Phaedrus tells him, for the speech is about love, or at least about desire. We quickly learn that it is a rhetorical and social *tour de force,* for in it the speaker argues to a young man that his proposal of sexual relations should not be turned down on the grounds that he, the speaker, does not love the boy; quite the reverse, Lysias' speaker argues, this is itself a good reason for granting him the favors he asks. The speech is in this sense a paradox, reversing deep cultural expectations, for in classical Athens the only thing that makes a liaison of this kind honorable rather than shameful is the devotion of the lover to the beloved.[4] In its complex and clever arguments this speech shows what the rhetorical skill of Lysias can achieve, and Phaedrus is stunned by its brilliance.

"Can anyone do as well?" Phaedrus asks when he has finished, thus

3. In working out the views expressed in this chapter I have found the following to be especially helpful: A. W. H. Adkins, "The Speech of 'Lysias' in Plato's *Phaedrus,*" in *The Greeks and Us: Essays in Honor of A. W. H. Adkins,* ed. Robert Louden and Paul Scholl-meier (Chicago: University of Chicago Press, 1996), 224–40; Harry Berger Jr., *"Phaedrus* and the Politics of Inscription," in *Plato and Postmodernism,* ed. Steven Shankman (Glenside, Pa.: Aldine Press, 1994) 76–114; Gerrit Jacob De Vries, *A Commentary on the Phaedrus of Plato* (Amsterdam: Adolf M. Hakkert, 1969); K. J. Dover, *Lysias and the Corpus Lysiacum* (Berkeley: University of California Press, 1968); G. R. F. Ferrari, *Listening to the Cicadas: A Study of Plato's Phaedrus* (Cambridge: Cambridge University Press, 1987); and C. J. Rowe, *Plato: Phaedrus* (Wiltshire: Aris and Philips, 1986). All Greek quotations are from the Oxford Classical Texts edition by John Burnet (Oxford: Oxford University Press, 1901).

4. See generally K. J. Dover's magisterial work, *Greek Homosexuality* (Cambridge: Harvard University Press, 1978). Here Lysias is arguing that the nonlover will paradoxically be more devoted to the boy than the lover, a position Socrates' second speech will answer.

making explicit what is nearly so already, that the relation imagined between Socrates and Lysias is that of competitors: here rhetorical competitors, more deeply competitors for the soul, perhaps in a sense the love, of Phaedrus. Socrates accepts the challenge, and makes a speech of his own on the same paradoxical thesis, and on somewhat similar grounds. For Lysias the main evil is that the passion of the lover will lead him to excesses that both he and the beloved will regret; for Socrates it is that the lover's passion is itself a form of madness or craziness. Socrates' speech is in praise of reason and moderation and balance in life, for him a kind of one-finger exercise.

But when he has finished, he is immediately overcome with a sense of his own impiety and wrongdoing—for is Love, *Erōs,*[5] not a god?—and gives a speech of another kind, on the other side, now celebrating the very madness in which the lover participates. This speech includes a famous myth, in which the human soul is presented as a chariot drawn through the sky by two winged horses, a good one and a bad one, managed by a charioteer. Each human soul once participated in the blessed life of the gods, Socrates says, beholding truth and beauty and all other good things as they actually are; but from that state it has fallen away, into the shell of a mortal creature, and has lost its wings. The great virtue and power of love is to remind the soul of what it saw and experienced in its earlier life, thus arousing desires that will stimulate it to grow the wings that will enable it to return to the life it once had. Love is divine madness in its best form. Socrates concludes this speech with a beautiful prayer to love.

In the second part of the dialogue Socrates and Phaedrus reflect critically on the three speeches before them, turning first to rhetoric, the art of speech and argument that Lysias practices and that Phaedrus admires. In what does it consist? Socrates argues, and convinces Phaedrus, that the art of speech cannot consist simply in the capacity to manipulate forms of speech, in cleverness of argument or anything superficial, but must lie in understanding the truth of what is spoken of, whether it is justice or beauty or whatever the subject may be. And since speech is a method of leading the soul, *psuchē,* in every case the nature of the soul itself must also be understood, and in particular the different forms of soul found in different people. The ultimate question

5. Here and occasionally elsewhere in the chapter, I follow an English term with the Greek work it is meant to translate. This is especially important with respect to *erōs,* for as we shall see there is another term for love, *philia,* with which it is regularly contrasted.

is not whether an act of speech succeeds in persuading others, especially the thoughtless, but whether it is good in itself, and this is always a question of knowledge and ethics, not merely of skill.

Then, by a transition that seems almost accidental, the topic shifts to writing. Socrates says that writing is always worse than speaking, though thought by many to be better; the reason is that writing cannot respond when it is criticized or questioned, but simply repeats itself monotonously. The true life of the mind can be found only in living speech, which can be imagined as a kind of writing not on material things but on the soul of another. The dialogue closes with another prayer, this one to Pan, in which Socrates asks that he may become "beautiful, *kalos,* within"; that whatever he has "outside" may be congenial to that which is within; that he may learn to count the wise man as rich; and that his own material wealth may be only such as a man of sensible mind can comfortably carry.

From one point of view, this is a potpourri: about whether the beloved should yield to the lover or the nonlover; about rhetoric; about writing; about the nature of the soul. Certainly if you tried to make this text tell us what "Plato thought" on a range of "subjects," it would lack coherence. Further complicating the question of subject matter is that of tone: much of the dialogue is arch and comical, other parts deeply felt, and a great deal of its meaning lies exactly here, in the specific tones with which Socrates and Phaedrus speak, to each other and to the reader. And what of the relation between these two men? Phaedrus is in a sense infatuated with Lysias; Socrates, as is revealed in an offhand remark at the end of the dialogue, has some undefined but admiring relation with Isocrates;[6] yet there is much that is erotic in their interaction with each other as well, and in some sense the whole dialogue is about the relation between them.

---

6. Erotic language is used to describe Phaedrus' infatuation with Lysias, but this is not a case of the classic kind of *erōs* of which the dialogue mainly speaks, which is that of an older man for a youth just reaching maturity. Lysias and Phaedrus were both historical figures, and only ten years apart in age; presumably their approximate ages would be known by Plato's audience. (The dates of the characters are these: Socrates was born about 469; Lysias about 460; Phaedrus about 450; Isocrates about 436; Plato about 429). Lysias spent most of his life in Thurii, in southern Italy; at the time the dialogue takes place he has just returned, as he did either in about 411, or as some maintain, a bit earlier. Only the relation between Socrates and Isocrates would have the appropriate difference in ages, and that, as we shall see, is no infatuation. For an attempt to construct possible historical dates for the dialogue, see Dover, *Lysias and the Corpus Lysiacum*, 32–34, 41–43; DeVries, *A Commentary on the Phaedrus of Plato*, 7.

Once we drop the expectation that the dialogue should be read as Plato's twisted way of telling us what he thinks on certain subjects, and accept the idea that the text has a life of its own which it is our aim to understand, the question of coherence begins to resolve itself, at least at a general level. Running throughout the text, from beginning to end, is the question: What attitude should Phaedrus have towards Lysias and his rhetorical accomplishments? He is infatuated with him, and with them, in more ways than one; Socrates holds out an alternative, himself and the kind of life he leads, for which his word is philosophy, "the love of wisdom," and which he wants Phaedrus to accept. This is not straightforward persuasion, however, like that which takes place in Lysias' speech—choose me, not him, for these reasons—because the lives of the two men are so different that there is no common language in which that difference can be adequately articulated and measured. But that difference is nonetheless the true and uniting subject of everything we read here.

What Plato tries to show is that the rhetorician is driven by a false love, the philosopher by a true one; the former creates false relations with those whom he addresses, especially when he writes; the philosopher creates true relations, especially in conversation. The passages on love and those on rhetoric thus have, despite appearances, a common subject. One point of the passages on writing is that the kind of relation that the philosopher aims to have with a person is an actual and present relation with another human being, not with an abstract or hypothetical entity, a "reader"; with another human who has a body, in fact, which if physically beautiful gives rise in one's erotic response to some of the instincts and motives of philosophy itself. This is about as far from the usual conception of a disembodied Plato as one can get; though there is an important paradox here, about which I speak below, for it is also of course true, against the force of the whole argument about writing, that Plato has written this text and left it behind him, for unknown readers.

The difference between Socrates and Lysias is not merely a difference between one set of propositions and another, asserted against a common background of shared motives and understandings; rather, the difference lies at the center of the self, in the way life itself and its most basic activities are imagined and pursued. We begin the dialogue in contact with a mind, that of Phaedrus, which, despite his evident virtues and abilities, has somehow got everything wrong. We as readers, and Socrates as his interlocutor, are brought into his world and come to share his way of talking and thinking. Plato's task in the dialogue is to move Phaedrus, and with him the reader, from this position to another, which at the outset cannot even be imagined; and which, even in retrospect, it is hard to remember, impossible to restate. ("The soul as a chariot drawn by winged horses?" the reader may ask; "I went along with *that*?") How the dialogue carries us from one position to another, how it defines the position it recommends, and then makes it disappear from the memory, these are our questions; and, as I have said, we shall pursue them both in general and at the level of the local and particular, with attention especially to the life of certain sentences. It is important to see that the major set pieces of the dialogue, the three speeches on love, are all preceded and followed by conversations between Socrates and Phaedrus, and that these interactions do much to define and redefine the meaning of the speeches themselves, creating the particular and shifting contexts against which they act.

Socrates and Phaedrus

The dialogue opens with a question from Socrates to Phaedrus, whom he has apparently just met: *poi kai pothen*, "Where are you going, and from where?" (More literally, "Whither and whence?") This tiny detail has great resonance, for while at one level it asks Phaedrus, sensibly enough, where he is physically going this morning, at another it asks a deeper question, spiritual or philosophic in kind: Where do you come from, where do you go, not only this morning, but in your life? That is in fact the central question to which the dialogue will be addressed. Phaedrus answers it in its most immediate sense, saying that he has come from the house of Lysias to the country, outside the city walls, in order to learn by heart the speech Lysias just displayed. As I have suggested, in what follows Socrates will make problematic the whole set of commitments out of which Phaedrus is operating when he does this. And at the end, after Socrates' prayer to Pan, the dialogue will conclude with the word *iōmen*, which means: "Let us go." The text is thus given its most fundamental shape by its beginning and its closing: the two men arrive separately and leave together.

Phaedrus tells Socrates that he has just come from the house of Lysias, where he heard a wonderful speech, in which Lysias argues that a handsome young man ought to sexually gratify the man who does not love him rather than the one who does. The appeal of this speech lies plainly in its paradoxical quality, its display of rhetorical skill in arguing for what seems impossible. Socrates marks his recognition of this, and his distance from it, in the gentlest imaginable way: *Ō gennaios,* "O splendid one!" If only Lysias would make a similar argument on behalf of the poor and old, he says, then he would be a public benefactor indeed. Socrates thus conveys his sense that this is a truly impossible position that cannot be taken seriously on the merits. But it is to be taken seriously in quite another way, as the expression of a certain kind of mind and a way of life that have great appeal for Phaedrus. Socrates is accordingly eager to hear it.

Phaedrus puts him off, saying that he cannot possibly remember the whole speech, which after all he has only just now heard for the first time. Socrates' response is crucial for the tone, and hence the meaning, of the conversation between them. He says:

Ὦ Φαῖδρε, εἰ ἐγὼ Φαῖδρον ἀγνοῶ, καὶ ἐμαυτοῦ ἐπιλέλησμαι. ἀλλὰ γὰρ οὐδέτερά ἐστι τούτων· εὖ οἶδα ὅτι Λυσίου λόγον ἀκούων ἐκεῖνος οὐ μόνον ἅπαξ ἤκουσεν, ἀλλὰ πολλάκις ἐπαναλαμβάνων ἐκέλευέν οἱ λέγειν, ὁ δὲ ἐπείθετο προθύμως. τῷ δὲ οὐδὲ ταῦτα ἦν ἱκανά, ἀλλὰ τελευτῶν παραλαβὼν τὸ βιβλίον ἃ μάλιστα ἐπεθύμει ἐπεσκόπει, καὶ τοῦτο δρῶν ἐξ ἑωθινοῦ καθήμενος ἀπειπὼν εἰς περίπατον ᾔει, ὡς μὲν ἐγὼ οἶμαι, νὴ τὸν κύνα, ἐξεπιστάμενος τὸν λόγον, εἰ μὴ πάνυ τι ἦν μακρός. ἐπορεύετο δ' ἐκτὸς τείχους ἵνα μελετῴη. ἀπαντήσας δὲ τῷ νοσοῦντι περὶ λόγων ἀκοήν, ἰδὼν μέν, ἰδών, ἥσθη ὅτι ἕξοι τὸν συγκορυβαντιῶντα, καὶ προάγειν ἐκέλευε. δεομένου δὲ λέγειν τοῦ τῶν λόγων ἐραστοῦ, ἐθρύπτετο ὡς δὴ οὐκ ἐπιθυμῶν λέγειν· τελευτῶν δὲ ἔμελλε καὶ εἰ μή τις ἑκὼν ἀκούοι βίᾳ ἐρεῖν. (228-a-5)

O, Phaedrus—if I don't know Phaedrus, I have forgotten my self as well; but neither of these is the case. I know [perfectly] well that in hearing Lysias' speech he did not listen to it just once, but repeatedly ordered him to perform it, and that Lysias eagerly obeyed. But for Phaedrus not even this was enough; and at the end he took the book in his hands and examined whatever he especially desired. He did this from the dawn, sitting there and speaking it out, until he went for a walk—as I think he did, by the Dog[7]—to learn the speech by heart, unless it was too long. He went outside the walls to practice it. Then, meeting one sick for the hearing of speeches—beholding him, beholding him right there—he was delighted at the prospect of having a partner in his rites, and called on him to lead the way. Upon being asked by this lover of speeches, *erastou tōn logōn,* to say the speech, Phaedrus acted coy, as though he did not wish to speak; but in the

---

7. "By the Dog" is a familiar Socratic expostulation, meaning roughly, "By God."

end he meant to speak after all, by force, even if the other did not
wish to hear him.

This brief speech does much to establish the tone of the whole: Socrates shows that he does know Phaedrus, for of course his suppositions
are entirely correct, and that he can cheerfully make fun of him, but he
does this in a fundamentally accepting and affectionate way. The passage is comic, but not unkind, in part because it shows how fully Socrates does in fact know who Phaedrus is. At the same time, it identifies
with great clarity where Phaedrus has come from, which was one of
the opening questions; and it does this through an act of the imagination, an argument from character: "I know Phaedrus, and the Phaedrus I know would have done this, and that"—an argument that is
confirmed by Phaedrus' silence.

What Socrates understands about Phaedrus is that he is totally absorbed in a certain version of the intellectual or artistic life, intoxicated
with it, even to the point of trying to deceive Socrates. This capacity
for absorption is itself a good thing, though misplaced; how to redirect
the mind and energy of Phaedrus is the central problem Socrates will
face in the dialogue. As he presents himself, Socrates in fact shares a
similar intoxication, for he is of course the one who is sick for the
hearing of speeches, and as we shall see, his susceptibilities are such
that he too needs correction.

Later in the dialogue Socrates will say that the successful maker of
speeches must have a knowledge of the general nature of the human
soul, *psuchē* (as in his great myth Socrates demonstrates that he himself has); in addition, however, he must know the differences among
various types of soul so that he can speak directly and effectively to
a particular audience, and it is this kind of knowledge that Socrates
is here demonstrating that he has about Phaedrus. He does indeed
"know Phaedrus." His definition of himself as "sick" for the hearing
of speeches is important too, for both Lysias' speech and his own in
response to it will define *erōs* as a species of illness; and his second
speech will redefine that illness as a form of inspiration. The suggestion
that Phaedrus would like to trick or force him into hearing the speech
of Lysias will also have resonance later in the dialogue, for it is closely
related to the idea of rhetoric itself and to the practice of seduction,
both of which are ways of getting others to submit to one's own will.
But the main element established here is the comic and affectionate
tone, here marked, even in translation, by such things as the exag-

gerated and overdramatic repetition, "beholding him, beholding him right there," by the stagey use of the third person, and by the odd combination of fantasy and fact—for Socrates is both imagining what happened and at the same time saying what is historically true, at least in the imagined world of this text.

Phaedrus is not quite through with his tricks; he says he will recite the speech from memory, but Socrates, seeing the text of the speech itself sticking out from his cloak, will not let him, and insists upon hearing the original thing. This insistence on reading will come to have a increased significance later in the dialogue, when Socrates argues against the practice and value of writing; here he is of course right to insist on the very words of Lysias, who is not present, since it is these words that have captivated Phaedrus, confirming in him the disease that it will be Socrates' object to cure.

The topic shifts now, somewhat strangely it may seem, to the landscape, for as Phaedrus says they must find a proper place for the reading, and where shall it be? Socrates suggests that they walk down the Ilissus in the shade of the trees until they find a convenient spot. Phaedrus points out a tall plane tree, some distance away, which has a grassy bank at its foot; then his mind moves to what he knows of this place, and asks whether it is not here that Boreas is said to have snatched up a young woman, Oreithuia, from the river. No, says Socrates, some way further down, where there is a ford and an altar.

There is much that could be said about this focus on the scenery—the background of their talk—as G. R. F. Ferrari has shown in his beautiful book, *Listening to the Cicadas,* which argues that much of the life of the dialogue consists of shifting relations of foreground and background. The three speeches on *erōs,* for example, are first foregrounded, as they are presented, then backgrounded as they are analyzed. Philosophy is in this way defined, Ferrari says, not as mythmaking nor as analysis, but as the activity of mind that comprehends both, in shifting alternation; this, in turn, helps explain why our memory of this text does not lead us to clear and restatable positions, but leaves us in something of the confusion that Plato's prose on occasion deliberately creates. I find all of this illuminating and right; of this passage I want only to observe that Socrates, who is often regarded as the ultimate urbanite, knowing nothing of the world outside Athens—and who will soon be so defined in this very dialogue—here shows that he knows more about the river and its locale than his supposed guide; a fact of which nothing is made, but it lies there in the background, challenging what is said in the foreground.

This brings us to the first of the sentences I want to read. Phaedrus asks Socrates whether he believes in the myth about Boreas he has just repeated. This question will come back again later in this dialogue, which has at its center the myth of the soul as the chariot drawn by winged horses, about which we must ask: How is such a myth to be read? In what sense can it be "believed"?

Socrates says that it would not be odd if he disbelieved the myth of Boreas, as the wise ones, *hoi sophoi,* do; [8] and that he could go on in their clever fashion, *sophizomenos,* and explain it away, saying that a blast of the north wind, *boreas,* threw the girl from the rocks, and that this is how the story arose. But once you start off on that track, Socrates says, it will lead to the rationalization of all kinds of things—people will ask you to explain the Centaurs, and Gorgon, and Pegasus—and I simply do not have the time for that. The reason is this: that I am not yet able to follow the Delphic command to "know myself," *gnōnai emauton;* this is the great object of life, and until I attain it it would be ridiculous to inquire into these other things.

A part of the beauty of this passage lies in its indirection, for Socrates does not answer the question put to him about his beliefs; instead, he says that the question focuses attention and energy in the wrong way.[9] As with many questions that are put to us, then, the right thing to do is to leave it alone. This is a refusal to compete on the offered grounds, a refusal to respond to a challenge on its own terms, and in it Socrates expresses an independence of such things. This is just the opposite of the way Phaedrus thinks: he will present Lysias' speech as a challenge to Socrates—can you do as well?—and he will similarly imagine Socrates' second speech as a challenge to Lysias, one that Lysias will not be able to refuse.

In his remark about the command of the Delphic Oracle, Socrates here asserts as primary a field of knowledge that is available to us all, namely, ourselves and our experience. But what does he mean by this? What kinds of questions would give shape to the investigation he describes?

Here is a sentence in which Socrates begins to show us how he thinks of these things:

8. This is, of course, a highly ironic phrase.

9. The question of belief is charged with external significance, as is Socrates' later speech in praise of the god *Erōs,* for one of the accusations made at his trial was that he did not believe in the gods that the city believed in (*Apology,* 24-b-6). Plato is here distinguishing Socrates from the Sophists, both in his lack of interest in disproving traditional myths and in his actual piety, of a kind, towards the Delphic Oracle and towards the gods themselves.

ὅθεν δὴ χαίρειν ἐάσας ταῦτα, πειθόμενος δὲ τῷ νομιζομένῳ περὶ
αὐτῶν, ὃ νυνδὴ ἔλεγον, σκοπῶ οὐ ταῦτα ἀλλ' ἐμαυτόν, εἴτε τι θηρίον
ὂν τυγχάνω Τυφῶνος πολυπλοκώτερον καὶ μᾶλλον ἐπιτεθυμένον,
εἴτε ἡμερώτερόν τε καὶ ἁπλούστερον ζῷον, θείας τινὸς καὶ ἀτύφου
μοίρας φύσει μετέχον. (230-a-1)

This is why I let these things [i.e., the explication of myths] go with a
brief farewell, believing the usual thing about them, and, as I just
said, I do not examine them but myself, asking whether I am a wild
beast more lustful and complex even than Typhon [a mythical mon-
ster], or, by contrast, a gentler and simpler being, by nature having
a share of some quality that is divine and not puffed up with vanity
[atuphos].

hothen de chairein easas tauta,
   for which reason with a brief farewell letting these things go,
peithomenos de tōi nomizomenōi peri autōn, ho nundē elegon,
   believing [or "accepting"] the usual thing about them, what I just said,
skopō ou tauta all' emauton, eite ti thērion on tunchanō
   I examine not these things but myself, whether I am myself a kind of wild beast
Tuphōnos poluplokōteron kai mallon epitethumenon
   more complicated than Typhon and more lustful
eite hēmerōteron te kai haplousteron zōon
   or on the other hand a gentler and simpler animal
theias tinos kai atuphou moiras phusei metechon
   in some divine and unpuffed up element a share by nature having.

("Unpuffed up" is *atyphou,* which also means, in a pun, "not typhon-
like," or "unbeastly.")

The drama of this sentence lies partly in its complex structure,
which is in outline this: first, two participial clauses ("letting these
things go," "believing the established thing"); then a relative clause
("what I just said"); then the main clause, beginning with the main
verb ("I examine") and concluding with the object ("not those things
but myself"); then a clause serving as a second object of the proposed
examination, ("whether I am *A*, or by contrast *B*"); then, in closing,
a participial clause ("sharing in some divine and unbeastly element.")
The sentence begins and ends with participles referring to Socrates,
both set in the nominative, and thus has something of the shape of
a circle or ring composition. The relative clause ("what I just said")
precedes its referent, which is easy in Greek, hard in English, and has
the effect of creating an uncertainty and then resolving it. Perhaps the

nerve of the sentence lies in its surprising pun, connecting *Typhon* with *atuphos* (unpuffed up).[10] The whole gives the distinct impression of a mind that can distinguish and construct, thus exemplifying the activities that much later in the dialogue will be held to characterize philosophic thought *(diairesis* and *sunagōgē).* It is a performance of rational thought at the level of the sentence.

Or so it seems. For beneath the elegant syntax the thought is most obscure: How, after all, is this examination to proceed? What can it have to do with the speech of Lysias? And if what Socrates says about not wasting his time on disproving myths is true, why is it not equally a waste of time to examine the speech of Lysias, for whom it will appear that Socrates has a deep contempt? What the sentence really seems to mean, but does not say explicitly, is that the reading of Lysias, to be of any value to Socrates, must be done in such a way as to be a reading of himself—whatever that would be.

As Socrates puts it, the question is whether he is an utter wild beast, which is a mildly comic and self-mocking suggestion, for nothing could seem farther from the truth. Yet the topic is serious, for at stake in what follows is what it means to be a human being in love, which is at least partly a matter of our animal nature and for some people seems to involve little more than a kind of beastliness. Socrates is asking, then, whether love, and we, can have a share in something else, something unbeastlike and even divine. But the suggestion and the question are gentle, to say the least, as gentle as the distancing expressed in Socrates' first response to hearing the theme of Lysias' speech—*Ō gennaios*—and it is in this gentleness and slight self-mockery, in its tone of voice, that the sentence has perhaps its most distinctive meaning.

Notice also that in this sentence Socrates foreshadows his great myth of the chariot and two horses, where he describes the soul as indeed having something of the divine, as well as something beastly. This sentence is, in fact, the first sketch of what will be the centerpiece of the *Phaedrus* as a whole.

The topic now shifts to the beauty of the scene in which they find themselves. Socrates delivers an exaggerated—puffed up?—panegyric on the tree, and stream, and grass, commending Phaedrus' skill as a guide, and drawing attention away from what he has just said.

---

10. Notice that in asking, "Am I Typhonic?" Socrates is using the material of myth as part of his interior investigation, as he will even more obviously do in his second speech.

It should now be apparent that Socrates' speeches are heavily marked in tone; he does not simply say something, but says it as part of a cultural and social gesture—one that is comic, or exaggerated, or making fun of someone, or accepting, or all of the above. The net effect is a kind of inherent uncertainty as to the status of whatever propositional meaning is asserted, accompanied by an increasing clarity as to the tone, or social meaning. In this, what Socrates says is closer to living speech, or a drama, than it is to more propositional or analytic kinds of writing.

The Speech of Lysias

The speech of Lysias, which comes next, is a striking work, perhaps most striking, as we shall later see, for something that is barely mentioned in the comments made by the others upon it. It is made on behalf of a man arguing that a boy should gratify him sexually, even though he does not love him. Then, as now, this is a paradoxical position at best, but it is further complicated by the nature of the practice of intergenerational homosexuality in classical Athens. In its idealized form, this relation consisted of an older man loving the physical beauty and moral potential of the young man, a younger version of himself; the young man could naturally not love the physical beauty of the older man in the same erotic way, but he could love his more complete and perfected moral nature. The older man was a patron to the younger one, offering practical advantages in the social and political arena, and something of a teacher as well, offering him a model of mature excellence as a guide to his own development. It was apparently considered shameful for the boy under any circumstances to submit to anal penetration (or to engage in oral sex); what was apparently permitted, though with such a lover only, was a kind of stylized masturbation, as portrayed on certain Greek vases.[11] It is, of course, not clear how often even in such ways these relations were consummated; it may be that for some people the whole thing was a kind of elaborate dance around powerful feelings, never resulting in sexual gratification at all.

It is a premise of the exercise that the speaker of Lysias' speech wishes to be sexually gratified by a young man, but in exactly what

11. See Dover, *Greek Homosexuality*, especially 52–53, 89–91, 103, 142–43. It is plain that one who submitted regularly to anal intercourse was beneath contempt. See *Gorgias*, 494-e-5. See also Claude Calame, *The Poetics of Eros in Ancient Greece* (Princeton: Princeton University Press, 1999), 137.

way is never revealed, for he consistently employs euphemisms at every crucial moment. Our attention is repeatedly drawn rather to his admission that he does not love him, *mē erōn*, for here lies the boldness of the rhetorical exercise; the fact that the speaker slides over the precise nature of his request remains in the background. Lysias was by profession a rhetorician who wrote speeches for litigants in Athenian lawsuits and I think one function of this speech is to be a kind of advertisement, demonstrating his skill at making an untenable position credible and persuasive. It is this skill that Phaedrus admires. In fact this speech is not meant to persuade a boy—there is no such boy [12]— but to impress his actual listeners with his rhetorical skill.

This is apparent from its shape and texture. It is written in rather condensed and sometimes difficult Greek, quite unlike Lysias' actual speeches to jurors, which are masterpieces of limpidity; and the arguments it identifies are for the most part not developed, but stand rather as argument headings, or topics. They are a display of the speaker's capacity for invention rather than for elaboration.[13]

Lysias' speech is built upon a comparison between the lover and the nonlover, showing that the advantage lies with the latter. Here are its main arguments: lovers regret afterwards what they have done, while, Lysias says, we nonlovers do not, for we plan it out in a coolheaded way like any other business; lovers look at what the affair cost them, in terms of lost labor, ruined friendships, wrecked businesses, and feel they have paid enough, while we do not incur these costs to begin with, and therefore have nothing with which to charge our partner when we are done; if lovers rank the beloved uncommonly high, as we do not, they will do the same with a successor beloved, forgetting the present one, while we place a constant and less exaggerated value on each; lovers themselves know they are sick with love, and it is foolish to bestow yourself upon a person in such a condition; if you make your choice only among lovers, the choice will be small, among nonlovers it will be large, so your chance of finding excellence is greater; if you fear reproach for what you have done, remember that lovers are likely to brag, nonlovers less so; on the same theme, if he is your lover, the fact that you keep company with him will give rise to suspicions, not so if he is not; after termination your situation will be much worse with a lover, for it will have been his effort during the affair to separate you

---

12. Unless Lysias has singled out Phaedrus (whose name means "shining" or "bright," and may imply handsomeness) and has designs upon him.

13. On the authenticity of the speech, see Dover, *Lysias and the Corpus Lysiacum*, 69–71; DeVries, *A Commentary on the Phaedrus of Plato*, 11–14.

from every other source of support, while the nonlover, not being subject to jealousies, will have welcomed the fact that you have other
friends, *philoi;* lovers want the body before they know the person,
and therefore cannot know whether they will wish to remain friends,
philoi, when passion is over, while we nonlovers begin with friendship,
philia; the moral influence of the lover is worse than that of the nonlover, for unsuccessful lovers are pained by minutiae and successful
ones overlook real faults, while only the nonlover retains the right balance of tolerance and judgment; if you think there cannot be faithful
friendship, *philia,* without love, *erōs,* then we could not value so much
our fathers or sons, or have faithful friends, *philous,* which is not so;
you should gratify not him whose need is greatest, but him who will
give the greatest return, and this is the nonlover.

Near the end of this passage comes the following sentence:

ἐὰν δέ μοι πείθῃ, πρῶτον μὲν οὐ τὴν παροῦσαν ἡδονὴν θεραπεύων
συνέσομαί σοι, ἀλλὰ καὶ τὴν μέλλουσαν ὠφελίαν ἔσεσθαι, οὐχ ὑπ’
ἔρωτος ἡττώμενος ἀλλ’ ἐμαυτοῦ κρατῶν, οὐδὲ διὰ σμικρὰ ἰσχυρὰν
ἔχθραν ἀναιρούμενος ἀλλὰ διὰ μεγάλα βραδέως ὀλίγην ὀργὴν
ποιούμενος, τῶν μὲν ἀκουσίων συγγνώμην ἔχων, τὰ δὲ ἑκούσια
πειρώμενος ἀποτρέπειν· ταῦτα γάρ ἐστι φιλίας πολὺν χρόνον ἐσο-
μένης τεκμήρια. (233-b-6)

If you are persuaded by me, I will keep company with you, serving
not only the present pleasure but the future benefit, not being weak-
ened by love but in command of myself, not taking upon myself
strong hatred on account of petty offenses but slowly creating slight
anger on account of large ones, pardoning all unintentional wrongs
and trying to avert intentional ones; for these things are evidence of a
friendship that will last.

ean de moi peithēi,
    If by me you are persuaded,
prōton men ou tēn parousan hēdonēn therapeuōn sunesomai soi,
    first, not only the present pleasure serving will I keep company with you
alla kai tēn mellousan ōphelian esesthai,
    but also the future benefit,
ouch hup’ erōtos hēttōmenos all’ emautou kratōn,
    not being weakened by love but ruling myself,
oude dia smikra ischuran echthran anairoumenos
    not taking upon myself strong hatred on account of little matters,
alla dia megala bradeōs oligēn orgēn poioumenos,
    but on account of large ones slowly making small anger,

tōn men akousiōn sungnōmēn echōn,
> for unintentional wrongs having pardon

ta de hekousia peirōmenos apotrepein,
> and intentional ones trying to avert,

tauta gar esti philias polun chronon esomenēs tekmēria.
> for these things are of a friendship *(philia)* to last a long time evidences.

I have had to change the word order a bit to fit with English conventions, but even from this translation you can see how balanced and structured this sentence is, built as it is upon a series of contrasts and parallels—present/future, pleasure/benefit, weak/strong, small/great (occasions for anger), small/great (anger), quick/slow (anger), intentional/unintentional, pardon/prevention—each cast in a clause or phrase with its own place in the sequence, and all adding up to a definition of Lysias' central term, *philia*. This is in form highly rhetorical, a display of real compositional skill: a peroration describing the character of the ideal partner and his relationship with the youth, and capturing much of the power and brilliance of the speech as a whole. A part of its significance for us is that one cannot help admiring the capacity of a mind that can make a sentence so modeled and balanced—the very capacity, or a part of it, that Phaedrus so admires in Lysias. But even when we first read it we may notice the emphasis on anger, a topic to which I return below.

Lysias' speech is in many ways an amazing display—when he has finished reading it Phaedrus cannot contain his admiration— but it is so in part because the skill of the rhetorician keeps the attention of his audience always where he wants it, on his argument and his own skill with words, so that we do not see what is in some sense directly before us, and, when seen, profoundly repellent. What happens if you read it as though it were a real speech, by a man to a boy, and ask what is meant by its primary assumption: that the speaker is one who does not love *(mē erōn)* the boy? The Greek word for love here, *erōs*, does not mean charity or affection or merger of identities, or anything like that; it means sexual desire. If the speaker has no sexual desire for the boy, what does he want from him? If he does have sexual desire, what distinction is he making when he says his desire is not *erōs*—is it then simply the desire for power over the boy, without the intoxication of sexual feeling? What he seems to be proposing, then, is not merely loveless sex, but sexless sex, impossible to ask or wish for; or, if that is too strong, desire of one kind, not of another—not the lover's bewitched obsession, but the impersonal desire for sexual gratification reduced to its core in our purely animal nature.

I think we are in fact to read the speaker as simply lying, disguising his actual erotic desire in order to enable him to make the very speech he does, which he hopes will lead the boy to choose him—even though this choice, of a lover, is itself condemned by his speech. The lie is of course meant to be perceived by Lysias' actual audience, for in it—and the paradox it entails—inheres much of the brilliance of the rhetorical performance. But the fact remains that on the conditions on which we are asked to imagine the speech taking place, Lysias' speaker is offering either deceit of the most patent kind or something even more awful, sex without desire simply for the sake of power. When we look at the speech as though it were actually made by a person seeking gratification from another, that is what we find, and it is a kind of hell. (Look at how deep the topic of anger is in the arguments summarized above, for example.) When we examine it as a display of skill by Lysias, having nothing to do with any claims made to any real boy, but merely meant to demonstrate his ingenuity, we find another kind of emptiness, similarly appalling.[14]

That even the speaker recognizes something of this is made evident both in his constant use of euphemisms to refer to the sexual gratification he has in mind and in his acknowledgment that one risk for the boy in the course he is urging upon him is shame and reproach. Likewise, he cannot avoid—most notably in the last clause of the sentence quoted above—the use of the central value term *philia* and its cognates, in a way that will necessarily reveal and define the true nature of his offer. For both in this sentence and throughout the speech, *philia* is the central term of value upon which Lysias' case rests. If what he asks is inconsistent with *philia* it should not be granted; if consistent with long-lasting *philia,* it should be.

Yet *philia* is a complex term. In one strain it means true friendship; not simply an exchange of pleasures and commitments, though including that, but actual friendship, a relation of mutual interest and concern and affection. In another strain, however, it means something rather different: participation in the network of political and social alliances that give one security and power, as we use our equivalent term when we speak of someone having "friends" in high places. In normal

14. For a reading of this speech that makes Lysias' speaker far more attractive than the hellish figure I describe, see Adkins, "The Speech of 'Lysias' in Plato's Phaedrus," 224–40.

use, and particularly as applied to the standard erotic relation between older and younger men, the two strains of *philia* are fused and interact, for both elements are present, as is, of course, *erōs* as well. In Lysias' speech, however, the pragmatic and political meaning is the only one possible, for the speaker has demonstrated his own incapacity for friendship of the other kind. In this very sentence, in fact, one sees the speaker claiming the power of anger and pardon; putting a primary value on self-control; and choosing by pleasure and benefit. Nothing could be further from the way he argues than true friendship. Every move is a calculation of self-interest; that is in fact its own claim to brilliance.

To one like Phaedrus who has not thought about these things, all this may not much matter; but to Socrates—whose effort it will be to enact friendship of a different kind—to Plato, and to the reader, nothing will matter more than the nature of true *philia*.

There is another mark of the hellishness of what Lysias offers, namely, that while he is rightly persuasive about the dangers of a relation with a lover of a certain sort, he assumes that the only alternative is a relation with him. He is here employing a standard seducer's line: You will do it with someone, why not me? Sometime, why not now? In contrast with all this, we are given Socrates within the dialogue, and Plato in writing it, both of whom, as we shall see, are acting out of friendship of a different kind, to which in fact it is their aim is to give a new and tangible definition.

In accepting such a speech as this as a model, and recommending it to Socrates as something splendidly done (234-e-6), Phaedrus is indeed showing us "where he comes from" and "where he is going," at least unless something else happens. He has got everything wrong, and has no idea that that is so. He seems to be unreachable.

Socrates and Phaedrus

The interchange between Phaedrus and Socrates that now follows is, to my ear at least, unpleasant, full of feints and moves on both sides that reflect a fundamental distance between the men. In response to Phaedrus' question, "Wasn't that wonderful?" Socrates at first agrees, so wonderful in fact as to strike him out of his wits, *ekplagēnai;* but he then goes on to say that the reason for this effect was not the speech itself, but Phaedrus' appearance as he read it, transported with pleasure, on which Socrates focused all his attention. Believing that Phaedrus knew more about "such things" than he did, Socrates says, he went along with him. Phaedrus reads this as a form of *paizein,* or play, and wishes Socrates would be serious, *spoudakein;* does he really think anyone could say anything that would be "more and better" than what Lysias said on this subject? In his response Socrates again dances around, archly saying something like this: "What? Are we now to judge it on the merits of what it said, and not as a display? I have nothing to say about that, since I attended only to the rhetoric of it; but even there I did think there were defects, especially in its repetition and a kind of youthful showing off, in its demonstration of the ability to say the same thing many ways."

Phaedrus responds with a direct challenge, "You are saying nothing," *ouden legeis;* of all the possible things to say on the subject Lysias has left out none, so that no one could say "more and better" on the topic. This is apparently Phaedrus' test of rhetorical excellence; Socrates meets this reiterated challenge in an oblique and irritating way, saying that he cannot agree, for he would be refuted by men and women of ages past who have done this very thing, that is, said more and better. When asked, "Which men and women?" Socrates answers with mock humility, saying in effect: "Oh, I am not sure: perhaps Sappho and Anacreon; but at any rate I am sure some have done so, for I myself feel I could say something different from Lysias, and not worse, and I know that I cannot be the source of such things, but must have got them from others." Phaedrus lets the identification issue pass and seizes on the implicit promise or boast that Socrates himself can do better; "If you can do this," he says, "I will set up a golden statute at Delphi in your honor."

One can see how little Phaedrus understands Socrates, and the *philia* he offers, when he thinks to tempt him with such an offer, which belongs entirely to *philia* of the other category. Though perhaps having its roots in an excess of enthusiasm, here expressed in conventional terms, his effort to induce behavior by a reward or incentive operates as a species of manipulation, not far removed from the idea of control and power at the heart of rhetoric itself, at least as represented here.

Socrates now backs away: Are you in earnest, *espoudakas,* because I attacked your beloved, and do you think I would really try to outdo him?—This is more than Phaedrus can bear. You must speak, he says, or we will descend to physical force; and I am stronger and younger than you; so speak willingly, *hekōn,* rather than by force, *bia.* This is an extraordinary moment, marking a true breakdown in their relations. Phaedrus is "joking," as I read him, but his joke nonetheless expresses a real determination to have his way. It is a transformation of the offer of a statue, a movement from incentive to force, and it is based on the same insistence on his own will, not his friend's wishes. It recalls Socrates' statement—in the speech quoted earlier, in which he said he "knew Phaedrus" and was certain that Phaedrus had taken the speech away to memorize it—that this Phaedrus, when meeting with one "sick for the hearing of speeches," pretended to be reluctant to speak but actually intended to do so, even if by force, *bia,* with a listener not willing, *mē hekōn.*

Socrates here responds by saying that he will be made ridiculous, *geloios,* if he enters competition with a good craftsman of speeches; Phaedrus repeats his gesture of threat, but in different terms, this time saying that if Socrates does not make the speech, he (Phaedrus) will never ever under any circumstances show or report to him any speech of anyone, here piling up the negatives in a marvelous display of his own skill with language: *mēdepote . . . mēdena mēdenos . . . mēte . . . mēte . . .*" The tone here, as I read it, recedes from the joking threat of force to a more genuinely comic and faintly apologetic self-exaggeration. Socrates yields, saying that Phaedrus has found out very well the way to compel a lover of speeches, *andri philologōi,* to do what he commands—thus making explicit that Phaedrus is here acting as a rhetorician upon him.

But, Socrates says, he will speak with his head covered, lest he see Phaedrus while he is talking, and lose his way out of shame, *hup' aischunēs.* What is this shame? Ostensibly, shame at performing so much worse than Lysias; but more deeply, shame at being forced or cajoled into something he does not want to do; and, as we shall see, shame of a deeper sort as well, shame at what he says. On the other hand, the very gesture of covering his head has an arch and self-conscious quality. In this speech he is thus both pretending shame, as a kind of joke, and actually experiencing it, perhaps to his own surprise.

Socrates' First Speech

Socrates' speech, supposedly in contrast to the speech of Lysias, is really a revised version of it, though couched for the most part in terms that are more congenial to traditional Socratic and Platonic positions. The fact that it is both highly familiar to readers of Plato and in some ways very close to Lysias' speech has the effect of putting into question the Platonic assumptions on which it proceeds.

Socrates begins with a passage of extraordinary simplicity: Once upon a time there was a boy with many lovers. One of these, who was in fact in love with him as much as any of the others, cleverly persuaded the boy that he was not in love, and made this the ground of his argument. (In saying this, though without highlighting it in any way, Socrates exposes the point made above about the impossibility at the core of Lysias' speech: the speaker must be in love, for the alternative is still worse; but this means that the speech is all the elaboration of a lie. No wonder Socrates hides his head.)

Socrates begins his speech to the imaginary boy by saying that they should, like rational people—and unlike Lysias, who began *in medias res*—begin with a definition of their subject, in this case *erōs*, or love. This articulates a need the reader will feel, though as we shall see Socrates does not do much to meet it; and it slides over another and deeper need, for a definition of *philia* and its relation to *erōs*. For that we must wait.

Socrates begins his definition of *erōs* by saying that each of us has two forces within him, an inborn desire for pleasure, *emphutos ousa epithumia hēdonōn*, and an acquired opinion, *epiktētos doxa*, that aims at the good. Sometimes these harmonize, sometimes pull in different directions: the name for the one is *hubris*, or violence, for the other *sōphrosunē*, or balanced judgment. Love, *erōs*, is the strongest of the hubristic forces, and the one most in need of restraint.

Now Socrates is off and running, for he can easily give a speech in favor of *sōphrosunē* and against *hubris*. In doing so he is building not only upon the idea, seen also in Lysias, that the lover is one who has lost his self-control, but also upon his own earlier remark that he wants to learn about himself, and in particular whether he is purely a wild beast, or has perhaps something of the divine as well. Notice also that in his talk of the soul divided between *hubris* and *sōphrosunē* he is on his way to the image to be used in his second speech, of the chariot and winged horses. But he is not there yet: his present way of imagining it defines *erōs* as the most prominent of the violent and hubristic forces; in the later version, one form of *erōs* will be the force that enables us to resist those very forces, recalling to us the experience we had of beauty itself before we fell into our present forms.

Socrates picks up the method of Lysias not only in condemning the lover's lack of self-control, but also in the kind of conduct he recommends, which is a species of calculation: in making the choice between lover and nonlover one should determine which course of conduct produces the better combination of harm and benefit, *blabē* and *ōphelia*. In this context he develops the argument, already sketched out by Lysias, that through his intolerance of independence and his jealousy of others the lover will tend to injure the boy. He will do this in respect to his mind, where he will keep him from philosophy; with respect to his body, where he will want him to remain weak; and with respect to his estate, where he will want him to be economically dependent. He will want him without marriage, child, or household: *a-gamon, a-paida, a-oikon* (240-a-6). Socrates closes with a wonderfully rhetorical passage of condemnation, building his accusations like a speaker in a law court, all against the lover: while in love, he is tyrannical and unpleasant; after falling out of love, he is untrustworthy, secretive, and ashamed; and once he has regained control of his mind, he wants nothing to do with what obsessed him when he was crazy. The friendship, *philia*, of the lover is false, for it is not attended with good will, *eunoia*. The boy should not gratify the mindless lover, *anoētōi kai erōnti*, but the nonlover who has a mind, *mē erōnti kai noun echonti*. "As wolves love, *agapōsin*,[15] lambs, so lovers are friends, *philousin*, to boys."

Socrates and Phaedrus

As before, what happens between Phaedrus and Socrates when the speech is over is at least as important as what is said in the speech itself. Socrates stops at the point marked above; Phaedrus not unintelligently says that this is only the middle of the speech he was promised, and that Socrates should go on to extol the virtues of the nonlover. In making this point about Socrates' speech he is making it as well, though he is not aware of it, about the speech of Lysias, which likewise did little to explain why the relation with the nonlover would have any real value, except by comparison with the demented lover. Socrates refuses to accept the challenge to go on, but in an offhand way says merely that we should assume that the nonlover is the opposite of the lover, having all the virtues the other lacks. This is a display of exactly the lack of seriousness with which Phaedrus taxed him in the last interchange between them, a demonstration that what he has just said is unmeant and unmeaning, the product indeed of compulsion. This is

15. The verb *agapousin* is even less sexualized than the words based on the *phil-* root, like *philia*. It is connected with the word *agapē*, of which the New Testament will make a great deal. Here its use is strongly ironic: "the kind of affection wolves have for lambs, that is the friendship of the lover for boys."

what it is like to yield to rhetorical force, and it all has an inconsequential and empty feel.

Socrates now concludes: "I am now going away, across the river, before being forced by you to do something more." This is at least as striking as Phaedrus' "joking" threat of physical force in the last interchange: it is an offer to terminate the conversation, and to that extent the relation between them, by physical action; it is a gesture expressive of deep dissatisfaction with what he has said and become. How are we to understand this?

As I read what has happened, Phaedrus has revealed that he is committed to a completely wrong way of thinking and acting, exemplified in his admiration of the speech of Lysias, and that he has no idea that this is so. This condition is not simply the consequence of an improper basic principle, or something like that; it is the whole fabric of his mind that is wrong. In conversation with him, Socrates has so far not been able to identify what is awry, or to correct it, but has himself surprisingly been caught up in it, giving a speech that is in the main a rewriting of Lysias' own. He does bring it closer to Socratic principles and attitudes, but only partially; it is as much or more a yielding by Socrates, and now it is his own defect of mind and imagination that he does not understand. He has become implicated in the world of Phaedrus— perhaps partly through Phaedrus' physical charms for him, for there is an element of the flirtatious here. All Socrates can do is to say, No more of that. The Delphic command quoted earlier, "Know Thyself," has acquired a new and somethat bitter significance.

But when he starts to cross the river he is stopped by his divine voice, *to daimonion,* which forbids him to leave until he has made expiation to the gods. No sooner does he hear this voice than he knows that he has done wrong; indeed, he says, even while giving the speech he vaguely felt, in the words of Ibycus, that he was acquiring honor from men by offending the gods. "It was a terrible speech," Socrates says, "terrible, *deinos,* both the one you brought with you and the one you made me speak." By "terrible," he says, he means "foolish and impious." The reason, he says, is that Love is a god, the son of Aphrodite, though none of this appears either in the speech of Lysias or his own; and if a god, he cannot be evil.

What is most striking here is Socrates' sense that the speech he gave, and the one given by Lysias, are in the deepest respects the same, not competitors at all; the same, and dreadful. He here disowns his speech, saying that it was really a speech of Phaedrus, which was planted in his mouth as if by magic—though in fact not by magic, as we know, but by compulsion and persuasion at the hands of Phaedrus, perhaps indeed by seduction at the hands of Lysias, whose speech tempted this response.

The proper mode of purification, Socrates says, is to do as Stesichorus did when he was blinded for libeling Helen, namely, to compose a retraction, or "palinode," taking it all back. That is what is called for here, for the speeches were both of them shameless, *anaidōs*—a very strong word. You can see this in a minute, he says, if you imagine that they were overheard by a person of good character who was himself in love, or ever had been. He would think from the way we characterized the conduct of lovers that we had been brought up among sailors. This is a crucial moment, for Socrates here invokes the view, for which there is strong cultural support, that *erōs* is not a bad thing but a fine one.[16] There are people who diminish or degrade it, true, such as sailors and by implication Lysias; but there are other possibilities and it is these to which we should attend. This remark is enough to bring to the surface the ugly and vulgar base upon which the speech of Lysias rests.

Socrates will make his retraction, he says, and do so with head uncovered, for now he has nothing to be ashamed of. He tells Phaedrus that he thinks Lysias should do likewise, and, in place of his earlier speech, write that a young man should gratify the lover and not the nonlover. Phaedrus, showing how little he has moved from the position at which he began, misunderstands Socrates to be issuing a challenge; he says that when Socrates has made his speech he will force Lysias to write one in response. (Notice the insistence on writing here; nothing is now made of it, but it will come back later with a new significance.) Socrates' response is full of weight: "This I believe you will do, so long as you are the person you are," implicitly holding out simultaneously the threat that Phaedrus will not change and the hope that he will.

Indeed it is a fundamental premise of the dialogue that we can and do change who we are, and that such change is in fact the object of an educative life, in conversation and in reading. But thus far, the transformation has been all the wrong way, and Socrates has his work cut out for him. How will he manage to give a speech in favor of the lover? What relation will he establish between *erōs* and *philia*?

16. For one account of the complexity and power of *erōs* in this world, see Claude Calame, *The Poetics of Eros in Ancient Greece* (Princeton: Princeton University Press, 1999).

Socrates' Second Speech

This time Socrates begins by telling the boy that the argument he just made against the lover—that he is touched with madness, while the nonlover retains his clarity of mind—would be well said if it were true that madness, *mania,* were always bad; but it is not. In fact many of our best blessings come to us through madness. Madness is present in the inspiration of the Delphic Oracle, in the prayers and purifications that dispel inherited curses, in the achievements of men inspired by the Muses, and so on. For example, if someone tried to make poetry without madness from the Muses, *mania Mousōn,* believing that with skill alone, *technē,* he could be a good poet, he would be deeply disappointed. [245-a-5]. It is not enough for the opponent of *erōs* to show that it is a kind of madness, then, but that it is a harmful one; and we, on the other hand, must show the opposite, that it is sent for our good. Our demonstration will be disbelieved by the clever, *deinois,* believed by the wise, *sophois.*

The Soul

Socrates begins by undertaking to explain the nature of the soul, *psuchē,* which is the first thing that must be understood. He argues first that the soul is immortal, for it is a source not an object of movement. Then he says, in effect: "To describe the form of the soul, its structure or quality, directly would call for an entirely divine and lengthy exegesis, and would be beyond my powers; but to say what it is *like,* by comparison or metaphor, that I can do." He then presents the myth that is the center of the entire dialogue: Let the soul, *psuchē,* be likened to the combined capacities of a pair of winged horses and a charioteer. Among the gods these horses are both good; but among human beings one is good, and from a good parentage, the other the opposite. This means that for us the task of the charioteer is a most difficult one.

This way of imagining things presents certain obvious questions. If the *psuchē* is immortal, for example, why are some creatures mortal? Socrates explains that by its nature the soul has no body, and lives in the upper air and oversees the whole world; but if a soul loses its wings, as many do, it descends and inhabits an earthly creature, now having a body that can die. Although the soul itself cannot die, then, the creature that combines soul and body can do so.

How is it that some souls lose their wings? Socrates' lengthy explanation begins with the fact that the gods, each with two good horses, patrol the heaven in orderly companies, each according to his own quality, while the rest—meaning the souls of human beings—follow as well as they can. For these the bad horses present real difficulty, since their tendency always is to descend; the gods by contrast ascend to the highest point to dine and feast, from which place they see even beyond the heavens.

This place beyond the heavens has never been made the subject of a proper hymn of praise by any poet, nor will it ever be. But this is what it is like—Socrates with self-conscious immodesty undertakes to tell us—for one must always dare to tell the truth, above all when speaking of the truth:

ἡ γὰρ ἀχρώματός τε καὶ ἀσχημάτιστος καὶ ἀναφὴς οὐσία ὄντως οὖσα, ψυχῆς κυβερνήτῃ μόνῳ θεατὴ νῷ, περὶ ἣν τὸ τῆς ἀληθοῦς ἐπιστήμης γένος, τοῦτον ἔχει τὸν τόπον. (247-c-6)

hē gar achrōmatos te kai aschēmatistatos kai anaphēs ousia
    For the without-color-and-without-design-and-intangible being
ontōs ousa, psuchēs kubernētēi mōnōi theatē noi,
    really being, by the steersman of the soul alone seen, by mind,
peri hēn to tēs alēthous epistēmēs genos, touton echei ton topon.
    about which is the genus of true knowledge, holds this place.

Or:

This place is held by Being itself, as it truly is, without color or shape or palpability, which can be seen only by the governor of the soul, the mind, and which is the only subject of true knowledge.

I hope you can see that there is in the transition from my nearly word-by-word translation to the still crude one that follows a movement in the direction of dead speech. In the second version it sounds all very self-assured and assertive and nontentative, as though Socrates is describing his cosmological theory in a classroom. "Being itself, as it truly is" sounds empty; the only thing one could imagine doing with such language is memorizing it for an exam. Something like this is I think a feature of virtually all translations of Plato into English: they make him sound like a systematic and conceptual philosopher, setting forth a theory—and a theory in this case that cannot possibly be true, so the reader reasonably asks, Why are we reading it?

In Greek, by contrast, the whole thing—this sentence and the myth of which it is a part—has at every stage a quality of inventedness or tentativeness, a working out not of what the soul "is," but what it "is like," with a self-conscious extravagance of imagination.[17] Thus the string of adjectives between the article "the" and "being" works as the beginning a list of things one might say; it could go on and on in principle forever, so whatever we do or say is marked as incomplete. These adjectives all begin with the alpha privative, meaning "not," so the very form of the words tells us that this is a form of speech that will undertake to tell us not how things are, but how they are not. It is marking out negative space, not asserting that a thing exists; it is telling us that our usual language, of positives, will not work. The phrase "being as it really is" is not a conceptual and boring formulation, but a neologism, a way in which Plato stretches the language to suggest what cannot be said: *ousia* ("being," as a noun) *ontōs* ("really," or "being," as an adverb) *ousa* ("being" as a participle)—all three words coming from the same verb.

The phrase about the steersman of the soul of course invokes the image of the primary myth itself, here working as a transformation of the "charioteer" we have already seen, in this case to be identified with "mind." The evident idea is that the *psuchē* has parts, living parts, in relations of tension, and that it is only one part that sees in the way described. "About which is the genus of true knowledge," or "which alone is the subject of true knowledge," does tell us something positive about the "being," answering the negatives of the first line, but not much, for knowledge and being are defined in terms of each other. In the final phrase, we get at last to the main verb, *echei*, or "holds"; this reminds us that everything that has preceded has been, like the string of adjectives, an extension of the undefinable subject, an extension that could in principle go on indefinitely. But however long it went on, we know that it would never end in clear specification; the sense of the sentence is that of a mind feeling its way out into the inexpressible, trying one and then another way to put it, never being other than suggestive, then bringing it all down to a momentary conclusion, before setting forth on another uncertain venture of language and imagination—a sentence, in fact, such as the one Emerson described in the quotation in chapter 5. Perhaps the worst thing about the English translation is that it erases the sense of extension piled on extension by

17. The word *soul* has for us all the wrong connotations, from nineteenth-century English pietism to popular psychology. "Self" would be somewhat better, but perhaps the *psuchē* is best thought of as "life-breath": that which makes the individual physical being alive and gives it self-awareness.

reversing the order of verb and noun: "This place is held by . . ." It can never have the quality of the Greek word order: "The not-*A* and not-*B* and not-*C* being truly as it is, seen only by *X*, the object of true *Y*, holds this place."

Madness

Socrates goes on to say that the *psuchē* in the place beyond the heavens beholds and feeds on justice itself, on beauty itself, not in the transitory forms in which we perceive these things but in their eternal natures. After feasting on these things, the soul returns to its place within the heavens, to feed the horses, and to rest.

Such is the life of the gods; Socrates thus reminds us of what we have perhaps forgotten, that he has here not been speaking of human souls, and that he has still not explained why such souls lose their wings. Now he tells us: these souls, divided as they are, cannot rise so easily or so far as the souls of the gods, but jostle one another in their course around the world, some of them peeping up above the heavens for a moment, then falling back, some never making it there at all. In the press and confusion, wings are broken, and souls fall to earth. If a soul follows a god so far as to see something of what is true, it will be safe from harm for the rest of the circuit; and if one could do that always, one would be always safe. But when a soul fails to see, and is weighted down with evil and forgetfulness, it sinks, ultimately to take corporeal form.

Human forms, both psychological and physical, are distributed according to the experience the soul has had in the heavens; and in a marvelously comic sentence we are told that the soul that has seen most will be planted in a man who will become a lover of wisdom or beauty, or one given to the Muses and to love; the next, in one who will become king; the third, in a businessman; the fourth, in a trainer or doctor; the fifth, in a seer or prophet; the sixth, in a poet; the seventh, in an artisan or farmer; the eighth, in a sophist; the ninth, in a tyrant. An unstated part of the significance of this sequence is that the rhetorician, whose central effort is to extend the range of his will, whatever it may be, is a close cousin to the tyrant, who does the same thing, though by force rather than persuasion.

The one who spends his life on earth justly will receive a better fate than one who does not, and will go from form to form, in thousand-year cycles, until its cycle of ten thousand years is fulfilled, when it becomes winged once more. But the one who leads a sincerely philosophic life, or loves a boy philosophically, will become winged after only three thousand years, at least if he chooses this life three times in a row. In all of this Socrates is evidently delighting in his power to rank the world by fiat, perhaps an act of tyranny of his own, and the whole has a comic, teasing, and slightly self-mocking air, as far from the didactic and puritanically condemnatory as one could well imagine.

This brings us to our next sentence, a difficult one, summing up what is said about the kind of madness, *mania,* we call *erōs:*

Ἔστι δὴ οὖν δεῦρο ὁ πᾶς ἥκων λόγος περὶ τῆς τετάρτης μανίας—ἣν ὅταν τὸ τῇδέ τις ὁρῶν κάλλος, τοῦ ἀληθοῦς ἀναμιμνησκόμενος, πτερῶτάι τε καὶ ἀναπτερούμενος προθυμούμενος ἀναπτέσθαι, ἀδυνατῶν δέ, ὄρνιθος δίκην βλέπων ἄνω, τῶν κάτω δὲ ἀμελῶν, αἰτίαν ἔχει ὡς μανικῶς διακείμενος—ὡς ἄρα αὕτη πασῶν τῶν ἐνθουσιάσεων ἀρίστη τε καὶ ἐξ ἀρίστων τῷ τε ἔχοντι καὶ τῷ κοινωνοῦντι αὐτῆς γίγνεται, καὶ ὅτι ταύτης μετέχων τῆς μανίας ὁ ἐρῶν τῶν καλῶν ἐραστὴς καλεῖται. (249-d-4)

So the whole argument about the fourth kind of madness, *mania,* comes to this: whenever someone sees the beautiful here below, he is reminded of true beauty; he becomes winged and flutters with the desire to fly, but he cannot; looking upwards like a bird, and having no care for the things below, he is thus accused of being possessed by *mania;* this is of all enthusiasms the best, and from the best origins, alike to the possessor and to the one sharing in it; and participating in this madness the lover *(erōn)* of beautiful people [and things] is called lover indeed *(erastēs).*

Esti dē oun deuro ho pas hēkōn logos peri tēs tetartēs manias
It is (and) therefore here the whole arriving argument about the fourth madness

This the first clause of a long sentence, and might be translated: "the whole argument about the fourth kind of madness arrives here at this point," implying a kind of "namely" or other phrase that will explain what "here" means. But the sentence in Greek has a wholly different shape, beginning with the verb to be—"is" or "there is" or "[it] exists"—followed by two particles, followed in turn by "here," which has as yet no plain function, followed by "the whole" in the nominative singular masculine: that gives us our subject, and the sentence now seems to read "the whole is here." But the whole what? Before that is clarified we have, in a way that may feel to us inserted, a present participle in the nominative singular masculine, "coming" or "arriving," and only then the "*logos,*" or argument. So it reads "the whole arriving argument is here": maybe best translated, "it is plain that the

whole argument arrives here." The last four words simply modify the
logos: "about the fourth madness." In what follows it becomes important that the clause ends with the "madness," for in Greek the next
clause begins with a relative in the singular accusative feminine, agree-
ing with *manias,* or madness, thus:

> *hēn hotan to tēide tis horōn kallos, tou alēthous*
>> which, whenever someone seeing the beauty here, the true [beauty]
>
> *anamimnēskomenos, ptērōtai te kai anapteroumenos*
>> remembering, becomes winged and fluttering
>
> *prothumenos anaptesthai, adunatōn de, ornithos dikēn blepōn anō,*
>> desiring to fly up, but being unable, looking up in the manner of a bird,
>
> *tōn de katō amelōn, aitian echei hōs manikōs diakeimenos;*
>> not caring about the things below, is accused on the grounds of being manically
>> disposed;
>
> *hōs ara hautē pasōn tōn enthousiaseōn aristē te kai ex aristōn*
>> thus it follows that this of all enthusiasms the best and of the best
>
> *tō te echonti kai tō koinonounti autēs gignetai, kai hoti tautēs*
>> both to the possessor of it and to the one sharing in it becomes, and that
>
> *mētechōn tēs manias ho erōn tōn kalōn erastēs kaleitai.*
>> partaking of this, this madness, the lover of the beautiful [people or things] is called
>> erastēs.

Notice that the sentence does not after all build on the relative *hēn,*
referring to "madness," in the way we expect; in fact it seems to collapse syntactically, and go off on another tangent. "Which madness?"
it first invites us to ask; and we are then given a story, thus: "which,
whenever someone, seeing the beauty down here and being reminded
of the true beauty [he has seen before], becomes winged and fluttering
with desire to fly but not being able to, looking up like a bird, not
caring for the things down here, is accused of being crazed . . ." The
demand of the relative in the accusative, that it be the object of a verb,
is simply never met. It is as though we have forgotten it. The new
clause is marked by "whenever"; its subject is "someone"; and its
main verbs are "becomes winged" and "gives cause to believe"—and,
just as the demand of the relative is not met, so too we have here a
dependent clause with no clear method of dependency.

In the remaining part of the sentence this difficulty is addressed in a
striking way: the *hōs* is another clause marker, either meaning "that,"
and referring all the way back to "argument," *logos,* in the first clause,
or meaning "thus" or "so" and indicating that what follows flows
naturally from the description of the winged and fluttering one; *ara* is

a particle meaning "it follows naturally"; *hautē* is a feminine singular demonstrative pronoun in the nominative, meaning "it"—this is the word that picks up the unanswered relative, matching it in gender and number, and thus means "this madness." The rest of the clause flows to our ears naturally except for the deferral of the verb to be, which I here advance, making the whole read: "Thus it follows that this madness is of all enthusiasms the best and from the best [sources or ancestry], both for the person who experiences it and for the one who keeps company with it." The final clause carries the punch: "and that because he shares in this madness the lover of beautiful people [or things] is called *erastēs*."

This kind of break in syntactic structure is called anacoluthon; its effect here is to disorient the reader, to raise you above the world and restraints of syntax just as the chariot and the soul are raised above the world and the heavens, into another place. You are in contact, this form says, not with a designed structure or artificially created experience, not with the product of professional rhetorical skill, but with a mind working as the mind actually does, shifting its forms of speech to meet the demands of truth and feeling. Yet of course, as the dramatic conclusion makes plain, this is the result of art after all; art above art.[18]

What is the tone of this sentence, indeed of the whole myth of which it is a part? I can well remember my own first exposure to this text, in a class at school, where I was taught that this is what Plato "believed": that the soul went through these phases and struggles, and that the moral duty of the young man was therefore plain—to be a good charioteer, controlling his evil impulses. And again and again in later life I have read accounts of Plato that assume that this, like similar passages in other works, is meant in some literal-minded way, which seems to me utterly impossible. For one thing, in this very dialogue, Socrates previously raised doubts about whether, or how, myths are to be believed. For another, he explicitly characterized the myth as an effort to say what the soul is like, not what it is, that is, as a kind of

---

18. The editor of the Greek text has tried to soften the effect of the anacoluthon by the use of dashes to set off what we would call a parenthetical; but this does not entirely regularize the syntax and is in any event anachronistic, an attempt to remove a problem the Greek was composed to present. And even if the anacoluthon could technically be resolved in such a way, the complexity and uncertainty of the sentence would still create very much the same sense of detachment from ordinary reality. Compare the sentence at page 161 above, describing the place beyond the heavens, and indeed the whole paragraph of which it is a part (247-c-2 to 247-e-6), which similarly carries the reader to a place beyond language, into a world for which ordinary uses of words and their connections will not suffice.

figurative speech. Finally, and even more important, the whole is written with a delicate mixture of the serious and the comic, a lightness of
touch that enables it to be at once ludicrous, as here, and wonderfully
beautiful, and it is in the music of these tones that much of its meaning
lies. Compare what follows, which reads in rough paraphrase something like this:

> Not many souls remember these things; but those that do are struck
> out of their wits whenever they see something that resembles what they
> saw there, and they no longer belong to themselves; though they do not
> know what they are experiencing, for they do not perceive clearly. Of
> the other pure essences in the place beyond the heavens—such as jus-
> tice and *sōphrosunē*—earthly manifestations are dim; but this is not
> so of beauty, which shines forth in the physical world with a clear and
> accessible light. (If we could see wisdom in such a way, the suffering it
> would occasion would be unendurable.)
>
> The man who does not remember is not stirred with feelings of rev-
> erence when he sees the physical manifestations of beauty (particularly
> in the boy), but simply wants to possess it, as beasts do.[19] But the one
> who does remember what he once saw trembles and sweats, as at the
> presence of a god; the heat melts whatever is blocking the pores
> through which his feathers sprout, and his feathers start to grow.
> Whenever he is with the beautiful boy, then, he experiences remem-
> brance and love and is drawn closer to beauty; whenever he is away,
> his pores dry up and shut off the feather-shafts within, and these push
> against the skin and throb with desire, driving him crazy with pain.
> Thus he devotes all to the god of love.

The preceding paragraph is too long to quote word for word, but
perhaps even my summary can suggest something of its extraordinary
tone: it is explicitly a fantasy, a way of imagining what love is like
by telling a story of prior perception and remembrance; the effect
of beauty is described in terms that are simultaneously spiritual—
for he is talking throughout of the soul—and physical, for the throb-
bing and itching and pain are all plainly sexual; simultaneously ludicrous—feathers and pores!—and beautiful; simultaneously zany and
serious, comic and deeply felt. It is written with a consciousness of

19. Remember here Socrates' question, whether he was a wild beast like Typhon, or
had some element of the divine, as well as the animal, within him; and my argument that
what Lysias proposes is sex stripped not only of *philia* in its better sense, but of *erōs*, and
thus a reduction to the purely animal.

its own qualities, explicitly as a way of working with language, and one's audience, to do what the language cannot in any simple way do. Much of the life of the prose lies in this complex and delicate mixture of tones; it would be completely false to portray this as a conceptual system or as a solemn account of the machinery by which the soul lives and grows, cast in a language thought to be adequate to the purpose.

Erōs

Socrates goes on to say that each soul chooses to follow a particular god through the heavens; people differ as the gods to whom they devote themselves differ, and they choose their beloved accordingly. Using their god as their standard, they naturally try to make their beloved increasingly like that god, and when they do, they benefit him. The desire of those who truly love thus becomes noble and good for the beloved, as well as for the lover, tending to produce happiness for him at the hands of the friend, *philos,* who is maddened with love, *erōs,* for the one he cares about, *philēthenti.* In such a man *philia* and *erōs* are united.

What about the physical aspect of sexual love? Here Socrates returns to the image of the horses, describing in a wonderfully explicit and amusing way the internal conflicts that sexual desire generates, the ignoble horse wanting to copulate instantly, while the other horse and the charioteer restrain him, out of reverence for the god, hauling him back to his knees. When the charioteer gains control, and follows the boy with love, the boy sees the effects of that friendship in his own life and is amazed at its beneficence; and he sees, too, love in the eyes of his lover, and, though he does not know what it is, becomes inspired by it, and himself falls in love, though in a weaker way, and wants human and physical contact. If the lover and beloved can resist the impulse to have sexual relations, and live in contact with love itself, they will lead a blessed and harmonious life, in command of themselves and coherent, enslaved with respect to that part through which evil enters the soul, free with respect to that part through which virtue does. On ending their lives, they become winged and light, and neither human *sōphrosunē* nor divine *mania* is able to provide greater good to men. And even if they do yield to the sexual side, they will live as friends, and although when they die they do not become winged, they will at least have the desire to become winged.

Such are the blessings that come from *philia* with an *erastēs.*

SOCRATES CONCLUDES with a prayer to *Erōs:* forgive what I said before and receive this with favor; do not remove your blessings from me, but let me be still more than before honored by the beautiful ones. If Phaedrus and I said bad things in the first speech, blame Lysias as the cause, and turn him to philosophy, "so that this lover, *erastēs,* of him [Phaedros] may no longer be divided in mind, as he now is, but simply direct his life toward love with philosophical speech," *pros erōta meta philosophōn logōn.*

The last sentence makes explicit the main point of everything Socrates has been doing, which is to try to help Phaedrus reconceive and redirect his life. Thus far he has done this through speeches, for that is the form set for him by the admiration of Phaedrus for Lysias. In the second half of the dialogue, however, he will proceed in another mode, in actual conversation, mind with mind, taking these three speeches as his subject. From performance he turns to criticism.

To pause for another moment on the speech we have just worked through, it is important to see that it is not a freestanding work, but acquires much of its meaning from the rest of the text, including the opening scene, the two other speeches with which it is naturally to be compared, the kinds of interaction between Socrates and Phaedrus that each speech stimulated, and the conversation on rhetoric and writing still to come. As Ferrari puts it in *Listening to the Cicadas,* the two halves of the dialogue, the first narrative and mythical, the second dialogic and analytic, imply one another; neither mode of thought and life is enough, standing alone; together, with all the tensions between them, they define the full philosophic life.

Socrates and Phaedrus

Phaedrus' response to Socrates' speech shows how far he still is from being the ideal audience the speech implies, and in this way defines Socrates' remaining task. First, he joins in the prayer only with a deep qualification—"if indeed that would be better for us"; then he expresses admiration for the speech, but in comparative or competitive terms, saying that he is afraid that if Lysias were to respond he would do so in a speech that would seem by comparison coarse and low, *tapeinos.* He sees the speech as a performance, that is, to be evaluated by still-unstated criteria of rhetorical excellence, not as a statement of what Socrates truly believes, to be responded to as such—not, that is, as what Thoreau would call "sincere."

The conversation that follows has some of the unstructured quality

of real conversation, shifting its subjects, leaving them open and unre-
solved. First, the idea of coarseness generalizes itself in the mind of
Phaedrus, who says that Lysias has recently been attacked for just this
quality, being called by one of the political people a logographer, or
speech writer—which he in fact was by profession, writing speeches
for litigants, which they would memorize and deliver as if their own
(as Phaedrus was doing with the speech on love). The relevance of the
accusation here is that it may lead Lysias, through *philotimia*—love of
honor or reputation—not to write a response after all.

Socrates pooh-poohs both the likelihood of this and the charge that
gives rise to it, saying that people like the politician in question in fact
enormously favor writing, and take great pride in their works—in this
case the laws themselves. The real point, for him and for Lysias and
for us, is not that writing itself is a shameful thing, but that writing
badly is so.

That raises the question: What is good writing? or How does one
write well? Shall we examine the speech of Lysias with this question in
mind? By asking these questions Socrates has worked the conversation
around to bring it to bear, without Phaedrus' quite knowing it, on
Phaedrus' own response to the speeches he has heard, the basis of his
admiration and criticism. What should one admire in a speech?

Phaedrus leaps at the chance to talk about these speeches, saying
that it is for such pleasures as reading and hearing these speeches that
life is best lived. Socrates in response invokes the presence of the local
deities, the cicadas singing in the trees overhead, telling a myth about
them: that they are the souls of men who were so intoxicated with the
Muses, when those beings first came into existence, that they danced
and sang without stopping to eat until they died, so much that the fact
of their death escaped their own notice. Now they are cicadas, repeat-
ing their life of song without food; but when they die, they report to
the gods, telling them which people on earth honor which of them, and
how well. If they see us snoozing in the heat they will think we are like
slaves or sheep; if they see us engaged in conversation, *dialogomenous,*
they may give us a good report.[20]

20. In doing this, Socrates once more confirms the value of the mythological imagination that was at work in his second speech. Notice, too, that the souls that became cicadas
were taken by a form of *mania* or madness, a devotion to the Muses that was too exclu-
sive and complete. The myth itself thus tells us that philosophy is not only a matter of the
Muses or myths, but also of a different kind of thinking, which it will be the aim of the rest
of the dialogue to exemplify. It is also a warning to Phaedrus that his enthusiasm may need
examination.

This is a wonderfully rich passage, full of humor and imagination; here I want only to say that this invocation of a critical and divine judge, the chorus of cicadas, invites us to see that the very conversation they are beginning, like writing, can be good or bad. The questions they are asking of the speeches can thus be asked of the conversation in which we are now engaged: What are the standards by which it should be measured?

Art and Knowledge

What is good writing in the composition of a speech, and what is not? The first requirement, suggests Socrates, is that the speaker know the truth of what he is talking about. Phaedrus doubts this, saying that he has been told that, in the field of rhetoric at least, one need know only what the majority in one's audience believes, for this, not truth, is the ground upon which persuasion rests.[21]

This question is crucial to what Socrates is doing—to what extent is your writing shaped by the preexisting views of your audience, to what extent by something else?—and it will come back at least three more times in the course of the dialogue. This repetition demonstrates among other things that the education of Phaedrus, or of any of us, is not simply a matter of pointing out what has not been understood, but involves transformation of the imagination and the self. Here Socrates' refutation is highly comic and easy: suppose we needed a horse to defend ourselves; neither of us knew what a horse was, but I knew that you believed a horse to be the domestic animal with the longest ears, and then made a speech praising the ass, saying how valuable it would be in war and so forth; would I not be simply ridiculous? In this as in every case, what we need to know first is the truth of things.

Socrates goes on to consider speeches in the law courts, where the topic is justice. Here the object of the speaker is to make the same thing seem just or unjust, depending on his role. This is a specific form of a more general practice, the object of which is to make one thing resemble another different thing as closely as possible, first in one way then another. To do this well, one must proceed by small stages from the way things actually are to the characterization one is urging upon one's audience; this, concludes Socrates, requires knowledge of things as they actually are, and not merely of people's opinions.

21. Compare the position of Gorgias in *Gorgias*, 460a–461b.

Then comes a sentence familiar to us: "One who does not know the truth, but seeks only the opinions of his audience, will thus produce a ridiculous and artless, *atechnon,* handbook, *technēn,* of rhetoric." Phaedrus, less than wholly persuaded, responds only "possibly so," *kinduneuei.*

There is another version of Phaedrus' argument, one that acknowledges that it is valuable to know the truth of things; the claim for rhetoric now is that even with that knowledge one will fail to persuade others if one does not have in addition knowledge of the art of persuasive speaking. But this is true, says Socrates, only if there is indeed an art, *technē,* of speaking well; and is there? Or is it only an artless practice, *atechnos tribē?*

Criticizing the Speeches

Socrates begins again, taking as it were a second pass at Phaedrus, this time focusing on the speech of Lysias, and his own speeches in response, to see which of them qualify as *technos* or *atechnos.* Remember, the question we are asking is whether there is any art or science of speaking that is different from knowledge of the truth; an art or science that even one who does know the truth will need. (An odd question indeed, one might think, to be raised by a speaker who could approximate the truth about the life of the human soul, and the role of love in that life, only in a glorious myth!) Consider, Socrates says, the beginning of Lysias' speech, which reads this way:

> You have already heard how I am circumstanced, and that I think it would be to our joint advantage if these things happened; here I argue that I should not fail of what I ask simply because I am not your lover, *erastēs*. Those who do love find that they repent . . . etc.

This is a fine moment, bringing back into our consciousness the speech of Lysias—including the voice in which it is written and the character that it defines—in a context in which its ugliness will be felt the more strongly for what we have read in the interim. Here it is subject to a question, about its intellectual quality, that makes it seem stupid as well. For it fails, Socrates says, to meet our most basic expectation, which—at least on matters like love, with respect to which people disagree—is that a speaker should begin with some way of defining what it is he is speaking about and has in mind. Nothing could be farther from this than Lysias' speech, which assumes everything, states nothing. It begins not at a proper beginning but at the middle.[22]

As for the rest of the speech, asks Socrates, does it not have the same disorganized character? Phaedrus stiffly replies, "You are kind to think me capable of knowing so precisely what he has done" (264-b-9). Socrates then presses Phaedrus no longer on this speech, but drops the subject, turning instead to the two speeches he himself composed, one against and one in favor of love. The second of these he summarizes briefly and inaccurately, saying that he distinguished between human and divine madness, one as a kind of sickness, the other as a divinely caused transformation of our accustomed modes of thought and life; that the four kinds of love he defined were that of the mantis or seer (inspired by Apollo), that of the religious mysteries (inspired by Dionysos), that of poetry and other arts (inspired by the Muses), and that of Love (inspired by Aphrodite); and that in this speech he engaged in collection *(sunagōgē)* and division *(diairesis)*, intellectual operations that are fundamental to rational discourse, in this case dividing love into two—in the first speech condemning the bad version, in the second praising the good one.

This is in fact a highly inaccurate account of what he actually said, which was much less schematic than he now claims, and the purpose of which was not to distinguish between two kinds of love, but to show how the same thing, the madness or distraction of love, could be viewed and understood as a good or bad thing. Socrates' supposed summary is in fact an addition to what he has said, in which he tidies up his earlier account, in some ways against its own power and beauty and meaning. It is an analytic account of a poetic expression, and it both adds to and subtracts from it, just as the poetic expression could be said to do with respect to an analytic account; the dialogue in this way places these two elements in tension, showing, as Ferrari claims, that full human intellectual functioning requires both—not reducing one to the other, nor assuming the priority of one over another, but in productive sequence and alternation.

Socrates does not pursue this point, but merely labels his own

22. What this comment brings to the surface is not just that the speaker in the speech of Lysias failed to define love, as an intellectually necessary stage to respectable speech or thought about it, but that, far more basely, he disguised through euphemism and indirection exactly what he was asking for, which was almost certainly not a respectable liaison between older and younger man, but sexual relations of a more shameful kind.

method as dialectic, distinguishing it from the rhetoric that Lysias practices and teaches, and thus raises once more the question whether rhetoric is an art. Or does dialectic in fact comprise everything that is artful or scientific in speech?

Surely not that, says Phaedrus; think of what is written in all the handbooks. Ah yes, says Socrates, running off a list of parts of speeches, such as *prooimion, diēgēsis, tekmēria* (preface, narrative, evidence), and methods, such as *gnōmologia* and *eikonologia,* (speaking with maxims and with images), all in a highly comic display of his own learning about the practices he is rejecting. How are we to look at all this? he asks. Compare the man who says he is a doctor because he knows how to make people warm or cool, or to induce them to vomit or move their bowels, or the person who claims to be a tragedian because he knows how to make long and short speeches, or frightening or pitiable ones; we would say that they did not in fact know medicine or tragedy, but the things you need to know first, before you know medicine or tragedy, for they do not know when to do the things they describe. They do not have the art in question, but a pre-art.

Phaedrus, at last, concedes the force of that argument, and says that the things taught in the manuals really do seem to be like that. But what about the art of the true rhetorician, *tēn tou tōi onti rhetorikou kai pithanou technēn* (269-c-9), and how and where do we acquire it?

Some of it is simply talent, Socrates says, but the part that is a *technē* depends on knowledge of the subject matter. Just as medicine requires knowledge of the body, so rhetoric does of the *psuchē:* its essential nature, its forms or types, and the way each is affected by different kinds of speech. Here Socrates is describing in an analytic way the kind of "knowledge" of the soul that rhetoric requires; but in the dialogue as a whole that knowledge is given a far richer and somewhat inconsistent expression in the great myth itself, which represents knowledge not as propositional truth, but as imaginative and affective in character, indeed as the object of love.

Phaedrus is convinced,[23] but sees that the labor of such an art would

23. I may overstate the change in Phaedrus. In "*Phaedrus* and the Politics of Inscription," Harry Berger argues that Socrates really has little effect on Phaedrus. My own sense is different: that Phaedrus has undergone a reorientation, but without really understanding how or why. I sense very little of the sour resistance that sometimes accompanies Socratic failure. On the other hand, it is to me odd, and works as a comment on Phaedrus' capacity of mind and spirit, that he is persuaded, if he is, by the kind of argument referred to in the text, and not by the stunning myth of the soul.

be enormous. Is there any way to avoid it? Here Socrates returns once more to his familiar topic, saying that some experts claim that you need not know the truth to persuade, but only what is probable, or what the audience believes to be probable, for this is what matters in the law courts. The trouble is that, as we just said, probability works by its resemblance to truth; and he will argue best about probabilities who knows the truth.

To do the kind of work he describes, Socrates says, is truly difficult, as Phaedrus saw, for it requires nothing less than a real education; and he who engages in it is best advised to do so not in order to achieve something in relation to men but to become able to say what is pleasing to the gods. Phaedrus, again the doubter, says:

> Παγκάλως ἔμοιγε δοκεῖ λέγεσθαι, ὦ Σώκρατες, εἴπερ οἷός τέ τις εἴη. (274-a-6)
>
> *Pankalos emoige dokei legesthai, o Sōkrates, eiper hoios te tis eiē*
>
>> Entirely well to me it seems to be said, O Socrates, at least if one is able [to do it]

Socrates, acknowledging the force of the doubt, yet stating the faith upon which he will base his life, responds:

> Ἀλλὰ καὶ ἐπιχειροῦντί τοι τοῖς καλοῖς καλὸν καὶ πάσχειν ὅτι ἂν τῷ συμβῇ παθεῖν. (274-a-8)
>
> *Alla kai epicheirounti toi tois kalois kalon kai paschein*
>
>> But also for the one who puts one's hand to noble things [it is] noble even to suffer
>
> *hoti an tōi sumbēi pathein*
>
>> whatever it should fall to him to suffer.

This crucial sentence has a simple structure, but an effective one: the juxtaposition of the two words for noble, the noble things that one attempts, *kalois,* and the noble of the complement—"it will be noble, *kalon*"—reinforces both terms.[24] This tends to fuse the fundamental strains that work within this family of words, for *kalos* can mean both externally good—handsome, beautiful, appropriate to a person of power and grace—and internally good, meaning morally right: it will be morally right to pursue the beautiful, beautiful to pursue the morally right.[25] The sentence stresses moral significance in another

---

24. *Paschein* and *pathein* are parallel too, one the present infinitive, the other the aorist infinitive, of the same verb.

25. When I say that it is beautiful or noble things that he pursues, that is I think the dominant meaning, for *tois kalois* is the dative plural of the extremely common *ta kala,* beautiful things. But it is also the dative plural of *hoi kaloi,* beautiful males, and this second meaning is also present, at least in shadow form.

way, for Socrates is saying that it is the attempt to do right, to live the right way, that matters, and that one should not expect any immunity from harm as a consequence—an obvious point to be made by a "Socrates" who is a character in a composition made after the death of the real Socrates, but a crucial one, an essential ingredient of moral maturity. Nothing is farther from the success ethic of the rhetorician, whose art is confirmed when he prevails upon an audience, disconfirmed when he does not. Socrates has brought Phaedrus to the point where he can begin to see the truth of such a sentence, and perhaps to make it his own; this is to have done much to transform him; and if we have followed as we ought, much to transform us as well.

Reading and Writing

In an important sense this is the real ending of the dialogue, for Phaedrus has at last been moved from his original position to one from which he can begin to see the value, as well as the difficulty, of the course Socrates has proposed. While, as we shall soon see, much remains to be done, the main thing has been achieved, namely, a reorientation of the mind and being of Phaedrus.

The remainder of the dialogue is not exactly a summary, for it is inconsistent with the idea of truth and conversation out of which Plato and Socrates function that anything as full of life as this text could be subjected to summary; rather, it is an experience for the reader that has some of the quality of a final examination. The text from the beginning has been trying to teach us how to read it, and now we have the opportunity to test what we have learned.

Socrates marks the shift by saying that enough has been said about the question whether speeches are the subject of a distinct art, *technē,* and if so what it is; what remains is the question of the fitting and the unfitting, *euprepeia* and *aprepeia,* in writing; that is, in what way it can be done well, and badly. In putting the matter this way Socrates takes as a given the idea that writing itself is neither good nor bad; the issue is how it is done. He thus picks up a point made earlier (at 258-d), where he said that it was plain that it was not shameful to write speeches, but it was shameful to do so shamefully and badly, *aischrōs kai kakōs.* At that point he first framed the question we are about to examine: "What is the way of writing well, and the reverse?" *(Tis oun ho tropos tou kalōs te kai mē graphein?)*

Socrates begins his examination with another marvelous myth, about writing, once more reaffirming, but in a complex and qualified way, the narrative and imaginative mode of thought. The story is that in Egypt there was a god named Theuth, who was the first to discover arithmetic and calculation and astronomy and draughts and dice. He went to the king of Thebes, Thamus, to whom he offered his arts, *technas*, saying that they should be given to the rest of the Egyptians. Thamus examined each in great detail as it was presented, to determine whether it really was good or not. Some he approved, others not. When Theuth came to writing, he was confident that this was good: he had found a "drug, *pharmakon*, of memory and wisdom." Not so, said Thamus; writing will in fact induce forgetfulness in those who use it, through lack of exercise of the memory; they will have to be reminded by these external marks, not remembering what they carry in themselves. You have found a drug not of memory, he says, but of reminding, which will create not wisdom but only the appearance of wisdom.

Phaedrus' response to this story is to challenge its veracity: "Socrates, you easily compose (make up) stories from Egypt, or wherever you wish," meaning by this: "I don't believe it." And of course neither do we, in the usual sense of belief. Phaedrus is raising once more a question that bears not only upon this myth—and the one about Boreas, with which we began, and Socrates' repeated invocations of the cicadas—but the great myth about the soul, and upon this very dialogue too, which is of course imaginary: How are such compositions to be read? In response to Phaedrus, Socrates invokes a comparison with the oracle of Dodona, where it is said that the first oracles were given by oak trees and rocks; and the people—who were not wise, *sophoi*, like you young men—made it their habit to listen to the tree and the rock, whenever they spoke the truth. It is not who speaks that matters but whether what is said is true.

Phaedrus instantly agrees, saying that Socrates rightly rebukes him, and that what Thamus says about writing is correct. This is a complex moment, for here Socrates is telling him, and us, how to read the great myth: not by reference to the authority of its author, but by whether it tells the truth about the *psuchē*, which in this case can be tested only by one's experience. The question is not whether your soul once actually had wings, but what your life is like, including your life of love; is it not truly like this? There can be truth in such a story, and Phaedrus is right to accept his rebuke. On the other hand, he misses the comic

tone of the new myth almost entirely, and goes too far when he leaps
to agreement with Thamus, for he is merely acquiescing in Socrates'
authority.

Socrates then puts the position again, in slightly different terms: that
one who thought that he could leave behind him a science, *technēn*,
in writing, or one who thought that in someone else's writing he had
something firm and clear—that real knowledge could be communi-
cated that way—would be mistaken, if he thought that written speeches
or words, *logous,* were anything more than a reminder for one who already knows. Socrates confirms what Thamus says in other terms, saying that a written text is like a painting of a person; they both seem to
be alive, but when you ask them a question they have nothing to say,
or only what they have already said, and then in always exactly the
same terms. The written text cannot adjust itself to its audience; nor
can it defend itself when questioned, but for this needs the real person
behind it.

Yet of this kind of writing there is a legitimate brother, one that is
written with understanding, *epistēmē,* on the soul of the person learning; a kind of writing that is able to protect itself, and knows when and
to whom it is necessary to speak or be silent.[26] Here Phaedrus can, for
once, show that he does indeed understand: "You mean the living and
breathing speech of the man who knows, of which a written version
one might justly call a kind of image." "Just so," says Socrates; he
concludes that writing is therefore a kind of *paidia,* or game, which
can be of real use in reminding us of what we once knew, but which is
not entitled to the serious zeal, *spoudē,* of dialectic—the practice by
which we find out the truth about things, including, as he told us at the
outset in his reference to the Delphic command, oneself.

Having agreed about this, he says, we can settle the other issues,

26. Harry Berger Jr., "*Phaedrus* and the Politics of Inscription," has convinced me that
I at first accepted too uncritically the image of "writing on the soul" as an unqualified good.
The image is, after all, one of imposition, with one person acting on the other—as Kafka,
for example, saw in "In the Penal Colony"—and this is deeply inconsistent with the relation
of mutuality required for dialectic. But I think these negative implications do not undo the
rest of what Socrates says: most writing does say the same thing always and it is unable to
defend itself, though one cannot quite say that of Plato's writing in this dialogue; likewise,
living interchange of mind with mind can produce a different kind of knowledge, not information but capacity for intellectual life—though the undertones of the image of "writing on
the soul" serve to remind us that this too can be done in an authoritarian and killing way.
What he says is true in a general way about writing and speech, but one ought not use the
medium to judge an expression's quality. The truth lies, once more, not on the surface of
what is said, but behind it, in the life of the mind, as that takes place in good or bad ways.

about whether Lysias' speech was written with *technē* or not; as for the definition of *technē,* that has been made clear enough. Phaedrus requires reminding, and Socrates gives a concise and complex summary: the *technē* of speech-making requires, first, knowledge of the subject matter; second, a capacity to define and analyze it into its component parts; third, knowledge of the nature of the soul, and of particular souls; and fourth, a capacity to address one's speech accurately to one's individual audience. As for writing, the great ground of reproach is thinking that there is some great certainty and clarity, *saphēneian,* in it, when it is only in living speech that full communication occurs. The question, then, is not only one of skill and understanding, but of attitude.

And here we get a wonderful Platonic sentence, too long to do in Greek, that sums it up.

> The one who believes that there is of necessity much *paidia* in a written speech on any subject, and nothing worthy of great zeal, *spoudē,*— and in nothing spoken, either, if it is spoken in the manner of the rhapsodes, who speak for the sake of persuasion, without teaching or questioning—but that the best of speeches are really reminders for those who know; the one who believes that clarity, completeness, and worth inhere only in things taught and said for the purpose of learning, and that are truly written in the soul, about just and beautiful and good things; the one who believes that these speeches are his legitimate children, both as he finds them in himself, and if any children or brothers have come into existence in the souls of others, and who says farewell to speeches of other kinds—such is the kind of person that you and I, Phaedrus, might pray that we become. (277-e-5)

Notice that Socrates has softened the opposition between writing and speaking: it is not that writing has nothing but *paidia,* but that it has much *paidia;* nor that writing is entitled to no *spoudē* at all, but not to great *spoudē.* It is not the case that writing has no value, but that it cannot be completely clear and finished, as one is likely to think; I take this as meaning that it will always require reading, or interpretation, and that its job will be done only when that has happened. The best writing, he says, is only a reminder to one who knows; but, above all in this dialogue, that is not a small thing to say, for, as you will remember, it is the function of love itself to remind us of what we once knew.

There is an obvious paradox here, which is that this speech against writing occurs in a written text. How far is what it says of writing true of Plato's own practice? Is it he really saying that we should treat this very text as a kind of amusement, and not as serious work? I think not, but rather that these remarks can be taken as a clue to the reader, a way of defining Plato's own aim in writing: to write in a way that is not liable to such charges; in such a way, that is, that his text does respond to the questions we have about it, and not in the same terms, for as we come back to it with increased understanding we see it saying, or doing, different things. Not that the text can ever achieve exactly what is achieved in actual conversation, in which Plato elsewhere says his true philosophy can alone be found; but it can approximate it much more closely than Socrates' account suggests. It does this, as I have been saying all along, by conceiving of its task not as the statement of a series of truths, but as the engagement of the reader in a set of activities— paralleling those in which Socrates engages Phaedrus—that will carry him towards a clearer understanding of his situation in the world, not at the level of propositions or reminders, but at the point at the center where he imagines himself, the world, and the meaning of his own actions.

Every passage in this dialogue is placed so carefully with respect to other passages, one complicating or answering another, that there are no simple statements of the truth that the reader can take away with him, or treat as reminders. The meaning of this text, then, like that of the other Platonic dialogues, does not lie in an intellectual system it is supposed to represent or recommend, but in the actual experience of tension and uncertainty and conflict that reading it entails, in the life into which it initiates us. It is part of its point that it disappears in the memory.

There is another obvious connection, this one with the speech of Lysias that started the whole thing off. This was of course written; and Socrates, you will remember, insisted upon the reading of the speech, rather than hearing Phaedrus' best recollection of it. This was an elevation of writing over speaking, for only in this way could they have before them the actual words of Lysias, the value of which was to be the subject of their argument. It is true that these words could not defend themselves, and when the opening lines were repeatedly examined, in the passage I discussed earlier, they looked worse and worse, deader and deader. On the other hand, writing is here shown to preserve something that memory does not; and when the writer is not simply absent but unavailable, as Plato himself is, we have much to be grateful for in that. It is only when one has a written text, after all, that it can be made the object of attention of the kind that Plato's writing demands and rewards. What is more, the deadness and sameness of Lysias' speech is established not by comparison with an actual living conversation, but with Plato's own writing. It is the life of Plato's writing that shows the deadness of Lysias' writing.

Finally, there is the question of tone. The myth about writing is enormously amusing, as we imagine this eager god presenting his inventions to King Thamus for approval, the king scrutinizing them with care, asking questions designed to determine their true worth, the god in turn arguing like a salesman for the value of writing, and so on. This passage treats myth-making, like writing, as a form of play, *paidia,* yet at the same time affirms its value, in the imaginative act, indeed in the play itself, which is such an important part of the relation between these two men, and has been from the beginning.

At the very end of the dialogue Socrates says that the person described in the sentence quoted above, the person they would wish to be, should not be called wise, *sophos,* for that is too much for a human being and belongs only to a god; rather, such a person may be called *philosophos,* or wisdom-loving. Socrates advises Phaedrus to speak to Lysias, not telling him what he should say to him—as though to write it—but in confidence that he will know what to say, and to do.

Phaedrus raises a parallel question about Isocrates, whom Socrates defines as his beloved, *paidika*—what of him? In a balanced, admiring, yet objective way Socrates praises his capacities, and says, in essence, that if he allows himself to be inspired by what is divine within him, he will achieve excellence; if not, not. This is what he shall report to Isocrates, his beloved, as a message from the gods of this place; in so doing he defines much of what he means by *philia* and perhaps *erōs* too.[27]

He closes with his famous prayer to Pan, asking that he may become noble, *kalos,* within; that what he has outside may be in friendship, *philia,* with the inside; that he may count the wise man, *sophos,* as rich; and that he may have only such gold as a man of balanced life and judgment, *sōphrosunē,* can carry.

The whole dialogue closes with an enactment of friendship achieved:

---

27. The reference to Isocrates is puzzling. Is Isocrates really to be considered Socrates' beloved? This balanced and sober and objective evaluation, and this hope, could then be taken as expressing philosophic love: it is by this kind of perception and judgment that the lover can make the beloved better. Another interpretation is that "beloved" here is to be taken metaphorically, to refer to one of whom Socrates is inclined to approve. Perhaps it is the reader to whom Socrates' admonition is really addressed.

SOCRATES: "Do we need to say anything more? To my mind we have prayed
   sufficiently."
PHAEDRUS: "Yet make the prayer for me too; for the things of friends *[phi-*
   lōn] are in common."
SOCRATES: "Let us go *[iōmen]*."

FROM ONE POINT of view this dialogue is an exploration of its own
question about writing well, and thinking well, from many perspectives and with many examples, including the speech of Lysias, the
two speeches of Socrates, and the conversations in which Socrates and
Phaedrus engage. Within the world of the dialogue, the aim is to subject one way of thinking to a critical process that reveals its emptiness
and shamefulness, and to establish another. The kind of life thus held
out by Plato for our admiration and imitation is extraordinarily complex and integrative: it includes competence at many different forms
of speech, from question and answer to narrative to myths to formal
speech-making; it includes the emotional and physical experiences of
sexual attraction, again in many forms; and it includes the precision
and grace with which tones of voice are created and shifted, especially the tone characteristic of this dialogue, at once comic and serious,
amusing and in earnest, or in the terms used by Socrates, a form at
once of *paidia* and *spoudē.* Likewise, it is the characteristic of the sentences we have read to represent not an idea or a proposition, but a
mode of thought, one that is simultaneously complex and tentative,
organized and exploratory. The activity of "writing well"—which includes speaking well, thinking well, claiming meaning for experience
well—has two dimensions, in both of which the artist must be capable:
relations with his language, and relations with others.

   In the case of this dialogue, a crucial part of the achievement of
Socrates, and hence of Plato, is the redefinition of the relation between
erōs and *philia.* For him *philia* is not reducible to a set of practical
benefits one receives in return for participating in the practices of *erōs,*
as it is for Lysias; rather, *philia* is friendship in its deepest and most
enduring sense, of which *erōs* is a central part. And *erōs* itself is not
reducible either to a kind of dementia or to functions purely animal,
nor is it simply an aspect of power, but is rather the central spring and
nerve that enlivens the soul and brings it back to its proper concerns,
including its proper relation to what is divine. To recall Socrates' first
inquiry about his own nature, it is not simply that he has within him
something divine, in addition to the animal, but that the divine and the
animal interact to make a whole person and a whole life.

The great myth is the center of this dialogue for it is a performed response to the question how one can talk about that for which we have no ready language. The answer is, by metaphor and invention; and not only that, by invention which simultaneously marks its impossibility—who could believe this stuff about sprouting feathers?—and its utter seriousness. It is beautiful, as well as true; and in reading it one can learn something about the practice of belief. For there is a sense in which the myth cannot possibly be true or the object of belief, yet another in which it is profoundly true; and it is believed as such things can be believed, for it changes the way in which at least some readers imagine themselves and their world.

This myth is a way of addressing a central question of life: How can one accurately and sensibly talk about that central aspect of the self out of which we all live, with respect to which alone "sincerity" is possible? This is the aspect of the self out of which Thoreau speaks and Huck and Odysseus act; it is the aspect with which we are in contact when we read these books, or any book written sincerely from a distant land. What is this part of the self? What kind of life does it have? What kind of career is possible for it, with what hopes, what dangers? These are the questions that the myth addresses, saying not that this is what our life *is,* as Socrates tells us at the beginning, but that this is what it is *like.* This myth is one of those rare human inventions that in a sense comprehends the whole of human experience, as in a different way the Bible does or Dante's *Divina Commedia.* But, unlike those, it is presented in an exaggerated, fanciful, and self-conscious way that defines the kind of truth it has, and does not have, with extraordinary precision.

This text works on us as readers very much as Socrates works on Phaedrus, by frustrating our desire to reduce it to a propositional scheme or to a learnable skill—to reduce it, that is, to "writing." It does this by making such reductions impossible, offering us instead an experience too complex and varied for any such representation. It stimulates a certain kind of life in the reader, and that life is, in the end, its meaning. It engages us in an intellectual activity that cannot be reduced to the calculation of costs and benefits, but is a form of love, the love of beauty and truth. With Phaedrus, we see that the mode of life held out for us is hard, impossibly hard; but this kind of life is about the greatest things, and, as Socrates says in the sentence quoted earlier, for one who attempts the noble, it is noble to suffer whatever that course brings. This is what enables him to say that it is not for the sake of acting and speaking with respect to men that it is right to work so hard to acquire this art, but in order to become able to say and to do what is pleasing to the gods (273-e-5).

℞

My maternal grandfather, who died when I was five, was an Episcopal priest in a small New Jersey town. I can remember him a little; he was a slightly built man, unassuming in manner, full of laughter and warmth and kindness. All my life people who knew him have spoken to me of him with love.

As I think now about what his life was like, what strikes me most is the sense that the demands of his position must have brought him to face, over and over, all the stages of human life: today a baptism, tomorrow a funeral, the next day a wedding. Again and again in the lives of his parishioners he must have seen joy become sorrow, sorrow become joy.

Such a life would be a discipline of the feelings and the mind; as I imagine it, his response to each event, in its ideal form anyway, would be deep and genuine—real happiness, real sorrow—but as time went on his feelings would also be qualified by what he had just seen and done, and by what he knew was coming. The life I imagine him leading would bring him to being at once engaged in the moment and removed from it, for he would see more and more of the larger patterns of which it was a part. All this would mean a gradual deepening of the self and mind.

Did his religion help my grandfather in this, by offering him a language and a set of practices and beliefs upon which a life could be founded, from which he did not have to turn away at moments of loss and crisis, in which he could locate himself at times of grief and happiness alike, at funerals and baptisms, and to which he could turn from whatever other languages made up his existence? If so, how did it work?

One possibility is that it was for him a dogmatic series of propositions, the truth of which he accepted on faith, that would enable him to locate any event or experience in a larger structure of thought and imagination. Everything that happens is an instance of some general truth; it has always been anticipated. This is the kind of coherence religion has often been thought to offer—a set of answers.

But this does not fit with my fragmentary sense of him. Might the materials of his religion have been instead for him a kind of language, a set of stories and phrases and rituals and gestures, materials of meaning as yet incompletely finished, that would enable him to address a moment not as though it were wholly foreseen and accommodated, but in a fresh way, as something new yet to which it was possible to speak? Not with the idea that his religion has for once and all given immutable coherence to all experience, but that it enabled him to make and find coherences, from moment to moment and day to day. The proof of its value would not then lie in the way experience conformed to preexisting propositions, but in his voice, in the shape of his gestures, in the responsiveness to others he could achieve—a life not of certainty but uncertainty, a life of art, and for that reason a life all the more.

PART THREE

SEVEN

Frost and Herbert: Poetry as Life

I want to begin this chapter by thinking further about a certain aspect of the last, namely, the great myth at the center of the *Phaedrus*. This myth, almost like a religion, offers Phaedrus, and the reader, a way of imagining the whole of human life, from before birth till after death. This is a way of thinking of the world and the self within it, and other people too, that is presented as coherent, a language to which one can return from the details of life to reform and redirect one's understandings and motives. It is offered as the kind of imaginative structure that can give life meaning in virtually every aspect, from intellectual conversation to physical love.

This myth has often been read, and understandably enough, as a kind of metaphysical statement of what Plato believes: once we were in touch with the Eternal Forms, now we no longer are, and philosophy is what brings us back into connection with them, all as though the myth repeated what seems to be the doctrine of the *Republic* and the *Theatetus*. But this kind of reading simply disregards the complex mixture of tones to which I paid so much attention in the last chapter; and it disregards something else as well, which is that in this version the most salient fact about the Eternal Forms, once beheld in the heavens, is that they are not available to us at all in this life, the only life we have. The point about Plato's doctrine of the Eternal Forms, in this dialogue at least, is thus not to assert the truth of their existence, which can after all never be known or observed while we live, but to define, by their absence, what human life, as we actually know it, lacks. The myth is a way of drawing attention to the fact that knowledge of the Forms is denied us. We must live on conditions of radical uncertainty; and it is to show us how this might be done without collapsing into incoherence or despair that the dialogue exists, that Plato's version of philosophy exists. The myth is offered not as a metaphysical doctrine upon which one can securely lean, or to which one can grant authority, but as an instance of the process of invention-in-conversation that the dialogue simultaneously exemplifies and recommends.

The aim of Plato's text is to work on the reader much as Socrates works on Phaedrus, by offering him a disorienting experience of controlled uncertainty and in this way stimulating independence of mind, in the way that conversation, or dialectic, at its best can do. This kind of philosophy is not the promulgation of a certain set of propositions about the world, but a mode of life and thought; its end is not a set of statements, but an end of a different sort, the transformation of the mind and imagination of the participant, both Phaedrus within the dialogue and us as readers of it. The process represented in the dialogue—philosophy itself—is one that by its nature has no termination until death, and the hoped-for return to the world in which beauty and truth and justice can be seen simply and clearly for what they are. For Plato there is no language—certainly not the ordinary Greek of the day, and no version of it that he or Socrates could manage to produce—in which the truth can simply be said. In his view we had better get used to that fact and start displaying our awareness of it in our speaking and writing alike.

In this chapter we return from Greek to English, in the form of certain poems by Robert Frost and George Herbert.[1] As we shall see, both of these writers make poetry that in important ways works like the kind of philosophy we saw in the *Phaedrus,* for it carries the reader to the edge of language, in this case our own, and from the point so de-

---

1. In my work on Frost I have been most helped by *Robert Frost on Writing,* ed. Elaine Barry (New Brunswick, N.J.: Rutgers University Press, 1973); Reuben Brower, *The Poetry of Robert Frost: Constellations of Intention* (New York: Oxford University Press, 1963); Richard Poirier, *Robert Frost: The Work of Knowing* (New York: Oxford University Press, 1977); William Pritchard, *Robert Frost: A Literary Life Reconsidered* (New York: Oxford University Press, 1984). The best edition of his works is *Robert Frost: Collected Poems, Prose, & Plays* (New York: Library of America, 1995).

On Herbert: the best editions of his works are *The Works of George Herbert,* ed. F. E. Hutchinson (1941; corr. reprint, Oxford: Clarendon Press, 1945), and *The English Poems of George Herbert,* ed. C. A. Patrides (London: J. M. Dent, Everyman ed., 1974). The critical works most useful to me have been: Chana Bloch, *Spelling the Word: George Herbert and the Bible* (Berkeley: University of California Press, 1985); Michael Schoenfeldt, *Prayer and Power: George Herbert and Renaissance Courtship* (Chicago: University of Chicago Press, 1991); Richard Strier, *Love Known: Theology and Experience in George Herbert's Poetry* (Chicago: University of Chicago Press, 1983); Joseph H. Summers, *George Herbert: His Religion and His Art* (Cambridge: Harvard University Press, 1954); Helen Vendler, *The Poetry of George Herbert* (Cambridge: Harvard University Press, 1975).

fined asks what I have been calling the deepest question: whether the writer can find a way of imagining the world and the self within it that will enable him to engage in coherent speech and valuable action. As was the case in the *Phaedrus,* this is a question about the possibility of meaning not only in the work of art itself, but in life.

I read these two poets together here not only because there are interesting and important comparisons to be drawn between the ways in which they work,[2] but also in order to exemplify a process deep in the heart of intellectual life, and of this book, but as yet unmentioned, namely, the process of reading one work, or set of works, in light of another. This is one of the ways in which we make our own minds, our own imaginations, and equip ourselves to face the problems of language and meaning that the writers themselves face. Reading one work in light of another is the reader's equivalent of metaphor, which Frost once defined as saying one thing and meaning another, saying one thing in terms of another. Our experiences of reading naturally shape each other, for every text derives much of its meaning—in a sense all of it—from its context, and we cannot help placing what we read in contexts partly of our own making, defined by our educations. The connections so established can be chronological, as one brings one's reading, say, of Donne to Yeats; or antichronological, as in my reading of Frost and Hebert, for I was familiar with Frost, who was once to me very much the ideal poet, long before I read Herbert with any care. What I say, then, has an irreducibly autobiographical element; this is not a mistake or embarrassment, for it is in fact part of my point that all of our readings have such elements, and that it might be good to make them more explicit than we usually do.

---

2. One might argue that Herbert had a significant influence on Frost's poetic practice—if not directly, for Frost was not a great reader of Herbert, then indirectly, through Emerson, who was in many ways Frost's master and who read Herbert with admiration throughout his life. One interested in establishing such "influence" might point to the similar rhyme patterns of "The Collar" and "After Apple Picking"; to the thematic similarity of the "The Storm" and "Tree at My Window"; and the closing phrases of "Prayer" (I)—"something understood"—and of Frost's sonnet, given its title by these words, "for once then something." (On Emerson and Herbert, see Michael J. Colacurcio, "'The Corn and the Wine': Emerson and the Example of Herbert," *Nineteenth-Century Literature* 42 [1987]: 1–28.) But that is not the way I wish to think about the relation between these two poets. Rather, I wish to look at the connections between these poets in a different way, from the point of view of the reader, or, more properly perhaps, of a reader; not as a matter of causation across time, but as an instance of the process by which one experience of reading shapes another.

I first read Frost while still in school, as natural successor to Thoreau, for he was, I thought, a nature poet. But he became central to my mind mainly as a result of the training in reading I received at Amherst College in the late 1950s.[3] This was a world in which English was widely regarded as the most demanding and rewarding field of study, with an almost mystical power, and close to the center of that field was Robert Frost. He was Amherst's poet, we felt: he had actually taught there many years before and he still visited the campus for a week or two every year, and sometimes even more frequently. And he was of New England, at least by transplantation—as we were of New England too, at least by transplantation. More even than Eliot he was for us the exemplar of what a poet could be. Part of this was his interest in form; part that he seemed to speak in ordinary language, the virtues of which were the subject of the great freshman composition course that transformed the minds of so many of those exposed to it (and an example of which appears in the passage between chapters 5 and 6). Frost could be seen, as Reuben Brower and others argued, as a poet of voices;[4] and "voice" and "tone of voice" were essential elements of our vocabulary, not only in the reading of poetry, but in thinking about our own writing; for we were taught that in writing we defined ourselves and acted on others, and that writing itself was in this important sense an ethical activity. The heart of what it has meant for me to come to Herbert by way of Frost is that the reading of Frost's poetry of voices has helped me hear the voices in Herbert better.

In what follows I shall assume in the reader a passing familiarity with the poetry of Frost and Herbert, but no more, and shall describe or reproduce the poems upon which I most depend.

Differences and Similarities

To start with obvious differences between the two poets, Herbert is a seventeenth-century Anglican priest who writes poetry exclusively about his religious life; Frost is a twentieth-century American who makes the world of nature in New England the material of his much more public poetry. Herbert's verse was not published during his life-

---

3. For other accounts of that world by those who experienced it, see Richard Poirier, "Reading Pragmatically: The Example of Hum 6," chap. 4 in *Poetry and Pragmatism* (Cambridge: Harvard University Press, 1992), and William Pritchard, "Ear Training," chap. 1 in *Playing It by Ear* (Amherst: University of Massachusetts Press, 1995), and "Foreshadowings," chap. 1 in *English Papers* (Minneapolis: Greywolf Press, 1995).

4. See Brower, *Robert Frost: Constellations of Intention, passim.*

time, but left in his will for a friend to publish or burn, as he thought best; Frost made a career of his poetry, one of the few in the century who made a living at it, and he was his own best publicist. It is not surprising to discover, then, that Herbert typically speaks out of the central experience of his inner self, to his God or to some version of Him, while Frost speaks less as a self than as a poet, or The Poet perhaps, and in a way that is far less directly revealing of inner struggles. Frost speaks not to various versions of his God, but to a reader as secure and universal as he himself seems to try to be. Despite his stance as an isolated rural figure, then, he works in a much more public and formal idiom than Herbert usually does.

Herbert writes from the inside out, or as Emerson says of him *ab intra*,[5] starting with internal experience for which he has no adequate way of talking and trying to make such a language in his verse. The images and metaphors he uses are often explicitly marked as efforts to say the unsayable; they are typically not arrayed in the form of a story, but connected by movements of imaginative and emotional association. (This is one reason it can be hard to memorize his poems.) Frost, by contrast, typically writes from the outside, beginning with a highly visualized event in the natural world—a spider on a heal-all, a deer swimming across a pond, the reflection of a face in the surface of a well, a dust of snow falling from a hemlock tree—and then expands upon it, finding meaning within it or claiming meaning for it, almost always against the possibility of no meaning at all. Herbert is in this dimension much more like the other great American poet, Emily Dickinson, than he is like Frost.

Yet there are important similarities between them as well. To begin with, they are both misread in a similarly sentimental way: Frost as the country sage producing verse of a greeting card banality, Herbert as the pious Anglican saint, writing poems of sweet devotion. Both of them are in fact as far from the sentimentality attributed to them as could well be imagined: Frost bleak and cold, Herbert terrified and alone, both of them undermining at every stage just the implications of their verse that are seized on in such misreadings.

But these misreadings are not accidental; they have a basis in the writing itself. Part of what misleads the reader in each case is what might be called the sententiousness of the verse. In Frost, this shows up

5. Ralph Waldo Emerson, *The Journals and Miscellaneous Notebooks* (Cambridge: Harvard University Press, Belknap Press, 1969), 7:157.

as the portentous voice of the Yankee sage uttering wisdom. "Something there is that doesn't love a wall"; "One could do worse than be a swinger of birches." In Herbert the analogous tendency is towards a moralizing sermon voice, which is seen most completely in his long poem, "The Church-porch," but it appears throughout his verse.[6] What the typical misreading of both poets misses is the degree to which the writer's sententious tendency is made problematic by the verse itself, made in fact the object of sustained poetic criticism.

A related point is that both poets, in different ways, are interested in the virtues of plain speech and natural diction: Frost trying to catch the rhythms of ordinary New England speech and cast them in the forms of verse; Herbert obsessed with the thought that the best verse, the best prayer, would be the simplest. As he says in the first of two poems entitled "Jordan": "Let them not punish me with loss of rhyme / Who plainly say, *My God, my King.*" For Frost the effort is to incorporate this diction and these rhythms directly into his verse; Herbert does this too, and does it beautifully and naturally. His great poem "The Flower" begins this way, for example: "How fresh, O Lord, how sweet and clean / Are thy returns." All this reinforces the idea that the truths these poets utter are in some way simple ones. Yet, as he makes plain especially in the two "Jordan" poems, Herbert sometimes feels that the very simplicity of voice and diction to which he aspires is inconsistent with his own commitment to poetic form and complexity. Frost sees a somewhat similar opposition between natural and artificial speech—between the "sentence sound," described in the letter to John Bartlett reproduced in chapter 4, and the demands of meter and rhyme—and makes of this tension a fundamental principle of his art. And both of them, in the end, are as far from simple as one could well imagine.

Both Frost and Herbert are consumed with what is for them the ultimate metaphysical or theological question: Who—or What—is out there? For Herbert the issue has less to do with the existence of his God, which he in some sense never seems to doubt,[7] than with His

---

6. Examples can be found in "Sundays," "Lent," and even in some of the very great poems, as at the ending of "The Flower" and "The Holdfast."

All quotations from Herbert and Frost are from the following editions: *The Works of George Herbert,* ed. F. E. Hutchinson (1941; corr. reprint, Oxford: Clarendon Press, 1945); *Robert Frost: Collected Poems, Prose, & Plays* (New York: Library of America, 1995).

7. Though in some poems, such as "The Search," the possibility is presented that God is so remote that He might as well not exist.

nature or quality: Is He a God of power or a God of love? Of justice or mercy? What relation, if any, has He with Herbert (or with the speaker of his poems)? For Frost the question is superficially less theological than metaphysical:[8] Is the natural world full of fellow feeling, as it seems to the Wordsworthian nature poet in him? Or is it cold, indifferent; random, maybe; or malign? This is the question of his famous "Design," and it runs through a great deal of his verse.

Both poets are also absolute masters of poetic form, among the greatest in the English language: Who else, except Yeats, can make verse that so continually meets strict and varying formal requirements, yet sounds effortless, as though the speaking voice naturally fell into such forms? And form itself has a deeply substantive meaning in the work of both poets: the very fact that language can be cast in the ordered forms of verse, that the sentence sound can work within the constraints established by the meter, that the right word rhymes with the right word, is for both poets, I believe, one of the strongest arguments, perhaps the strongest argument, that something like grace is at work in the world. For whatever may be true of the universe more generally, here in the poem is enacted the possibility of order and beauty; and for both poets the sources of this order and beauty are in the world, in the materials of language, not simply made up by the poet. In "Paradise," for example, Herbert discovers that he can make a poem in which the last word of the first line of each stanza loses its initial letter in the second, its second letter in the third, and it all works out: "Charm, harm, arm; grow, row, ow; start, tart, art." Or in "Heaven" that the last word of the line can come back, reduced, in an echo that affirms a source of meaning in the language and in the world: "Shall it persever? Ever." But these are only extreme instances of the more ordinary yet still profound fact that it is possible to think in words that rhyme, in sentences that run in metrical forms. Nothing we know would make this likely, but it is so, a fact of poetry, to which different poets will of course give different meanings. For each of these poets it becomes an affirmation of what he most doubts.

The initial points of similarity, then, are these: that each poet is susceptible to sentimentalized misreadings; that these misreadings are in sense invited by the poet's tendency towards the sententious, in Herbert's case towards the sermon voice, in Frost's that of the Yankee sage; that each is simultaneously committed to simplicity of thought and

---

8. But see "A Masque of Reason" and "A Masque of Mercy."

diction and to a complex and artificial art that seems—sometimes to the poet himself—inconsistent with it; that each is consumed with the ultimate question of the character of God, or of the universe; and that each poet finds in the possibility of poetry itself perhaps the best ground for a hopeful response to this question.

There is still another similarity, related I think to each of the others, which I later develop at greater length, namely, that both of these poets are self-conscious in the extreme about the ways in which their claims of meaning, their constructions of the universe and themselves, have tendencies towards falsity. They are both highly aware, that is, of the deceptiveness of their languages and of their own desires. Their art in this sense carries them, and us, to the edge of language, to the point where it is remade. And they both know that what they then make can be false or empty or misleading. While it is true that the possibilities of poetic meaning are a ground of hope for both, then, it is also true that for both the very act of writing—or speaking or thinking—is deeply perilous, involving the danger of false feeling and false thought. This fact indeed defines a central subject for both poets.

The Delusive Imagination

I begin with Frost's most famous, or infamous, poem, "The Road Not Taken," which has made it into the canon of greeting card and calendar literature. We all know that the poem describes the choice of one path over another in the woods; but it is less widely recognized, I think, that it does this in two different and competing ways:

> Two roads diverged in a yellow wood,
> And sorry I could not travel both
> And be one traveler, long I stood
> And looked down one as far as I could
> To where it bent in the undergrowth;
>
> Then took the other, as just as fair,
> And having perhaps the better claim,
> Because it was grassy and wanted wear;
> Though as for that the passing there
> Had worn them really about the same,
>
> And both that morning equally lay
> In leaves no step had trodden black.
> Oh, I kept the first for another day!

> Yet knowing how way leads on to way,
> I doubted if I should ever come back.
>
> I shall be telling this with a sigh
> Somewhere ages and ages hence:
> Two roads diverged in a wood, and I—
> I took the one less traveled by,
> And that has made all the difference.

As the choice is first represented, the speaker sees no ground for it at all. He simply makes his choice, without any articulated basis—"then took the other." Once he has done this, however, he instantly starts to explain and justify himself, personifying the road and moralizing the choice: he took the second road "as just as fair, / And having perhaps the better claim, / Because it was grassy and wanted wear."

This is the imagining mind at work, claiming or finding or constructing meanings where there are perhaps none at all. The speaker is here starting to characterize the two roads, and his choice, in ways that will lead him at the end of the poem to utter a portentous and sentimental conclusion. But now, at this stage in the process, he can check this tendency and return to the careful observation of what is there. For he recognizes that, despite his claims, there is in fact no real difference between the paths: "Though as for that the passing there / Had worn them really about the same . . ."

The initial voice of realistic, particular, and unselfimportant description thus starts to fall into sentimental and moralistic pretension, but catches itself just in time. Yet, out of this very experience perhaps, the speaker foresees that the day will come, maybe in old age, when he will no longer catch himself, but fall victim to the tendencies of mind he has at once exhibited and resisted, a time when he will claim for himself a false heroic role as a latter-day Thoreau, marching to a different drummer:

> I shall be telling this with a sigh
> Somewhere ages and ages hence:
> Two roads diverged in a wood, and I—
> I took the one less traveled by,
> And that has made all the difference.

The sentimentality of this conclusion is marked for us by the heaviness of the repeated "I—I," by the lameness of the concluding word, which does not quite scan—the reader hovers uncomfortably between "differ-ence" and "diff'rence," neither of which is exactly right—and most of all by the prior description of the choice, which falsifies the claims being made here.[9] Yet the power of what I am calling Frost's sentimentalizing voice is so strong as to blur all this for the reader, to carry us as well as him into the land of the Hallmark card. The sentimentality is rejected, yet its uncanny power is at once acknowledged and performed.

This is not just a piece of sentimentality, then, nor just a joke on the reader, but a deeply serious and worrying poem that does much to explain why Frost writes and from what position he does so. Think of the poem in terms of time: the past is the time when the speaker started off to sentimentalize, but managed to catch himself, just barely; the future is the time when, as he imagines it, he will succumb to the tendency. What then is the present? The moment of anxiety, at which he confronts both past and present, himself and his language; the poem is a way of keeping alive a present capacity for thought and self-criticism, against a future in which it may be lost.

With this poem we can compare Herbert's well-known "Life," which I think also takes as its subject the self-delusive power of the speaker's imagination.

> I made a posie, while the day ran by:
> "Here will I smell my remnant out, and tie
> > My life within this band."
> But Time did becken to the flowers, and they
> By noon most cunningly did steal away,
> > And wither'd in my hand.
>
> My hand was next to them, and then my heart:
> I took, without more thinking, in good part
> > Times gentle admonition:
> Who did so sweetly deaths sad taste convey,
> Making my minde to smell my fatall day;
> > Yet sugring the suspicion.
>
> Farewell deare flowers, sweetly your time ye spent,
> Fit, while ye liv'd, for smell or ornament,
> > And after death for cures.

9. Earlier the same voice made another sentimentalizing gesture, which was also checked: "Oh, I kept the first for another day!" This is a claim that the choice is no choice, that he can always come back; but it is followed by an acknowledgment of reality: "Yet knowing how way leads on to way, / I doubted if I should ever come back."

I follow straight without complaints or grief,
Since if my sent [scent] be good, I care not if
It be as short as yours.

The speaker here first says that he collected some flowers and "made a posie" of them; he did this as "the day ran by"—that is, as a response to, or in acknowledgment of, the passage of time. "Here will I smell my remnant out, and tie / My life within this band." This is an attempt to face mortality by constructing an artwork of flowers and merging himself with it; but it fails, for the posie withers and dies. Like Frost's speaker, the speaker here first makes a claim of meaning beyond what the world will bear, then corrects it by reference to his experience.

The meaning-claiming side of the mind is not defeated by this, however, but turns it all into a lesson: "My hand was next to them, and then my heart: / I took, without more thinking, in good part / Times gentle admonition." No terror, no anxiety even of the kind implied in "while the day ran by," but a conclusion meant to be comfortable: "Who did so sweetly deaths sad taste convey / Making my minde to smell my fatall day; / Yet sugring the suspicion." Defeated in one attempt to face death by an act of imaginative creation, it tries another, turning the death of the flowers into a comfortable sermon.

Perhaps warned or troubled by his own observation that his suspicion is sugared, the speaker shifts to another conventional poetic gesture, bidding the flowers farewell: "Fit, while ye liv'd, for smell or ornament, / And after death for cures" (referring both to herbal medicine and to the kind of "cure" of his anxiety that the dying flowers are made by his imagination to achieve). At the end he asserts without conscious conflict his conclusion: "I follow straight without complaints or grief, / Since if my sent be good, I care not if / It be as short as yours."

The farewell to the flowers thus suggests a farewell of another kind, to himself, though even this is made harmless by the speaker's capacity to formulate its meaning in a benign way. But he gives it all away with the powerful "if": "if my sent be good." That is of course the real question, and it invites its correlative: If his scent is not good, what then? That is the issue, and the conclusion is far from comfortable. The surface complacency of this ending thus occludes the most likely and most threatening possibility.[10]

The phrase that best guides one's rereading of this poem is "with-

10. Recall the ending of "Vertue," where, apparently in consolation for the loss and death found in the natural world, the speaker says:

out more thinking," for it accurately describes the speaker's own state of mind: in making the posie, in declaring that he will merge with the flowers, in learning from their death a gentle lesson of his own mortality, and in resting at the end in a formulation marked by the poem itself as a false one, in all of this the speaker is avoiding thought—thought of just the kind the poem stimulates in its reader.

Both "The Road Not Taken" and "Life" are thus written against the poet's own tendency to say things that are too easy, that in one sense or another he knows to be false: in Frost the speaker is on the edge of self-consciousness, almost but not quite realizing the degree to which he will delude himself, while in the Herbert poem the speaker seems to be unaware of his performed self-delusion. But in both cases the poem itself makes the reader aware of what the speaker sees either dimly or not at all, inducing by a kind of structural irony a self-consciousness in the reader—"more thinking"—that it is one of the aims of the poem to create. In this way it brings us to the edge of language, where we can begin to see and to mistrust such seductive formulations.

Yankee Sage and Christian Sermonizer

The voice that Frost resists in "The Road Not Taken" is a version of his most characteristic one, that of the Yankee sage. It runs throughout his verse, sometimes under control as here, sometimes not. Think of "Birches," with its image of the boy climbing the birch to swing it to earth again. "I'd like to get away from earth awhile / And then come back to it again and begin over. . . . One could do worse than be a swinger of birches." Or of "Directive," the poem about finding the Holy Grail and oneself: "And if you're lost enough to find yourself / By now . . ." Or in "Mending Wall": "Before I built a wall I'd ask to know / What I was walling in or walling out, / And to whom I was like to give offense. / Something there is that doesn't love a wall." And so forth.

> Onely a sweet and vertuous soul,
> Like season'd timber never gives;
> But though the whole world turn to coal,
> Then chiefly lives.

The speaker, caught up in his satisfactory theologizing, glides over a question the poet presents us with: What of the soul that is not "sweet and vertuous"? Or: How can you make your own soul "sweet and vertuous," or even know whether it is these things?

As I say, this voice is Frost's most characteristic one, a kind of declaiming; yet the poetry not only uses it but commonly takes it, and its flaws, as one of its central subjects. It is repeatedly subject to criticism. For example, in "Mending Wall," the voice just quoted is answered by another, "Good fences make good neighbors"; the speakers limit each other by answering each other, and the poem thus puts both utterances into question. And in "West Running Brook" the man's somewhat long-winded theoretical speech about the meaning of the brook is answered by his wife, in quite another key. Yet sometimes Frost himself gets swept away by it, as he foresees he will in "The Road Not Taken."

There is still another dimension to the puzzle, also made apparent by "The Road Not Taken," which is that in such phrases as I have quoted there is both truth and force. We remember them: however true the criticism, there is truth in the criticized as well. The issue is thus more complex than I have yet proposed, and I shall soon return to the ways in which Frost works on this problem.

But I want to turn first to the analogue in Herbert to Frost's voice of Yankee wisdom, namely, what I have called his sermon voice. The strongest and clearest version of this voice is in "The Church-porch," which consists mainly of advice cast in quite conventional terms from an older to a younger man. For example:

> Lie not; but let thy heart be true to God,
> Thy mouth to it, thy actions to them both:
> Cowards tell lies, and those that fear the rod;
> The stormie working soul spits lies and froth.
>> Dare to be true. Nothing can need a ly:
>> A fault, which needs it most, grows two thereby.

Versions of this voice of doctrinal and moral truth appear throughout his verse, and it is deeply problematic for Herbert. From one point of view what it says is true, nothing truer; it represents the truths that he struggles to accept and to which he refers, in Izaak Walton's account, when he describes his verse as representing the "spiritual conflicts" between his soul and his God.[11] From another point of view, however, his verse shows that virtually nothing that is true can be said in such a

---

11. See Izaak Walton, *The Lives of Dr. John Donne, Sir Henry Wotton, Mr. Richard Hooker, Mr. George Herbert* (1670; Menston, England: Scolars Press, 1969), 74.

voice, in such language; the real truth lies in the inadequacy of all our languages, mirroring the inadequacy of the human mind and heart.[12] "Thy word is all, if we could spell" ("The Flower"). The truth of our situation can be captured, if at all, only in the tension-ridden and evanescent verse he writes at his best, not in any declamation of this kind. The sermon voice is also wrong in another way, theologically, for it is by nature authoritarian and tends to be punitive, and it represents a God who is those things too. Herbert's deepest struggles will in fact be not with the God so defined, his "bad" against God's "good," but with his own tendencies to use a voice of doctrinal and moral truth to define his God as authoritarian and remote, against a truth he also sees, that He is a God of love.

Of neither poet can we say that the verse reflects in some direct way the thoughts or feelings of an integrated self. Rather, for both, poetry expresses the workings of a divided self, in a language that is itself deeply problematic. Like the *Phaedrus,* this poetry has as an essential part of its subject the way the speaker can go wrong in writing it, and not merely aesthetically but at the center of his being and imagination.

Frost: The Claims of Meaning and Nonmeaning

In Frost the perils of sentimentality and false sagacity are not merely personal, as one might think from "The Road Not Taken," but come to have a theological or metaphysical significance. The reason is that his poetic reflections on his own tendency towards falseness also become a way of reflecting on the universe itself, a way of asking whether it actually has the kind of meaning we constantly and perhaps falsely attribute to it, or is by contrast mute and meaningless. Is his desire to discover meaning in the world deluded? Or will it be rewarded by what he finds? He thus moves from his position on the edge of language to asking what I have called the deepest question, which is whether he

---

12. There is an exception of a kind: presumably for Herbert the language of the Bible, and of the prayer book, are adequate for the purposes for which they are composed. But this does not change the point, for we use those languages only as readers not writers. One cannot simply adopt them when writing a poem or a letter or a sermon, for now they become ours, and flawed as we are flawed.

There are moments in Herbert when he seems to have achieved a sense of adequacy of expression, as in "The Call" and perhaps the end of "The Temper" (I). But this is not a position he can maintain from poem to poem. It is no sooner attained than it is lost. For a fuller account of this kind of movement, see my *"Book of Starres": Learning to Read George Herbert* (Ann Arbor: University of Michigan Press, 1994), especially 78–79, 123–24, 134–35.

can find or make a satisfactory way of imagining the world and himself within it.

Take as an example his poem, "Range-finding":

> The battle rent a cobweb diamond-strung
> And cut a flower beside a ground bird's nest
> Before it stained a single human breast.
> The stricken flower bent double and so hung.
> And still the bird revisited her young.
> A butterfly its fall had dispossessed
> A moment sought in air his flower of rest,
> Then lightly stooped to it and fluttering clung.
> On the bare upland pasture there had spread
> O'ernight 'twixt mullein stalks a wheel of thread
> And straining cables wet with silver dew.
> A sudden passing bullet shook it dry.
> The indwelling spider ran to greet the fly,
> But finding nothing, sullenly withdrew.

The poem begins with the speaker extending his imaginative sympathy to the world. This gesture draws attention to the double pathos of the situation, in which damage is done first to sentient nature by thoughtless man, followed by much worse, damage to a "human breast." The whole trope depends upon the speaker's sympathy for nature, which implies a reciprocal return, a community of sympathy between man and nature: "The stricken flower bent double and so hung."

But the next line begins to suggest a doubt: "And still the bird revisited her young." From one point of view this is charged with feeling, as we imagine the bird, like a human mother, still managing to live in the wreckage of battle; yet there is another possibility, that the bird is simply indifferent to the destruction. The next actor, the butterfly, first pathetically seeks "in air his flower of rest," the flower that has been destroyed by the bullet, but then quickly recovers: "Then lightly stooped to it and fluttering clung." The death of the flower—and by implication of more than the flower, the human breast—is of no real moment to him after all.

The speaker has been imagining this scene on the assumption, common in romantic poetry, that we live in a world of mutual fellow feeling; it is the resonance of the fall of the flower, or the man, in the feelings of others, that gives it its meaning. But as he writes another possibility emerges, that these assumptions are simply false, false and sentimental.

The last half of the poem, set off from the first by the strongly marked couplet and the new rhyme-scheme of the quatrain that follows it, responds to this discovery in two ways: first by speaking of the world of nature in a distant and impersonal way, "On the bare upland pasture there had spread / O'ernight twixt mullein stalks a wheel of thread / And straining cables wet with silver dew." The speaker here no longer represents nature as human and comprehensible, but as an apparently unmotivated external process, as though it were as remote as science makes it. Then, as the phrase "straining cables" begins to suggest, he shifts again, personifying nature once more, making it like us. But this time it is not benign and kindly, but like us rather in its malignity: "A sudden passing bullet shook it dry. / The indwelling spider ran to greet the fly, / But finding nothing, sullenly withdrew." The tearing bullet, which will kill a man, has been reduced to "nothing."

This poem thus catches the mind's struggles with its own inclinations and formulations, first trying to see the world as a web of sympathy, then correcting that to distant indifference, then in turn correcting that to malignity. The poem finds no place of rest among these formulations, but presents them as alternate and unsatisfactory possibilities. The movement of the poem is toward this aspect of the truth of our situation.

A similar tension is at work in many of Frost's poems, for example the well-known "Design," referred to in chapter 5, which begins in a sense where "Range-finding" leaves off, with a creature that is both endearingly human—"dimpled"—and repulsive: "I found a dimpled spider, fat and white." [13] What happens, we discover, is that this white

13. Here is the full text of "Design":

I found a dimpled spider, fat and white,
On a white heal-all, holding up a moth
Like a white piece of rigid satin cloth—
Assorted characters of death and blight
Mixed ready to begin the morning right,
Like the ingredients of a witches' broth—
A snow-drop spider, a flower like a froth,
And dead wings carried like a paper kite.
What had that flower to do with being white,
The wayside blue and innocent heal-all?
What brought the kindred spider to that height,
Then steered the white moth thither in the night?
What but design of darkness to appall?—
If design govern in a thing so small.

spider has caught a white moth on a white flower. The question with
which the speaker concludes is the question of order and meaning in
the universe:

> What brought the kindred spider to that height,
> Then steered the white moth thither in the night?
> What but design of darkness to appall?—
> If design govern in a thing so small.

The alternatives the speaker here considers are that nature is malign,
governed by evil design, or that it has no order, no meaning at all,
at least in any matter as small as this. He does not even consider the
possibility, with which "Range-finding" begins, of a community of
sympathy. The point of the poem is not that one alternative is true,
the other not, but that our situation is one in which we cannot help
thinking in these ways, both of them, each of which is answered by the
other.[14]

In "The Most of It" the isolated speaker watches a living being
crash into the water on the other side of the lake and swim towards
him. He sees in this event an embodiment of the idea that nature lives
and is concerned with him, that it reaches out to him, as fellow to
fellow—as though he expects this creature to join him as his secret
sharer. But it proves after all to be only a deer, who "stumbled through
the rocks with horny tread / And forced the underbrush—and that was
all." The imagined fellow feeling dissolves into brute fact and force.

By now Frost has brought us a long way from the problem of sentimentality as I originally defined it, for to speak of the "sentimental"
assumes that there is another, unsentimental and true, alternative: that
the paths really were the same, for example, and that no choice worthy
of the name could be made between them, or that the spider is truly
indifferent or malign. But in the series of poems just mentioned, there
is no such alternative. The truth is that we are caught between, or
among, languages that are all unsatisfactory. Even the denial of mean-

14. I am indebted here to Randall Jarrell, "To The Laodiceans," in *Poetry and the Age*
(New York: Vintage Press, 1955), 34, 42.

A more amusing version appears in "The White-Tailed Hornet," in which the speaker
describes the way in which, when you disturb it in a barn, the hornet with unerring instinct
stings you on the most sensitive place on your nose, thus demonstrating the competence of
nature, the effectiveness of natural selection, and hence the order of the universe. Yet on
another occasion, the story is wholly different, as are its cosmic implications: in your house,
the hornet is lost and awkward, unable to do what it was made to do, suggesting a kind of
randomness and radical incompetence in the natural world itself.

ing does not work. When the speaker in "The Most of It" concludes "and that was all," for example, he is in one sense right, but in another sense wrong; for in addition to that dismissive phrase there is the poem itself, beautifully shaped and ordered, which within its own compass enacts the very possibilities of meaning he seems to deny.

The point, then, is not simply that we are given to false sentimentalities, against which we should guard ourselves, but that the very process of imagination at the center of our minds simultaneously deludes and creates. A claim of meaninglessness can, after all, be as sentimental as a claim of universal fellow feeling, as incomplete and false. For Frost, as for Plato, no language is adequate to the meaning of events in the world; the closest thing to adequacy we can have is a poetry—or a philosophy—which locates us in the tension between our own deepest commitments and our deepest uncertainties.

The attribution of meaning to nature or to the universe is not simply a foolishness, then, an error from which we can extricate ourselves by thinking, or by poetry, but as deep a tendency as exists in human nature. Frost's poetry of doubt necessarily affirms its own processes of imagination and creation. We are thus caught between two impulses: on the one hand, to see meaning in the world—to find it and claim it—and on the other to doubt, not to see it, or to see meaninglessness. It is not that one is true and the other false, one inherently sentimental, the other inherently factual: we are simply in the situation in which two truths, two tendencies of our nature, both exist with equal force and reality.

How is it possible to think this double way, and how can it be good? As one analogy I have thought of what we would hope that a person running for president would think about the importance of his campaign and election. To run at all, he has to think that it matters supremely who will be elected, that his administration will do better than any other—that the election, in Frost's language, will "make all the difference." But if he believed this completely, 100 percent, he would be insane; at the same time that he believes it, then, we want him *not* to believe it, to realize that his contribution will be small, that the other person may not be so bad, that he will face lots of situations in which there is no good choice at all, and so on. Yet if he believed only this, he could never run for president.

Much the same thing could be said about our engagement in other essential but impossible activities: in voting, in teaching our classes, in writing our books, even in starting out on our marriages. It is not that we should have a balanced view, midpoint between extremes, but that both of the competing voices should be loud within us, in a full-throated way, though varying their relation from moment to moment: the voice that says that we can do it and that it really matters, and the one that says that we are caught up in processes beyond our control and understanding.

This doubleness is a form of moral and psychological maturity, towards which Frost's verse leads him and his reader. What it catches, and makes the topic of explicit thought, is the radical tension in human life between the claims of meaning and nonmeaning. Frost works out of a set of uncertainties about the world, himself and his language, that he cannot resolve; but he expresses this irresolution in an activity that makes the irresolution itself both conscious and explicit. Poetry is a necessity for this mind, an integral part of its life; not something he chooses to do, but what existence means for him.

For one more example of the way Frost can mark the achievement of his own imagination as false and fictional at the same time that he shows us how true and important it is, consider "Mowing." [15] Here the speaker imagines his scythe whispering as he mows. "What was it it whispered? I knew not well myself; / Perhaps it was something about the heat of the sun, / Something, perhaps, about the lack of sound." The speaker thus imagines another speaker, his scythe, and listens for its meaning; he is uncertain, but knows that "It was no dream of the gift of idle hours, Or easy gold at the hand of fay or elf" of which it spoke: "Anything more than the truth would have seemed too weak / To the earnest love that laid the swale in rows." Nothing fancy or poetic, then; plain and true speech, like that yearned for in Herbert's "Jordan"; and what it whispers is: "The fact is the sweetest dream that labor knows." Yet of course this poem is not the sound of a scythe, nor

---

15. Here is the text of this early poem:

There was never a sound beside the wood but one,
And that was my long scythe whispering to the ground.
What was it it whispered? I knew not well myself;
Perhaps it was something about the heat of the sun,
Something, perhaps, about the lack of sound—
And that was why it whispered and did not speak.
It was no dream of the gift of idle hours,
Or easy gold at the hand of fay or elf:
Anything more than the truth would have seemed too weak
To the earnest love that laid the swale in rows,
Not without feeble-pointed spikes of flowers
(Pale orchises), and scared a bright green snake.
The fact is the sweetest dream that labor knows.
My long scythe whispered and left the hay to make.

a series of facts, or factual truisms, but a poem, full of fancy and imagination and beautiful patterns of rhyme and sound, all of which are
necessary to their own meaningful denial or qualification. The process
of claiming meaning, which has in Frost its sentimental and sententious forms, and is by him often criticized on such grounds, is at the
same time the impulse from within that produces what is most valuable in life, including that criticism itself.

Herbert: False and True Meaning

What happens when, after such an experience of Frost, we turn to Herbert? First, like Frost, Herbert is consumed with a cosmic question,
though for him the issue is not so much, What is out there in the universe?, but Who is this undoubted God? Is He a God of Power or a
God of Love? And who is Herbert in relation to Him: a creature to be
punished for his sins, or to be made to suffer by whim? Or is he the
object of love, and his suffering really a kind of gift? Or is he simply
nothing at all to this figure, "a crumbe of dust" ("The Temper")? All
of these possibilities and more are enacted in Herbert's verse: one can
find a punitive God in "Justice" (II), for example, an incomprehensible
God in "Justice" (I), a God who forbids him to worship the beauty of
Mary and the angels in "To all Angels and Saints," a remote God in
"The Storm," a loving presence in "Love" (III), and so on. Herbert
himself is sometimes the sententious moralist or doctrinaire theolo-
gian, sometimes the broken soul, sometimes the courtier or art poet,
sometimes full of ambition of pride at his achievements, sometimes
raked with self-abuse.

Second, again like Frost, Herbert takes as his subject the perils and
defects of the very poetic processes by which he pursues these ultimate
questions of identity and relation. Herbert's speakers too go wrong, all
the time and in a thousand ways, and his verse is in large part about
the ways in which they do so. Yet the heart of the problem for him is
even deeper in the self than it is for Frost, and in two related ways. Part
of it is a radical epistemic uncertainty: he cannot be sure of what he
seems most to know. Consider, for example, the following plainly autobiographical poem, "Affliction" (I):

> When first thou didst entice to thee my heart,
> > I thought the service brave:
> So many joyes I writ down for my part,
> > Besides what I might have
> Out of my stock of naturall delights,
> Augmented with thy gracious benefits.

I looked on thy furniture so fine,
                    And made it fine to me:
Thy glorious houshold-stuffe did me entwine,
                    And 'tice me unto thee.
Such starres I counted mine: both heav'n and earth
Payd me my wages in a world of mirth.

What pleasures could I want, whose King I served,
                    Where joyes my fellows were?
Thus argu'd into hopes, my thoughts reserved
                    No place for grief or fear.
Therefore my sudden soul caught at the place,
And made her youth and fiercenesse seek thy face.

At first thou gav'st me milk and sweetnesses;
                    I had my wish and way.
My dayes were straw'd with flow'rs and happinesse;
                    There was no moneth but May.
But with my yeares sorrow did twist and grow,
And made a partie unawares for wo.

My flesh began unto my soul in pain,
                    "Sicknesses cleave my bones;
Consuming agues dwell in ev'ry vein,
                    And tune my breath to grones."
Sorrow was all my soul; I scarce beleeved,
Till grief did tell me roundly, that I lived.

When I got health, thou took'st away my life,
                    And more; for my friends die:
My mirth and edge was lost; a blunted knife
                    Was of more use then I.
Thus thinne and lean without a fence or friend,
I was blown through with ev'ry storm and winde.

Whereas my birth and spirit rather took
                    The way that takes the town;
Thou didst betray me to a lingring book,
                    And wrap me in a gown.
I was entangled in the world of strife,
Before I had the power to change my life.

Yet, for I threatned oft the siege to raise,
                    Not simpring all mine age,
Thou often didst with Academick praise
                    Melt and dissolve my rage.
I took thy sweetned pill, till I came where

I could not go away, nor persevere.

Yet lest perchance I should too happie be
                    In my unhappinesse,
Turning my purge to food, thou throwest me
                    Into more sicknesses.
Thus doth thy power crosse-bias me, not making
Thine own gift good, yet me from my wayes taking.

Now I am here, what thou wilt do with me
                    None of my books will show:
I reade, and sigh, and wish I were a tree;
                    For sure then I should grow
To fruit or shade: at least some bird would trust
Her houshold to me, and I should be just.

Yet, though thou troublest me, I must be meek;
                    In weaknesse must be stout.
Well, I will change the service, and go seek
                    Some other master out.
Ah my deare God! though I am clean forgot,
Let me not love thee, if I love thee not.

Here the speaker tells the story of his life, which is of course a version of Herbert's own. As he tells it, in the only terms available to him, the story begins in happiness and ends in misery. It is a story of affliction, moving from joy to pain. But, as the poem also makes plain, to speak this way is actually to misrepresent the nature of his experience. The pleasure—"At first thou gav'st me milk and sweetnesses; / I had my wish and way"—in fact confirmed him in a kind of infantile self-centeredness; the pain helped him escape from it to a state in which he can desire to be of value to another, if only a bird. And his difficulty is not only in his misunderstanding; as one who thinks in terms of joy and pain, loss and gain—as we all do, as we all must do—Herbert's speaker is asserting the priority of his own will and preference over his Lord's. To live is to sin.

In this, as in many of his poems, Herbert demonstrates a radical uncertainty about his capacity both to perceive and desire correctly. He cannot trust his perceptions, his feelings, or his language.[16] Herbert's

---

16. Thus "The Holdfast" strips from the speaker the possibility of any action, any claim, even the claim of impotence; leaving him with an inadequate phrase, "that all things were more ours by being his," which at one level makes no sense, at another asserts afresh just the self-interest the poem is supposedly written against. Or think of Herbert's translation

poetry addresses these uncertainties in the self and in the universe mainly by making them his explicit subject, in an effort at self-transformation. This is the aim, for example, of "Affliction" (I) itself: to carry him from the language of joy and pain to another kind of gesture, all that is available when the will has been stripped away: "Ah my deare God! though I am clean forgot, / Let me not love thee, if I love thee not." The affliction of which the speaker complains reduces him to the core of his being, the last thing he can give up; but this turns out to be his capacity for love, the best thing in him. The reduction of which he complains is thus in a sense a benign one, a healing transformation, which receives its completion in the poem itself.[17]

But the transformations worked by his poetry are not always of this kind. Sometimes they are incomplete, as in "Love Unknown," where the speaker's interlocutor tells him the truth but he himself cannot quite see it. Sometimes there is a transformation, but it is in the wrong direction: in "Sepulchre," for example, which begins with a gesture of natural and authentic sympathy—"O blessed bodie, whither art thou thrown? / No lodging for thee, but a cold hard stone?"—and ends somewhat grimly, locating love not in his heart, as it begins, but outside it. "The Temper" manifests two contrary tendencies, in a kind of double transformation. It begins with a sense of helplessness, as the speaker feels himself swung from heaven to hell; it moves next into a question, Why do you do this to me?—"Wilt thou meete arms with

---

of Psalm 23, which is normally read as one of the great expressions of trust in our literature. This is what Herbert says:

> The God of love my shepherd is,
> > And he that doth me feed:
> While he is mine, and I am his,
> > What can I want or need?

Herbert converts the psalmist's gesture of simple trust into a question, apparently with only one possible answer—"nothing." But the question is rendered real by the half-stated conditional: "While he is mine . . ." And what happens when I am no longer his? And the central terms here, "mine" and "his," though essential to human thought, necessarily assert the claims of the self against its God. They are undone, not so much by this poem as by others: "The Clasping of Hands," for example, which chimes "mine" and "thine" until they seem to merge in a loss of identity.

17. For similar instances, consider "The Thanksgiving," where the poet-speaker is brought at the end to recognize the limits of his art, in a breakdown of the will and mind that is at once a collapse and an achievement; "Gratefulness," in which the speaker of a simple prayer first feels it to be manipulative, and works his way afresh through the situation, enabling him to speak at the end in a way he could not at the beginning; "Christmas," where an ordinary voice of narration becomes capable of a song of praise and love; and so on.

man?"—then into a prayer, that the speaker be allowed to "roost and nestle" in his Lord's protection. His initial sense of puzzle and distress is thus first transformed into a challenge to his Lord; this in turn frees him to express his dependency as a species of trust:

> Yet take thy way; for sure thy way is best:
> Stretch or contract me, thy poore debter:
> This is but tuning of my breast,
> To make the musick better.

He concludes with a moment of imagined felicity: "Thy power and love, my love and trust / Make one place ev'ry where."

But in this very gesture he claims a kind of equality with God—"Thy power and love, my love and trust"—that cannot be stable; and the beginning of "The Temper" (II), which follows next, undoes the whole thing:

> It cannot be. Where is that mightie joy,
> Which just now took up all my heart?

Herbert's verse, like Frost's, is a way of dealing simultaneously with his radical uncertainty about the nature of the universe, and its God, and with his awareness of his own capacities for self-delusion. For both writers poetry is a method of thought and self-correction, in Herbert more than Frost a method of self-transformation; but in both even this method is unreliable. It may lead the poet into claiming meaning where there is none or denying it where there is. In Herbert the second possibility is especially present: the danger that he will claim no meaning where meaning exists, or a false meaning, or that he will depreciate himself beyond what the truth requires. Just because "The Temper" (II) comes second, for example, does not mean that it is right: the effect of the two poems is to leave the reader and the speaker poised between alternatives.

Consider "To All Angels and Saints," where the speaker explains his refusal to adore the beauty and gentleness of Mary and the saints by saying that his "King" forbids it. Here he defines his God as a God of power and justice only, as a will that simply must be obeyed. He thus strips from Him, and gives to Mary and the saints and angels, divine qualities of kindness and love, in this way constructing the deity to fit with his own need for a punitive power in the world. Or think of "Decay," where the speaker, talking to his God, describes the course of theological history as a decline from the "sweet dayes" when "thou didst lodge with Lot" and were present in the world "at some fair oak, or bush, or cave, or well." [18] Now, by contrast, "thou dost thy self immure and close / In some one corner of a feeble heart." You shrink into the heart, that is, and risk defeat at the hands of sin. For the speaker this is the story, as the title suggests, of "decay"; but for the reader it is the story of progress, of God's move inward, into the heart, where his momentary defeat at the hands of sin will ultimately be a triumph of love. The self-delusion here, and in "Love Unknown" as well, lies in failing to see the positive meaning of the story the speaker tells; in this context the denial of meaning is a denial of his God as well.

"Whitsunday" presents much the same issue. It begins, as so many poems do, with a touching gesture or prayer:

> Listen sweet Dove unto my song,
> And spread thy golden wings in me;
> Hatching my tender heart so long,
> Till it get wing, and flie away with thee.

The speaker here asks to be entered, and hatched, and seeks to "flie away with thee," in all of this, expressing a remarkable degree of confidence and trust in the Holy Spirit he addresses. But this doesn't happen, or not instantly; he then recoils, and universalizes his situation:

---

18. Here is the full text of the poem:

> Sweet were the dayes, when thou didst lodge with Lot,
> Struggle with Jacob, sit with Gideon,
> Advise with Abraham, when thy power could not
> Encounter Moses strong complaints and mone:
> Thy words were then, *Let me alone.*
>
> One might have sought and found thee presently
> At some fair oak, or bush, or cave, or well:
> Is my God this way? No, they would reply:
> He is to Sinai gone, as we heard tell:
> List, ye may heare great Aarons bell.
>
> But now thou dost thy self immure and close
> In some one corner of a feeble heart:
> Where yet both Sinne and Satan, thy old foes,
> Do pinch and straiten thee, and use much art
> To gain thy thirds and little part.
>
> I see the world grows old, when as the heat
> Of thy great love, once spread, as in an urn
> Doth closet up it self, and still retreat,
> Cold Sinne still forcing it, till it return,
> And calling *Justice,* all things burn.

"Where is that fire which once descended / On thy Apostles?" Once the stars and sun did joyful obeisance to the spirit: "The starres were coming down to know / If they might mend their wages, and serve here." But now you have withdrawn: "Thou shutt'st the doore, and keep'st within." [19]

But in doctrinal terms this is a mistelling of the theological story, which is that the Holy Spirit was sent by Christ, when He ascended, to take a permanent place among us. In this sense the speaker denies the reality, or at least the presence, of the very form of God to whom he is praying, apparently because his prayer was not instantly answered in a way he could perceive. He explains the absence of his God by reference to the martyrdom of the Apostles, the cutting of the "pipes of

19. Here is the whole of "Whitsunday":

>   Listen sweet Dove unto my song,
>   And spread thy golden wings in me;
>   Hatching my tender heart so long,
>   Till it get wing, and flie away with thee.
>
>   Where is that fire which once descended
>   On thy Apostles? thou didst then
>   Keep open house, richly attended,
>   Feasting all comers by twelve chosen men.
>
>   Such glorious gifts thou didst bestow,
>   That th' earth did like a heav'n appeare;
>   The starres were coming down to know
>   If they might mend their wages, and serve here.
>
>   The sunne, which once did shine alone,
>   Hung down his head, and wisht for night,
>   When he beheld twelve sunnes for one
>   Going about the world, and giving light.
>
>   But since those pipes of gold, which brought
>   That cordiall water to our ground,
>   Were cut and martyr'd by the fault
>   Of those, who did themselves through their side wound,
>
>   Thous shutt'st the doore, and keep'st within;
>   Scarce a good joy creeps through the chink:
>   And if the braves of conqu'ring sinne
>   Did not excite thee, we should wholly sink.
>
>   Lord, though we change, thou art the same;
>   The same sweet God of love and light:
>   Restore this day, for thy great name,
>   Unto his ancient and miraculous right.

gold" that were a conduit for the Spirit, implying that this action deprived the Spirit of a way into the world. But this is an odd result, to say the least, making this aspect of the Divinity subject to such human control. Perhaps we are to read the speaker as coming to see this, for at the end of the poem he recoils once more, this time from his unconscious denial and forced explanation into a gesture very different in feeling:

> Lord, though we change, thou art the same;
> The same sweet God of love and light:
> Restore this day, for thy great name,
> Unto his ancient and miraculous right.

But, as we have seen, in the story the speaker tells it is "God" who changes, not "we": He is either disabled or withdraws when the "pipes" are cut, and in either case is not a reliable presence, not a "sweet God of love and light" in any way from which we can benefit. I was at first inclined to read this stanza as a merely doctrinal assertion, a denial of the significance of story the speaker has just told and in that sense forced and empty. But I think we can also, and perhaps better, read it as a retraction of his failed and in some sense incoherent effort to explain what has happened, a denial of the story but now in a positive sense, in that he recaptures the sweetness and authenticity with which he began, thus reaffirming his capacity to trust even in the face of dis appointment. On this view, the first stanza makes a lovely prayer, which is not answered; the body of the poem tries to explain this fact, in a way that does not work; at the end the speaker abandons his effort at explanation, and the sense of injury or confusion that motivated it, and returns to the gesture with which he began, but now in a deeper and more mature way.

OR SO I SAY. WHO am I, you may well ask, to assert that this, or that, is the meaning of Herbert's poem? How can that be a sensible response to a poet who makes as vivid as he does his sense of the uncertainty of his own perceptions, feelings, and language?

Here we are at the center of the experience Herbert's verse offers us. I would put it this way: As we read poem after poem, we not only learn the language in which this verse is composed, its characteristic terms and movements and oppositions, we also come to understand the person who composed these poems, one after the other, and the nature of his struggle to understand the world, its God, and himself. It is our prior knowledge of his other poems, and of him, that helps us attune ourselves to this one. And as we proceed we can see that his question about his Lord—whether He is a God of justice or mercy, of punishment or love—is really a question just as much about himself: Can he imagine himself as able to recover what he once knew now that he seems to have lost it, as able to give depth and reality to his most fundamental gestures when they have come to seem empty or false? I think the question at the center of it all is not whether his Lord is a God of love, but whether he can imagine that he himself, with all his faults of mind and character, is loved. As readers of the book we know of course that he can, for at least in my experience it is not possible to read through this sincere and intelligent and scathingly honest verse of self-searching without in some sense feeling love for the person who speaks to us in such a courageous and open way. As for Herbert's own internal drama, the normal precondition to the recognition that one can be loved is the recognition that one can love, and Herbert's verse gradually establishes his confidence in his own capacity of that kind, from "Affliction" (I) to "Whitsunday." When we come to "Love" (III), the last poem in his book, it is because it at last speaks for us, saying what we know from our own experience to be true, that it has the incredible power it does:

> Love bade me welcome: yet my soul drew back,
>   Guiltie of dust and sinne.
> But quick-ey'd Love, observing me grow slack
>   From my first entrance in,
> Drew nearer to me, sweetly questioning,
>   If I lack'd any thing.
>
> "A guest," I answer'd, "worthy to be here":
>   Love said, "You shall be he."
> "I the unkinde, ungratefull? Ah my deare,
>   I cannot look on thee."
> Love took my hand, and smiling did reply,
>   "Who made the eyes but I?"
>
> "Truth Lord, but I have marr'd them: let my shame
>   Go where it doth deserve."
> "And know you not," sayes Love, "who bore the blame?"
>   "My deare, then I will serve."
> "You must sit down," sayes Love," and taste my meat":
>   So I did sit and eat.

BOTH FROST AND HERBERT make their poetry to a large degree out of the impulse to criticize their own tendencies towards false feeling and false meaning. In Frost's case the criticism is followed by the recognition that the impulse he is criticizing—that which claims meaning for experience—is at the center of his being. It cannot simply be rejected, but must be used, again and again, with all its perils. In Herbert's case the criticism of his own perceptions and formulations is reinforced in the first instance by the voice of Christian doctrine, which insists upon the defects of his mind and will that naturally flaw them; but this voice too turns out to have its vices, its punitive and authoritarian versions, and it must be corrected, just as his tendency to speak out of the self's experience of pain and pleasure must be corrected; both are by stages transformed to a view that accepts his own nature and recognizes what his God, as he comes to understand Him, has from the beginning been trying to tell him, yet he has been unable to hear.

Like Frost's, Herbert's poetry is thus written out of a double sense of its own impossibility and necessity. The sources of impossibility are in the self, in the language, and in the imperfect knowability of the Deity, to whom and about whom he speaks. There is no pure heart, no simple speech, no unflawed human action. All we have is the possibility of this kind of poetry. Again as with Frost, this poetry comes from the center of his life. His writing is the struggle of existence for him; in Thoreau's terms it is as sincere as it is imaginable that speech could be, and hence distant too.

For both poets the greatest source of hope and confidence lies in the activity of poetry itself, in the possibilities of beauty and form that it offers—and possibilities of truth too, truth of the special kind that interests both of them and Plato as well, namely, the movement towards greater recognition of the facts of our situation, where there are no nonproblematic statements of what is true, or none available to us. With Frost it all depends upon the miracle that his words, cast in sentences of meaning, are also meters and rhymes, and the further miracle that there is, sometimes at least, a tension between two forces, the force of doubt or dismissal and the force that drives the making of the poem—a tension that creates a new kind of life. For Frost it means something crucial about the nature of the universe that this is so. He once said in an interview that you can hear people talking through a wall and know something of what they are saying from the tone of the sentence itself, even when you miss the words.[20] I have a sense that this is how he hears his own verse, as though in its sounds are meanings

20. Robert Frost, "Robert Frost, New American Poet," in *Robert Frost on Writing,* 152–53. Compare his letter to John Bartlett, quoted above at page 112.

that have their source elsewhere. Much the same is true of Herbert as well, as "Paradise" and "Heaven" indicate, and, beyond that, as we recognize when we see that the work of his poetry is to remake his life at the center, transforming him in the deepest way. The poetry of both of these men brings us into the presence of sources of meaning beyond our understanding.

❦

In late March during my seventh grade year we had a week's vacation. This was a welcome break from school, but it promised little else; and partly out of boredom, partly out of a self-conscious desire to discover something about the world into which I was growing up, I decided to spend it learning what I could about our government. Each day, with a friend I talked into joining me, I went downtown to Hartford, on the bus, and explored a different institution: the legislative assembly of the state capitol, where I could understand almost nothing of what was going on; the FBI office at the post office, where the men took my fingerprints, locked me briefly in a cell for the fun of it, and showed me the map on which they kept track of major crimes; the city police station, dank and dirty, where we were introduced to the police court judge, and saw him in action, in what seemed to me a mysterious exercise of power; and finally, by good luck, the state courthouse, where a series of trials were going on. Of one I only remember that it involved some issue, vaguely sexual, that the adults there thought we should not be exposed to; I could not follow the proceedings in any event, and after a time we left. Then to another room, where a trial was going on about an automobile accident. We saw witnesses being examined, we pieced together the outlines of the story, then we heard the closing arguments. It was wonderful.

The facts of the case were these: on Easter morning a man taking some documents to his employer's second office out in the country decided to let his sixteen-year-old son, still without a license, drive the car. The boy ran the car off the road and hit an elderly woman on her way to church, injuring her severely. One question was whether the father was negligent in letting his son drive at all, or in failing to supervise him; another—

really between insurance companies—was whether his employer was liable if he was. This was an interesting question: the man was running an errand for the company as their employee, but his decision to use the time to teach his son how to drive was obviously his own. How was the question to be framed, how argued? Watching the lawyers on both sides, I saw an opportunity for thought and speech and argument of the most exciting kind. I was fascinated.

This experience was repeated when years later I was thinking about going from English graduate school to law school. I went to hear a moot court argument involving a complex question of state tax and administrative law and was astonished at the range and power of the arguments available. I had expected this to be resolved in a technical and uninteresting manner, by a dry-as-dust reading of some rules found in an old book with yellowing pages, but I quickly saw that instead it required argument about the most interesting and important things: about the meaning of language, including the way language means; about the purposes of the tax laws; about the relations between the citizen and the government; about the kind of respect that one agency of the government owes to judgments reached by another; and so on. The argument always had justice—and whatever justice could be made to mean—as its subject, and it seemed to me to involve everything, to call upon every capacity of mind and imagination. And it had to be shaped, in time as spoken, on the page as written, and directed to a particular audience or a set of audiences; in those ways at least, perhaps more, it had to be a work of art. I was entranced, and went back to hear other arguments, struggling to follow them, imagining myself making them.

Here was a profession that was set up on the idea that each side would have equal time to talk; that the judge or other audience would hear you out; that you could make whatever arguments seemed to you right; that you could do whatever you could to reformulate the language to make it say the truth from your perspective; and do all this in the interests of people who could not adequately speak for themselves.

In law school itself, I read each case, or tried to, as a piece of the real world, the world in which I wanted to make my way, and my question was what I could learn, or figure out, about life there from this evidence. My focus was always on language and expression: What could one say, here, as a lawyer for the shipowner, or there, as lawyer for the injured child, and how would you respond to either? I wanted to learn what could be said and what could not, how to make legal statements and arguments of my own. "Your honor, in this case . . ."

This world of language was always emerging out of silence, what was said out of what could not be said: the wrenching pain of the broken arm, the grief of the parent, the fury of the cheated man, and so on. I could begin to see that law was a system for the translation of mute and inexpressible experience to another plane, where it acquired significance of a new kind. It was a way of giving meaning to life.

EIGHT

The Life of the Law as a Life of Writing

In the passage that just precedes this chapter I describe my own first exposure to law, which I saw as a fascinating activity of mind, a way of engaging with language and the world. Suppose we were to take that young law student as representing a certain stage in the making of a lawyer—a stage a bit like that represented by Thoreau at Walden, full of a sense of unlimited possibility—and ask, What happens when such a one grows into the life of the law? I hope that in exploring this question we may be able to bring into the practical life of the present the large themes and questions presented by the great works from the past that we have been reading. To this end I shift my method slightly in this chapter, asking the reader to imagine himself or herself a lawyer, or law student, facing the questions the law presents its practitioners.

If you were thus to imagine yourself as the young lawyer or law student I describe, setting forth into the world, I think you would find yourself, like Huckleberry Finn, quickly meeting constraints of the most serious kind. To start with, the laws with which you must work are written by others, and they may of course be foolish, corrupt, or immoral. Think for example of the laws of human slavery in our collective past, and other laws of our own day: those that permit the continued degradation of the natural world upon which we all depend, for example, or those that fail to treat all of our children as people of equal worth and value, or those that permit our penitentiaries to be cesspools of crime; or, less dramatically, those that seem simply stupid or ill drafted. You may come upon certain rules of law or judicial decisions with which you profoundly disagree, others with which you simply differ. But in either case as a lawyer you must take them as authoritative, or challenge their authority only in certain established and limited ways.

What is worse, whenever you go to work with the materials of the law, trying to bring about a result that meets your client's interests, that makes sense from his point of view, there is always someone on the other side, challenging almost everything you say, trying to undo what you are doing. And when you go to court you must face the reality that judges and jurors can have all the limitations of human beings, from stupidity to dishonesty to mere self-importance or inattentiveness; yet it is to these people that you must speak and make your case. And what about the outcomes of the cases in which you are involved, or those that you invoke as authority? You will often think these plainly wrong, or unjust. In any event, even when the "right" side wins, there is almost always a loser, a person or entity whose voice and perspective are silenced, and what is to be said about him or her? In everything you do you must recognize that the law is part of a culture and a national political community that are far from ideal, in which you are implicated, yet of which you may in important ways want to be critical.

In addition, in our day it is easy to imagine the law as a rather mechanical institutional system, designed by social architects or engineers to achieve certain results in the world, say an increased gross national product or safer highways or effective schools. This perspective invites one to evaluate law by testing actual against designed outcomes, or by proposing different outcomes and ways to achieve them. To the extent the lawyer thinks in this way—the way of much social science—she may find herself conceiving of her own role in mechanistic terms too, as though she were really a cog in a machine of social control whose main virtue is efficiency of operation, rather than a mind confronting the realities of human experience and the difficulties of talking about it, and of shaping it, in language. This mechanistic image of her life is reinforced by the common and necessary way of talking about law practice in accounting terms, as a business whose end is profit.

Not all of these external limits or constraints are as serious or dramatic as those facing Huck Finn, but some of them are or can be, as the slavery example itself suggests. Suppose you really were a lawyer in a world in which human slavery was supported—defined, implemented, enforced—by the law, and by lawyers: How would you face that fact? Are there any analogues to slavery in our own world? Certainly people who represent the poor and weak often feel that they are up against an impossibly powerful set of political and intellectual forces that render them helpless, their clients unheard.

Finally, and in a sense much worse, is the fact that many of the constraints or defects we must face are at work in our own minds and

characters. How do you as a lawyer regularly imagine the human beings about whom you speak: as having what motives, what values,
what capacities, what experiences? How do you imagine the larger
world of which you are part, and yourself within it? Are these ways of
imagining adequate to your own sense of the possibilities of human
life? Without quite knowing it you may find yourself speaking a language that trivializes or dehumanizes others, or yourself; and how can
you be sure that has not happened? Other people, after all, often take
an extremely dim view of the ways lawyers talk and think.

Your own mind and values are put into question in another way
too, for you will often discover—or think you discover—that the law
is wiser than you are, drawing distinctions you have not thought of,
complicating what seem at first to be easy questions, leading you to
recognize their real difficulty, and so on. The very cultural forces you
want to be free to resist may in fact have much to teach, and you cannot be sure in any particular case what response is the right one. The
criticism you want to make proves more difficult than you at first imagined. And what happens when the legal culture changes, as it surely
must? You face then the twin questions faced by Odysseus: Can you
adapt to the new world, learn to speak its language, to make the moves
that carry persuasive force? And what happens to you when you do so?

I say all this, obvious as most of it is, simply to make clear that the
lawyer or judge is deeply limited and powerfully constrained in her
efforts to respond wisely and decently and intelligently to the cases that
come before her. These restraints are partly external, in the world, and
partly in her own mind and imagination. But this is not the end of the
story, and to show some ways in which it is not is the point of the rest
of this chapter.

What I suggest, briefly, is this: that the lawyer is not, as we sometimes think, only a cog in a system of social administration, nor simply
a profit-maximizing service provider, but a person who meets, who
can learn to meet, the moment at which the language of the law—a
language that has justice as its aim—is applied to experience, the moment at which it must confront other languages. Despite, or perhaps
partly because of, the constraints described above, this is a moment of
opportunity for thought and speech of a most complex and important
kind. The lawyer and judge live constantly at the edge of language, the
edge of meaning, where the world can be, must be, imagined anew; to
do this well is an enormous achievement; to do it badly, a disaster of
real importance, not only for the lawyer or judge but for the social

world of which they are a part, including the particular people whose lives they affect.

In reading the *Phaedrus* I put the question, What is it like to read Plato? Here I am asking, What is it like to do law, to read and speak this language? What kind of language is it, with what restraints, what enablements, and how can one learn to speak it well, as lawyer or judge? How does the law invite one to imagine the world and oneself within it? In particular, is the kind of thought we have been observing in others as we work through this book—in Thoreau and Twain, Frost and Herbert—also possible in the law?

These are obviously questions not for a single chapter, but for a life—my life—and here I cannot offer a complete response; but I do hope to suggest a line of thought that will connect what the lawyer does with what we have seen other writers to be doing. In what I say I shall for the most part assume that the reader is not a lawyer, though there may be moments that are not wholly accessible without a legal education—but that is part of the point. Like Greek, law is a language that must be learned.

Imagining the Life of a Lawyer

I want to begin by asking you to imagine what you think the life of a lawyer is like. One picture you may have is that of the person who knows the sets of rules promulgated by legislatures, courts, and agencies, how to find them, and how to read them in such a way as to tell his clients what they may and may not do, or to predict with accuracy what a court or other lawyer will do. In fact, and as I try to show with an extended example below, that kind of work is a relatively small part of what a lawyer does. The rules of law with which he deals are for the most part simply not sufficiently clear and specific to be applied in a mechanical way to the experience of his client. Or, to put it slightly differently, while in any real case there will be some rules that are so clear that no one can really argue about their application, there will be others that are open to real and serious contest, and it is upon the latter that the lawyer focuses most of his attention. I might sum it up this way: Of course the lawyer usually knows more than his client about the law, and in some sense has thus already thought about the issue his client presents; but there is always, or almost always, something new and distinctive and problematic about what the client brings him that requires further thought, and often thought of a deep and uncertain kind.

A second general point is this: that the lawyer always faces the uncertain relation between what can be said in words—legal words or any words—and the raw experience of his client: the pain of the injury, the fear of financial disaster, the inner certainty that the patent will make a fortune, the confidence reposed in another who has proved unreliable, and so on. One way to think of the law, in fact, is as an intervention into a world that works largely in nonlegal terms, and for the most part well enough, but that has now suffered a crisis or breakdown calling for its help. The parties were driving in different directions on the road when one hit a patch of ice and skidded into the other; or one sold a major piece of manufacturing equipment to another that now no longer seems to work well; or the couple got married with the highest of hopes but now find themselves, against every expectation, involved in messy divorce proceedings; or the two friends want to start a business together and have no idea how to do it.

In each case we begin with the life of the world that precedes the lawyer's involvement, where the parties are competent at shaping their own existences; there is then an event that leads one, then the other, to go to a lawyer; there then ensues a lot of activity, mainly in language—reading, talking, writing, advising, arguing, explaining; this is in turn followed by an action, or a refusal to act, by the court or by the lawyers in negotiation, and a return to the world of ordinary life, either changed by what has happened, or unchanged. It thus always is—or should be—a question for the lawyer what relation exists or can exist between the language of the law, the language in which he talks and functions, and the experience and life of the world. Does the law have an adequate way of expressing what happened in the past? Of shaping what will happen or should happen in the future? How do we know? How in the end is one to manage the relation between the language of the law and the kind of human experience that cannot be directly expressed in it?

A third general point is that the lawyer must perpetually face the relation between legal language and other languages—other ways of representing the situation or the actors in it, other ways of imagining human motive and experience, other ways of shaping the future. In the courtroom and negotiation alike other languages and voices are regularly translated into the law, always with some distortion, sometimes to good effect, sometimes to bad. Sometimes the law itself changes as a result, but in the end it systematically excludes voices, narratives, languages—ways of thinking and talking that it finds irrelevant to its concerns or of which it does not approve. It is thus a constant question for the lawyer how to manage the relation between law and other languages.

In each of these respects—in the uncertain meaning of legal language, in its uncertain connection to human experience, and in its uncertain relation to other languages—the lawyer regularly lives on the edge of language, where his task is to be conscious of it, aware of what it does, and ready to try to remake it.

Think for example what it would be like to have someone come to you and describe the collapse of a commercial deal, perhaps a partnership or a long-term contract, for which he had once had great hopes, but which has now proven a disaster. How completely could you capture in your own mind what happened in the world, what its significance was, and how would you think about what ought to happen next? How adequate do you suppose the legal language of partnerships or contracts would be to this situation? The language of accounting or economic theory? What place would the voices or languages of the parties, or of outside experts on technical issues, have in what you said or did? This set of questions could be asked about virtually any case—a divorce, an accident, a crime—and they are present not only when the law looks back on past experience, as it does here, but when it tries to shape experience for the future, by drafting a partnership agreement, for example, or a prenuptial contract, or a divorce settlement.

Such in rough outline are some of the structural difficulties the lawyer must face: How is she to do these things, and how do them well? To explore these questions I consider next an extended example in which I ask you to imagine yourself as a lawyer in a particular case. I suggest a series of questions that would occur I think to most lawyers, not with the idea that you should be able to answer them but as a way of giving further definition to the nature of life in the law.

A Graduation Prayer Case

Suppose that you are a lawyer in Providence, Rhode Island, and that a man you know slightly, Daniel Weisman, calls to make an appointment for him and his daughter, Deborah, to talk to you in your office. When you ask him what it is about, he tells you that when she graduated from her public middle school last month, a rabbi read formal prayers before and after the ceremony; he and she think this was wrong, and want the practice stopped.

They are due in your office tomorrow. What questions do you plan to ask them? What questions do you expect them to ask you? How do you hope the conversation will go on these matters?

Conversations with Daniel and Deborah

Here is what we shall assume you already know, from your dimly remembered course in constitutional law: that the First Amendment provides that "Congress shall make no law respecting an establishment of religion, or prohibiting the free exercise thereof"; that the Supreme Court has applied this provision, which was originally effective only against the federal government, to the states, including subdivisions like the City of Providence; that some years ago the Court held school prayers unconstitutional, but it has also permitted prayers in the state legislatures. It recently held, in a case arising in nearby Pawtucket, that a nativity scene was a permissible part of a municipal Christmas display.

You are also likely to have your own intuitive reaction on the merits of the case: thinking either that the inclusion of prayers in public school graduations is a plain violation of the separation of church and state, just what the Constitution exists to prohibit; or that this practice is plainly all right—we have had graduation prayers for ever, and nothing could be more innocuous than such a thing. One question, to which we shall return, is what you, as lawyer, or as judge when the case reaches court, should do with these initial responses, which we all have: Should you try to disregard them, or deny that you have them? Act on them directly? or what?

One line of your questioning will in fact be directed to the complication of these responses. For you do not yet know what form the prayer took, whether prayer is in fact a regular practice at Providence's public school graduations, or whether the principal or school board knew the rabbi was to offer a prayer, or discussed the possibility with him; and answers to these questions may affect your initial response, one way or the other. For example, if you are at first inclined to think the prayer a violation of the First Amendment, you may soften your view if you discover that it was volunteered by the rabbi, without warning to the principal; if you are inclined to think the prayer is not a violation, you may shift your view if you discover that it was drafted by the principal or the school board, or by the rabbi under guidelines they provided, or that the prayer was highly sectarian. These are important factual questions, and you can see how you would pursue them by questioning the Weismans and others.

As a lawyer you will also have another set of questions, very different from these, having to do with the motivations and interests of your clients, and questions that do not admit of such ready factual resolution. The most basic one is this: Why are they coming to you in the first place? You are a professional who earns your living by giving legal advice and representing people in court. Are they prepared to pay your usual fees to bring this suit, and if so, why? People put up with all kinds of offenses and injuries, all the time, without going to law about them. So what is going on here?

One possibility is that they think that they are civil liberties plaintiffs, that you are a good civil liberties lawyer—after all, you are a member of the American Civil Liberties Union (ACLU)—and that you will accordingly represent them for free, either out of commitment to their cause or as a way of establishing your reputation in a highly visible case. This possibility raises questions about you: Are you in fact willing to do this for free, or for a reduced fee, and why? (What are the dangers to the case or to you, in addition to any lost income, if you represent someone who is not paying you? How would this fact affect your relationship with them as you try to manage the case?)

If they are prepared to pay your fees, this still presents the question, Why are they willing to do this? To ask this question is not just psychological prying on your part; it relates to a central issue in the case, if it becomes a case—namely, the nature and intensity of the injury Deborah suffered. Exactly how has she been hurt, and how much? These uncertainties of motivation present a serious challenge to your ability to manage the conversation, for this line of questioning has no easy set of factual answers but requires judgment on your part, and the process of investigation is difficult to say the least.

There is another and even more problematic stage to the inquiry. It is Deborah's rights that have apparently been invaded, yet she is a minor and cannot sue in her own name, or make the client's decisions required in the case. In these respects her father acts for her, as he would in an ordinary personal injury case too. But there is a question here not so visibly present in the personal injury case, which is whether he is really acting for her, out of her sense of injury and her need for redress, or out of his own feelings, perhaps out of his own wish to be a plaintiff in an important civil liberties case. Who is your client really? (Are you obliged to make a judgment on this matter? Even if not obliged, do you think you should, or want to do so? If so, how do you inquire?) You can see that this makes a call on your capacities for tactful management of a conversation of the most demanding kind. Nothing in law school prepared you for it; but this is part of being a lawyer.

Thinking about why the Weismans are in your office will bring into focus another question, not so much of motivation and psychology as a practical one: What relief can the law possibly afford them? Damages are not likely to be significant, and will be hard to prove.

So what might the law do for them? An injunction preventing the prayer from taking place will hardly do, since that event is now in the past. Could you somehow use this case as a ground for seeking an injunction against the Providence School Board for future graduations? But how is that appropriate relief to Deborah—and even if appropriate, is it available? You know that the judicial power of the United States is limited to "case and controversies" arising under federal laws (or involving citizens of different states), and that this language has been interpreted from the beginning to prohibit what are called "advisory opinions," that is to say opinions not rooted in the facts of a particular case. The Court has evolved a set of subsidiary doctrines, meant to ensure that the constitutionality of state and federal statutes—or programs or other official actions—will be tested only in a case (a) in which the plaintiff has suffered an injury that is distinct from the injury suffered by the general public in simply knowing, or believing, that an unconstitutional law is on the books; (b) in which the court has the power to offer meaningful relief; and (c) in which the relevant facts can be fully developed, and the law argued, through an adversary process in which both sides have significant incentives to prevail, hence to do a thorough and careful job of informing the court. After all, in every such case the plaintiff represents not only himself but all others similarly situated, and the Court wants that act of representation to be fair and reliable.

What this means about Deborah's case is that it is not clear how the case can be framed: for what happened in the past, no relief may be possible, and what might happen in the future, at her high school graduation—assuming she stays in the Providence schools—may be too remote and uncertain to provide a basis for a case and controversy now. This is a puzzle that has to be thought about.

Finally, at the center of your concerns, in this conversation and later ones, is the ground of her objection to the prayer itself. What did Deborah experience at the middle school graduation, and what are her feelings as she contemplates a possible repetition of the prayers at her high school graduation? Exactly what happened and what was bad about it? Did she feel that she was excluded from a larger group, forced to reveal her own private religious commitments, or made the object of unwanted attention? Or was the problem more internal, a violation of her conscience, if for example she stood up with the others to honor prayers she did not accept? Or was she just offended at the display of religiosity? Not that her feelings or attitudes are the only thing that matter, but they may be important clues to understanding the case.

You may also want to explore her attitude towards the possible consequences of the suit on her relations with her classmates. Is she ready for whatever animosity or irritation that may produce? How do you present this question to her, how judge her response? (What role should Daniel have in these conversations: How do you describe that, and how do you present your decision, or the issue, to Deborah and Daniel?) You may discover from these conversations that her situation is in significant ways different from her father's: he may have different objections to the prayers and a different attitude towards the social cost of the suit. If he does, you will face a difficult practical and ethical question, that of defining your relation with your client and her father. Who will make the decisions that a client has to make?

Many of these questions may not seem at first to be "legal" questions, in the sense that they do not seem directed to the knowledge or interpretation of legal rules, but, as we shall see, that impression is somewhat misleading, for all of the questions relate to the way you will imagine and frame the case; and in any event, they are "legal" in another sense, namely, that they can be taken to represent a large and crucial element of a lawyer's life, and one in which it is very important that he or she do a good job. I hope you can see, even from this sketchy represention, that these lines of thought and questioning would be difficult and interesting to pursue, no doubt leading on to others equally difficult and interesting. The management of a case of this kind, even where the facts are fairly simple and not much controverted, takes hours and days and weeks of thought and writing. This is where the lawyer lives.

The Facts of the Case

Let us next assume that the following emerges from your conversation with the Weismans. At her graduation from middle school, the program listed the Invocation and Benediction as parts of the ceremony, and referred to the rabbi by name as the person performing them. Just prior to the Invocation came the Pledge of Allegiance, for which the students and their families all stood up, as usual; they remained standing for the Invocation, and likewise stood at the end of the ceremony for the Benediction. The Weismans' understanding is that the practice of such prayers is quite widespread in Providence. The principal told them that this was consistent with school board policy, and that the rabbi had been given, by the principal, a copy of a set of guidelines for nondenominational prayer prepared by the National Conference of Christians and Jews.

They obtained from the rabbi a copy of his prayers, which were as follows:

INVOCATION

God of the Free, Hope of the Brave:

For the legacy of America where diversity is celebrated and the rights of minorities are protected, we thank You. May these young men and women grow up to enrich it.

For the liberty of America, we thank You. May these new graduates grow up to guard it.

For the political process of America in which all its citizens may participate, for its court system where all may seek justice, we thank You. May those we honor this morning always turn to it in trust.

For the destiny of America, we thank You. May the graduates of Nathan Bishop Middle School so live that they might help to share it.

May our aspirations for our country and for these young people, who are our hope for the future, be richly fulfilled.

AMEN

BENEDICTION

O God, we are grateful to You for having endowed us with the capacity for learning which we have celebrated on this joyous commencement.

Happy families give thanks for seeing their children achieve an important milestone. Send Your blessings upon the teachers and administrators who helped prepare them.

The graduates now need strength and guidance for the future; help them to understand that we are not complete with academic knowledge alone. We must each strive to fulfill what You require of us all: To do justly, to love mercy, to walk humbly.

We give thanks to You, Lord, for keeping us alive, sustaining us and allowing us to reach this special, happy occasion.

AMEN

It is important to pause and consider these prayers. How do you react to them as you first read them: as admirable and serious attempts to mark a life-changing moment in the lives of these children and at the same time to respect the various religious views of the children and their parents, ranging from atheism to Catholicism to orthodox Judaism? As "religious" expressions, and if so in what way? As "secular," and if so what do you mean by the term? As a kind of pabulum, watered-down pieties of no particular force or importance? As you read and reread the prayers, you will want to imagine them from as many points of view as you can, trying to get a sense of their meaning to others, and perhaps in this way changing their meaning for you. For whatever the judge or judges may say, they too will be responding to this language, reading it one way or another, and you will have to be alert to figure out how they are doing so.

Notice too that it is not entirely clear which reading of the prayers most fits your case: if they are perceived as pabulum, someone may say that they are innocuous; if they are perceived as seriously meant, someone may say that this is what makes them valuable. One question in particular you should be prepared to answer as attorney for Deborah is this: If these prayers are held unconstitutional, how can the school and the parents and the children mark the uniqueness of the occasion, which is after all a natural one for reflecting on the larger character and purposes of human life? Or will you have to argue that the First Amendment means that the event can be given no gravity or transcendence?

Conversations with the Attorney on the Other Side

Assuming now that you have decided to take the case, you will need to talk with the lawyer on the other side, frequently and at length. What are the issues you should address as you plan these conversations? It is crucial to establish good relations of mutual trust and confidence with the opposing lawyer, as it is with the client, but how is this to be done? This is a major question, essential to the lawyer's professional life, for which law school may once more have offered no preparation whatever.

The answer will lie mainly in understanding with some clarity what your objectives are, what the objectives of the other lawyer are likely to be, and how, if at all, they may be harmonized. If there are differences that cannot be resolved, they may require a judge's action, but this does not have to be thought of or presented as a failure of any kind, certainly not as the occasion of threat or fear. So what do you think you and the lawyer on the other side can agree to about this case, what will have to be left to the court?

Let us assume that the school board wishes to defend the right of the schools to include prayers in their graduation ceremonies, and will thus not simply agree to stop the practice. That issue will therefore go to court, but we still cannot predict the board's strategy in litigation. One possibility is that they will want to win this particular suit any way they fairly can. If so, you can expect them to raise every reasonable obstacle, and perhaps some unreasonable ones too. Certainly they will attack Deborah's right to bring an action for injunctive relief for a conjectural harm so far in the future. On the other hand, it is possible that they will be happy to bring the general question of the propriety of graduation prayers before the court for its resolution. If the school board is elected, this may be a particularly attractive option, at least if the electorate is divided on the issue, for it will remove responsibility for a controversial choice from their shoulders.

From your point of view, the second option is far better, for if this is the board's position, they may be willing to cooperate in the development of the case, for example by describing the practice of prayer as it exists, identifying the people who have given prayers over the years, perhaps even providing the texts of the prayers, and so forth. Much of this information could of course be compelled through what lawyers call "discovery"—that is, depositions, demands for documents, and the like—but that would be expensive, and this is certainly a case in which cost is an issue. It will be much better if they volunteer the information than if you have to drag it out of them.

Even more important is the help they might be able to give you on the issue raised above, whether all the elements of a judicial case and controversy are present here. If the prayers at Deborah's middle school graduation were unique or aberrational or against school policy, it will be very hard to persuade a court that you have a real controversy about the high school graduation to come in two or three years' time. If, on the other hand, they are instances of widespread policy, which the board plans to follow indefinitely in the future if permitted to do so, the court may be much more confident that Deborah faces a real threat of a repetition of the prayers and thus be willing to entertain a suit for injunction now.

What this means is that you will want to work out with the other lawyers, if you possibly can, an agreed statement of the facts in which the board will identify the policy under which the prayers were given and affirm its commitment to continuing it. If, as I say, the board is eager to have the general question resolved by someone else, they may be happy to cooperate. (Does this mean that one aim of your conversation with their lawyers may be to put before them the reasons why that might be in the board's best interest?)[1]

Another issue brings us back to the question raised above, about the character of this suit in the first place. Is this to be seen as simply a private action in which you help Deborah and Daniel protect their personal interests? Or is it a great public case, in which the participation of others ought to be encouraged, such as the ACLU, which regularly opposes governmental conduct that could be thought to be an establishment of religion, or, on the other side, certain other public interest or religious groups? Such groups would not be formal parties, but might ask leave to file briefs as *amici curiae,* or friends of the court. Will you want to oppose or support their motions to that effect? If they are granted, will you want to discuss strategy with those who want to argue that the prayers are invalid? The obvious problem is that their interest will be in the general constitutional question, not in the particulars of Deborah's case, in the kind of injury she has received, or in the kind of relief that is appropriate to her. The participation of others may thus lead to a redefinition of the case, and a loss of your control over it. What may have seemed a lawyer's dream come true, a major constitutional case, may become something very different, if you—and your clients' interests—are muscled aside by others. On the other hand, their support may be helpful, as indeed may the publicity that might follow. How, then, are you to think about this question? Does it matter what Deborah and Daniel themselves want? After all, they—or one of them—may be delighted at the idea of being a plaintiff in a famous case raising a general question. On the other hand, it might be in their best personal interest to consider a negotiated solution, tailored to their objections about the specific graduation that awaits them.

---

1. Is there something ethically troubling about such an agreement, namely, that it is a kind of collusion in which the lawyers for the opposing parties agree to present the case in such a way as to maximize the likelihood that it will be seen to constitute a case or controversy within the court's jurisdiction? (Should that question be argued out in an adversary way, or is it enough if the agreed statement of facts is, so far as the lawyers can tell, true? How are you to think about such a question?)

Conversations with the Court

Suppose now that you and the lawyer for the school board have drafted an agreed statement that recites the following facts: that prayers have been offered at every middle school and high school graduation in Providence for the past ten years; that over 90 percent of them have been given by Christian clergy; that in each case the clergyperson has been given a copy of the Guidelines for Nondenominational Prayer composed by the National Conference of Christians and Jews; that in each case the Invocation and Benediction has been listed in the program, which invariably begins with the Pledge of Allegiance; and that the school board intends to continue this policy in the future, in particular at the high school graduation that would in the ordinary course of things be Deborah's. You present this statement of facts to the court, who considers and rejects the argument that there is no case or controversy (or never considers it at all). In any event, the court is now prepared to face the First Amendment merits of the case.

As you think about it ahead of time, how do you imagine the formal conversations you and the lawyer on the other side will have with each other and with the court on this issue? What will you say, what will the other side say? What questions do you expect the court to have, and how will you answer them? (However you imagine the argument on the central issues proceeding, what will its form be: oral, written, or a combination of both? Do you want it to be formal or informal?) It is to these questions that the rest of this section is addressed.

To begin with what must be the most important legal authority, the language of the First Amendment itself, it is plain that it does nothing to resolve the difference between the parties. It tells us that "Congress shall make no law respecting an establishment of religion," and on that point all will, as they have to, agree; but it does nothing to tell us whether these prayers are, or should be regarded as, such an establishment. As Socrates said in the *Phaedrus* of writing more generally, the amendment just sits there, reiterating itself, unable to respond to the questions we have of it.

But we have more than the language, we have a set of cases decided under it, and here your research uncovers two somewhat inconsistent lines of authority. In the first, favorable to Deborah, the Supreme Court has consistently prohibited prayers as part of the public school curriculum. The first such case, decided in 1962, held that it was an impermissible establishment of religion for the New York state public schools to begin each day with a prayer, selected by the regents of the system, that read: "Almighty God, we acknowledge our dependence upon Thee, and we ask Thy blessings upon our parents, our teachers, and our country." This is a "nondenominational" prayer, and it was said that the participation by students was voluntary, but the Court struck it down as an establishment nonetheless. Similar decisions have invalidated readings from the Bible, recitations of the Lord's Prayer, moments of silence meant as moments of prayer, and the like.[2] These cases would support the conclusion that the graduation prayer was invalid.

But there is also a contrasting line of authority, partly judicial, partly rooted in the traditional practice of other branches of government. The first Congress—the one that approved the First Amendment—hired a chaplain, and to this day sessions of Congress begin with a chaplain's prayer. The Supreme Court itself begins its sessions with the cry, "God save the United States of America and this Honourable Court." The Justices of the Supreme Court are sworn in on Bibles, as is the president, who almost always includes a prayer as part of his inaugural address, a practice that runs back to George Washington's day. The military services employ chaplains, and have done so for a long time. The Thanksgiving proclamation is typically in the form of a prayer, at least in part.[3] Some of these practices have received explicit

---

2. See *Engel v. Vitale,* 370 U.S. 421 (1962); *School District v. Schempp,* 374 U.S. 203 (1963); *Wallace v. Jaffree,* 472 U.S. 783 (1983).

3. Here is President Clinton's 1998 proclamation:

> Thanksgiving Day is one of America's most beloved and widely celebrated holidays. Whether descendants of the original colonists or new citizens, Americans join with family and friends to give thanks to a provident God for the blessings of freedom, peace and plenty.
>
> We are a Nation of people who have come from many countries, cultures and creeds. The colonial Thanksgiving at Plymouth in 1621, when the Pilgrims of the Old World mingled in fellowship and celebration with the American Indians of the New World, foreshadowed the challenge and opportunity that such diversity has always offered us: to live together in peace with respect and appreciation for our differences and to draw on one another's strengths in the work of building a great and unified Nation.
>
> And so at Thanksgiving we must also remember to be thankful for the many contributions each generation of Americans has made to preserve our blessings. We are thankful for the brave patriots who have fought and died to defend our freedom and uphold our belief in human dignity. We are thankful for the men and women who have worked this land throughout the decades,

approval from the Court; with others it is obvious that the Court will not attempt to interfere. In recent years the Court held that the Nebraska legislature did not violate the amendment by beginning its sessions with prayers offered by a chaplain paid with state funds, even though some of these prayers were highly sectarian in content. *Marsh v. Chambers,* 463 U.S. 783 (1983). A somewhat similar case approved the inclusion of a nativity scene in a Christmas display made by the City of Pawtucket. *Lynch v. Donnelley,* 465 U.S. 668 (1984).[4] These precedents would support the validity of the graduation prayer.

---

from the stony farms of New England to the broad wheat fields of the Great Plains to the fertile vineyards of California, sharing our country's bounty with their fellow Americans and people around the world. We are thankful for the leaders and visionaries who have challenged us through the years to fulfill America's promise for all our people, to make real in our society our fundamental ideals of freedom, equality and justice. We are thankful for the countless quiet heroes and heroines who work hard each day, raise their families with love and care, and still find time and energy to make their communities better places in which to live. Each of us has reason to be proud of our part in building America, and each of us has reason to be grateful to our fellow Americans for the success of these efforts.

NOW, THEREFORE, I WILLIAM J. CLINTON, President of the United States of America, by virtue of the authority vested in me by the Constitution and laws of the United States, do hereby proclaim Thursday, November 26, 1998, as a National Day of Thanksgiving. I encourage all the people of the United States to assemble in their homes, places of worship or community centers to share the spirit of goodwill and prayer; to express heartfelt thanks to God for the many blessings He has bestowed upon us; and to reach out in true gratitude and friendship to our brothers and sisters across this land who, together, comprise our great American family.

IN WITNESS WHEREOF, I have hereunto set my hand this seventeenth day of November, in the year of our Lord nineteen-hundred and ninety-eight, and of the Independence of the United States of America the two hundred and twenty-third.

WILLIAM J. CLINTON

4. Other examples of this tradition include the invocation of the Deity in the Declaration of Independence, and in the Constitutions of many of the states; the Pledge of Allegiance with its reference to "God"; the phrase on our money, "In God we trust"; the reference in the Northwest Ordinance of 1787 to the importance of "religion." From some points of view the clearest example of this kind of establishment may be the universal practice of exempting church property from local taxes, upheld in *Walz v. Tax Commission,* 397 U.S. 664 (1970). And compare the "charitable deduction" available for gifts to religious organizations—and not just for their works of charity, but for their most purely religious activities. A gift to a monastery to support the monks in a life of prayer would qualify, for example. To take another example, clergymen and divinity students have normally been exempt from the draft, as have those whose conscientious objection meets certain standards, including a basis in "religious belief."

What are you to do with these competing lines of authority? Obviously it would be easiest for you if the court were simply to throw out the second line, which affirms legislative prayers, and rely solely on the first line, prohibiting school prayers. But this is not likely on the part of a lower court, to say the least, nor even in the Supreme Court, though it would in some sense have the power to discard one line of authority or the other. Is the Court really to tell Congress that its chaplain, which it has had since its beginning, is unconstitutional? Or, on the other hand, that a public school may begin its day with prayers read by a teacher or principal? The Court has produced these conflicting lines of authority for real reasons, even if it cannot wholly explain them.

Instead of choosing between them, then, both you and the lawyer representing the school board are faced with the task of creating an argument, written or oral, that gives place to both of these conflicting or opposing lines of authority—a little as Coleridge says a poem achieves "a balance or reconcilement of opposite or discordant qualities." How is this to be done?

The simplest way is to maintain that while both lines of authority should be kept intact, one of them should be preferred to the other. In this mode you would argue, for example, that the manifestations of religious belief found in inaugural addresses, Thanksgiving Proclamations, legislative prayers, the Pledge of Allegiance, and slogans on our money should be given much less weight than the language of the amendment (as you read it) and the reasons supporting it, as these have been defined in the school prayer cases. You would concede that the practices just mentioned should be allowed to continue in force, but only because they are trivial in impact and significance (since they are neither intended nor understood as serious expressions of commitment to a religious view of the world); or, if not trivial, because they have a unique historical authority, which—being merely historical—ought not be extended beyond them. Beyond that, you might argue that the continuation of most of these practices is supported by the fact that their invalidation would present in acute form the problem of separation of powers—the Court telling Congress what to do in its own halls, for example, or the president how to draft his own inaugural address—a problem not present in Deborah's case. You would in short be urging the trial court to admit the inconsistency in the two lines of authority established by the Supreme Court; to hold that the aberrant tradition should be permitted to remain—partly for institutional reasons, partly for historical ones; but to refuse to extend it, since it is inconsistent with the basic values of the amendment.

On the other side, the lawyer for the school board could be expected to argue to the opposite effect: that the uninterrupted practices of the nation, running back to the time of the passage of the First Amendment, are an important and living source of authority with which the courts should interfere most reluctantly. It is the school prayer cases, then, that should be limited in their force: they should be allowed to stand, perhaps because of the element of legal compulsion—children are required to attend school—or because of the impressionable age of those subject to it, but they should not be extended beyond their present scope.

Both these arguments are reasonable enough, but they are in two ways imperfect or incomplete. First, notice that even if you succeed in persuading the court to prefer in a general way your line of authority over the other, that does not necessarily decide the case. That is, even if the court agrees that the tradition of public religious ceremony ought to be severely limited, as you are arguing, it might still find the prayers offered here to be within that tradition: after all, we have had prayers at public school graduations, all over the country, ever since we have had graduations; and as the lawyer for the board argues, the reasons supporting the school prayer cases—legal compulsion and impressionable age—are not present here.

The school board lawyer faces her own version of the same problem: she could persuade the court that the tradition of public prayer should be given prime authority, but still lose on the grounds that these particular prayers do not fall within that tradition, since they do not go back to the time of the founding or anywhere near it. After all, public education became an important part of our national life only in the latter part of the nineteenth century. Moreover, these prayers do not take place in a public place but in a school, or in a space rented by a school, where the Supreme Court has been especially concerned with the possibility of religious indoctrination.

The second way in which the arguments are imperfect is that they do not really succeed in harmonizing the two contrasting lines of authority. Perhaps it is impossible to do that, but there is nonetheless great pressure first on the lawyers, and then on the court, to find a way to imagine the relevant and authoritative past in such a way as to make sense of it as a whole. Is there a principle, not merely a set of practices, that can justify the different results in the two kinds of case? Can you offer a way of imagining the First Amendment, that is, that will explain the two lines of authority and enable the court to decide in a reasoned way whether this case, or another one, falls under one heading or the other? Here, as often, the argument is a deep challenge to the lawyer's imagination.

Coercion and Endorsement

To begin with the school board's lawyer, she is likely to argue, as I suggest above, that what distinguishes the school prayer cases from all others is the element of coercion, overt or covert, particularly in light of the impressionable age of the students. Her proposed principle would be that when coercion is present, there is a violation of the establishment clause, otherwise not. In support she would observe that in the school prayer cases children are required by law to attend school; that they are of an age when they are likely to be deeply affected by the practices of their teachers; and that the prayers are typically repetitive, having their full effect only as they are heard year after year. None of these things is true of Deborah's pending high school graduation, where attendance is not required, the students are young adults, and the event happens only once in the life of most students, or, if more often, still with the greatest infrequency. This is no more objectionable than hearing the mayor talk at a prayer breakfast, or the president ask the blessing of the Almighty on our land and its people.

How are you to respond on Deborah's behalf? First, no doubt, by arguing that coercion is not the right test, for the evils against which the establishment clause are directed go far beyond that. Suppose that the federal government in fact established a Church of the United States, complete with government-drafted prayers and hymns, and with government-paid pastors: that would plainly be invalid, but where would the coercion be? In the tax money used for these purposes, perhaps, but that argument could be dealt with by allowing the taxpayer to check a box if he were opposed to this use of his money, and no one would think that such an exemption would make the Church of the United States constitutional. But to say this is not enough: How are you to articulate a principle of your own, one that will work as you wish it to?

Here you, and I, are right at the edge of the law, for no one has I think succeeded in answering that question adequately. The view towards which the Supreme Court has been working, though used as a ground for decision only once, is one that speaks in terms of "endorsement," the idea being that the government may not "endorse religion."[5] But it is hard to square this language with the obvious endorsements expressed by the traditional prayers described above, from Congress itself to the president, or the endorsement implied in the municipal crèche scene that the Court approved in *Lynch v. Donnelly*. There is thus required another distinction, expressed in another term—the Justices have chosen "acknowledgment," in default of anything better—to describe what the government *may* do, for example in scheduling winter holidays to coincide with Christmas. The asserted principle is that the government may not endorse, but it may acknowledge.

But this reasoning obviously requires much by way of explanation. In the first place, just why is an endorsement bad? Who is hurt by it, and in what way? And how is an invalid "endorsement" to be distinguished from a valid "acknowledgment"?

In thinking about these questions one possibility is to focus on the present day, and its values, and to say that the vice of endorsement is that it makes people feel excluded or marginalized by their different religion, or their nonreligion. This could be thought of as a peculiar emotional harm, of the sort that might be the ground for a tort action; or, rather differently, as a political harm, for one premise of democracy is that we are all equal participants, and any governmental designation of an "in group" is injurious to democratic life, entirely aside from any purely emotional costs. As applied to Deborah's case, the claim would be that she experienced exactly the sort of marginalization on religious grounds against which the amendment is directed.

Another possibility, though fraught with peril, is to define the term *endorsement* by reference to the meaning of the amendment at the time it was originally passed. The reason this is perilous is that the times have so deeply changed. One line of argument originally made in support of the amendment, for example, was that its passage was neces-

---

5. See *County of Allegheny v. ACLU*, 492 U.S. 573 (1989). Notice that if government action can be seen to prefer one religion over others, that is an independent ground of invalidity. Is there such a preference in Deborah's case? This is one of the nice points about the facts, for in the graduation that actually took place the prayer was composed and read by a rabbi, a member of a minority religion, and the prayer itself was crafted to avoid any sense of preference for one of the major American religions or another. Yet one might still find preference, either by thinking of the impact of this kind of nondenominational prayer on those religions not represented in it, for example Buddhism or Hinduism or certain religions of Native Americans, or by looking at the practices of the school board over the years, which may well have favored Christians over Jews, Catholics over Protestants, and so forth.

sary to protect religion from the corruption of government, a position not often expressed today. Another difficulty is that at the very time that the amendment was passed to prohibit the federal government from establishing religion, many of the states in fact had established religions, complete with taxes to pay the salaries of clergy and to meet the expenses of the church, laws requiring attendance at church, and so on. At the time this presented no problem of coherence, for the Bill of Rights applied only to the federal government; but after the adoption of the Fourteenth Amendment, which prohibited the states from interfering with "life, liberty or property without due process of law," the question became salient. As a way of giving that language some substantive content, the Court has turned to certain of the first ten amendments, including of course the First Amendment, as establishing "fundamental rights" with which the states may not interfere without strong justification. If the First Amendment was originally meant as a declaration of general value (that establishment is always a bad thing), what the Court has done works well enough; but not if the amendment was meant rather as a jurisdictional measure, saying in effect that establishment is neither good nor bad in itself, but a matter for the states to decide. If this is the right reading of history there is much for those who would apply this language to the states still to explain.

A final difficulty with "endorsement" as a theory of recovery in this case (though not "coercion") is that it is not clear how it relates to the case and controversy requirement: What is the nature of the harm that is supposed to be inflicted by endorsement, and what showing of that harm need a prospective plaintiff make to establish a case and controversy? (Or in this field will the Court decide questions that are more abstract in kind than it usually does? If so, why should it do so?) These are of course especially salient questions in Deborah's case, when her high school graduation, the only one at issue, is still rather remote.

For our purposes we need to pursue this line of thought no further. It is enough to have some sense of the way in which the argument complicates itself, layer upon layer, leading to considerations of history, of the basic understandings of democracy, of the often conflicting reasons that support a prohibition on establishment, then and now, and of the peculiar history of our Constitution, which came to regulate the relations between the citizen and the state in a serious way only after the Civil War.

BUT IT MAY BE VALUABLE to return to the point that would be raised by the lawyer for the school board, that the primary factor that distinguishes this case from the school prayer cases is the absence of coercion. She is here conceding that coercion is bad (as almost anyone would); this means that if we can establish coercion we can prevail in this case without making a way through the thicket of First Amendment theory and history just described.

How, as Deborah's lawyer, would you make such a case? What difficulties would you face and how would you address them? To start with, the "coercion" test seems to invite a highly particularized inquiry into what actually occurred at Deborah's middle school graduation, and we would like to know exactly what did happen there. What was the tone and atmosphere of the event? Is the fact that most of the students and parents stood up for the Invocation proof that others were coerced to do so, against their will? What were the sanctions or pressures or consequences that produced the alleged coercion of Deborah: disapproval of bystanders, marginalization within her social group, or what? And suppose she was pressured into standing: Exactly why is that a bad thing? Standing could be read simply as a compelled expression of respect for the religious views of others, not as a compelled religious statement or performance of her own. In any event, how is this compulsion any more offensive than the equal or perhaps greater compulsion to stand for the Pledge of Allegiance (with its reference to "God") which you can be confident the Supreme Court will not strike down? To say that the problem is "coercion" thus seems to involve us in an ever-expanding series of questions, relating both to the definition of coercion itself and to the particular circumstances of the case.

What is worse, as we have already noticed, Deborah' s graduation from middle school is in the past, and not really the subject of this lawsuit; the important question is not what happened then but what will happen at her high school graduation, for which specific plans have presumably not been drawn up. If the issue is coercion, and coercion is seen as a highly specific question of fact, this may strengthen any reluctance the court may feel to decide the question now, and lead it to postpone the whole lawsuit until the facts are much clearer.

How can this line of thought and argument be addressed? In the next few pages I want to propose a response, not with the thought that it is necessarily right or conclusive, but simply to show something of the way in which one lawyer's mind might work here.

Let us begin by thinking about the fact that the First Amendment not only prohibits establishment of religion but also interference with the free exercise of religion. This creates a deep tension right at the heart of things, for every prohibition of an activity on the grounds of establishment—like school prayer—is an interference with someone's exercise of their religion; likewise, every protection of free exercise—the right of the Amish to take their children out of school, or of a Sabbatarian applicant for unemployment compensation to refuse work on Saturday—is something of an establishment. This tension is complicated further by the facts that the First Amendment also protects freedom of speech, and that virtually every restriction on religious practices is also an interference with speech, every protection of religious practice a protection of speech.

Here is a way to suggest the oddity of the situation the language of the amendment creates. Suppose that the principal, instead of choosing the rabbi to make the Invocation and Benediction, had asked a notorious racist to speak to the graduates and their parents; assume further that he gave a speech espousing the doctrines of Aryan supremacy, praising Hitler and the South African apartheid regime. This would have been infinitely worse than the rabbi's prayer, one can assume, for Deborah and perhaps almost everyone in the audience; but it would have presented no constitutional question at all, except perhaps the question of the speaker's right to continue without interruption (or the constitutionality of a racial incitement statute under which he was later prosecuted). In this case the law would in essence have said to those who felt injured and outraged by the speech: "There is nothing we can do; in our country we bend over backwards to allow people to say whatever they want; and we take the greatest pride in doing so. The fact that you are in a sense compelled to sit and listen to this is in this context irrelevant, once the decision to let the person speak has been made. This is tough, but life is tough; you have available to you the most powerful instrument of all, which is your own capacity for speech in response. If he says something profoundly objectionable or hurtful, you should point out the flaws in what he has said. Your remedy is speech itself, and the political process." [6]

Why should there be such a difference when the speech takes the form of a prayer? What is there about the Invocation that might lead to a different kind of analysis, and to a different result, from the speech?

At one level, of course, the answer is easy, which is that the First Amendment speaks directly to the establishment of religion, and if re-

6. It is also true that free speech doctrine recognizes what it calls a "captive audience," and that an argument for the protesting students or parents could be based on such grounds. See *Cohen v. California*, 403 U.S. 15 (1971); *Lehman v. City of Shaker Heights*, 418 U.S. 298 (1974).

ligion is not involved neither is that part of the amendment. There will be difficult cases requiring a judgment as to whether or not a particular practice involves "religion," but the example of racist speech as I have given it is not one of these. But this says nothing about *why* the amendment should treat religion and speech so differently, and hence does nothing to help with the decision of this case. To help with this question, imagine one more case: the racist speaker in the example just given fills his speech with references to the Bible and the plain edicts of God. Does that change the result? Or is this still to be regarded simply as speech, and beyond the amendment's prohibition?[7]

At least one argument that what the rabbi did is in an important way different from the racist speech, even racist speech resting on a theological basis, might be based on the special nature of an act of public prayer. The rabbi is here not speaking *to* the audience, but *for* it; that is the implication of the act; and, we would argue on behalf of Deborah, she is entitled not to have the school speak for her in violation of her religious (or antireligious) views. But this does not quite get us home, for a speaker of the kind I was just imagining, the racist, could also purport to speak for the school and its students: "We have had enough of this phony sentimental liberalism, this denial of plain scientific and theological facts. We reject . . . we insist . . . ," and so on.

But the rabbi is not just speaking, he is praying, and praying on behalf of the community of which Deborah is a part. This is different and perhaps it is fair to say that there is in this practice an element of compulsion, arising not from a requirement of the law that Deborah herself act in a certain way, not even from social pressure as that term is usually meant, but from the very social practices of invocation and benediction as we know them, which are collective acts. There is not a legal or social compulsion for Deborah to do something, exactly, but she suffers something, namely, a kind of forced participation in this practice. This participation is a social fact, not dependent upon her intention, and there is no real way for her to dissociate herself from it effectively, certainly not without risking embarrassment and odium. She wants to be part of this community; after all, it is her school—her teachers, her classmates and their parents—but does not want to be part of this community at prayer.

This suggests that there really is something different, and on one

---

7. On the relation between religion and speech, see *Rosenbloom v. Rectors of University of Virginia*, 515 U.S. 819 (1995).

scale at least worse, when there is a prayer of this kind, no matter how nonsectarian or inoffensive, rather than a detestable speech. The injury suffered is not just a sense of offended sensibilities, or exclusion from the majority; and the element of coercion is not—as the opinions seem to think—reducible to the question of the degree of pressure she feels to conform, but inheres in the practice itself.[8] The harm is an injury to religious identity.[9]

Judging Meaning

Much more, of course, would need to be said to develop this line of thought fully, but notice this in particular about it: if the court were to take such a view, it would be resting its decision not on the particular types and degrees of compulsion present in this school at this time and place, but upon its own perception of the meaning of a common social practice, here that of collective prayer. This might mean that the court could avoid examining the particular details of the middle school graduation, and that it would be less troubled by the remoteness of the high school graduation. But the question still remains whether this question of general social meaning is one the court ought to feel itself entitled to decide, and if so why, and by what procedures.

Is this a question of fact, for example, upon which the testimony of experts or others might be offered? Who would qualify as an expert on such a question: a psychologist, a journalist, an historian of contemporary religion? A rabbi? A priest? If there are experts on one side you can expect them on the other, and this raises the question how the clash between them would be managed and resolved. Should the views of ordinary citizens, say other parents and teachers, also be admitted? Who should decide what should be the effect of a disclaimer in the program, saying for example that "standing during the Benediction is understood not as participation in the prayer, but only as an expression of respect for those who do participate"? Then, to return to the

8. This argument as akin to the "coercion" argument, but it would not require a finding that in the particular case a particular plaintiff experienced something, difficult indeed to define, called "coercion," but would find the requisite force and impact in the act of prayer itself.

9. The line of argument I am tracing out suggests that if she were an atheist, or simply hated religious observances, or rabbis, that might not be enough, for she would not have suffered the kind of injury that makes the prayer invalid. This in turn is to see establishment questions as questions of religious liberty. The opposition of the atheist to the prayer is not religious, the argument would go, but a kind of speech.

first question, who should decide the meaning of the act of collective prayer: the jury, the court, or the school board itself?

One might argue that questions of the meaning of a social practice like prayer, for constitutional purposes at least, is properly for the court, ultimately for the Supreme Court, because it is not only a factual but in a certain sense a normative question too. The Court would not be saying—because it could not—that it has measured the degree of psychological coercion present in every graduation prayer case in the country and determined that it always flunks some constitutional standard; rather, it would be both making its own judgment about such probabilities and at the same time shaping expectations for the future—saying that in America we know a practice called collective prayer, that it has the features we have described, and that we should accept this account of it as true. This the Court should not do, and really could not, if its factual judgment were not self-evidently correct in a large range of cases, and to a large range of observers; but there may be exceptions too, instances where its generalization is false, and when the Court disregards these it is not just reporting on facts but engaging in an act of the prospective and normative imagination. It is saying, "Let us imagine this part of our common life this way; and having done that, let us regulate it as follows."

It may be surprising, but the Supreme Court, and other courts too, do exactly this all the time: when the Court strikes down confessions taken without *Miranda* warnings, for example, on the grounds that the atmosphere of interrogation is inherently coercive and deliberately made so by investigating officers, it is imagining the process of interrogation in a way that no doubt has some factual support, but is also undoubtedly untrue as to some interrogations, perhaps many, which are not in any fair sense of the word coercive. Or consider the practice of the search warrant, which the police must under some circumstances obtain from a judge before carrying out a search: this requirement is supported in part by a certain way of imagining what the judge typically does in reviewing a warrant application, namely, to subject the zealous officers to reasoned judicial control, bringing the law itself to bear upon the process by which it is enforced. But in practice this may not happen. Often, at least, the police will obtain warrants from magistrates or judges known to be sympathetic to them, and unlikely to raise difficulties; and when they do raise difficulties, it is often with the aim not of protecting the citizen but of making sure that the warrant is supported by adequate probable cause and will thus survive later scrutiny.

Assuming that there is, as I suggest, a significant gap between the way in which the Court imagines the warrant process and the way the process actually works, does this mean that the Court is wrong to insist upon it? I think not, and for two kinds of reasons: practically, for the warrant process still freezes the officers' testimony at a point before they actually confront the citizen; symbolically, for there is a social meaning in the fact that the officers acknowledge, by the production of the warrant, that they are subject to forces superior to them, in fact to the law itself. The Court is thus creating one of the symbols or practices by which the government can be seen to limit itself.

Deciding and Writing

Let us take all that I have said as only one way of imagining the issues in the case and starting to think about them. Other lawyers would focus on different aspects of the case and see them somewhat differently. Much of the interest of the law, and much of the importance of the process of thinking that lies at its center, in fact resides in these very differences. For the law is not a mere mechanical working out of premises to conclusions, but an arena in which opposed ways of thinking meet in contest, first in the minds of the lawyers themselves and then in their opposing arguments to the court.

In particular, I have addressed only briefly, and in some cases implicitly, certain questions deep in this branch of the law: how to imagine religion itself, its value and its dangers; how to conceive of the two clauses of the First Amendment, and the role of the Supreme Court, and lower courts too, in interpreting them; what theory of the First Amendment the Court should adopt, if any; what attitude should it take towards its own precedents; and how far, if at all, it should defer to the judgments made by the school board or the principal in approving prayers of this kind. My hope here is not to have presented anything like a comprehensive view of a case, or a field of law, but rather to have given some sense of the kind of intellectual and imaginative life that the lawyer leads. If you want to see for yourself what the Supreme Court did with a case like the one we have been imagining, turn to *Lee v. Weisman,* 505 U.S. 577 (1992). You may be interested to see to what extent your own thinking has anticipated the reasoning you see there.

But one matter does deserve further attention. What happens after you and the lawyer for the school board have decided upon your arguments, given them shape, and presented them to the court? The obvious answer is that the judge will decide the question before her, of course, but the question remains: What can be said about how she does this, or ought to do it? Does she, or ought she, decide the case by the logic of the stronger arguments? As her instincts of justice dictate, educated as they are by your arguments? Do you think she could even tell you what she does if you were to ask?

Here, at the point of legal judgment, we necessarily have a human decision, with all that that entails, and like other such decisions its roots and nature and quality are all to some extent hidden from us. In ordinary life we know that we can try to explain why we moved to North Carolina, or became a teacher of Russian, or bought the house on the edge of town, but also that our efforts will always be incomplete. If we are alive to our own processes of thought, we will know that nothing we can say will completely and accurately describe or explain them. The same is surely true of judges: they can tell us that they paid serious attention to the arguments, imagining them as fully and sympathetically as possible, listening seriously to both sides, and even that their own inclinations shifted as the argument proceeded; they can then give us what they think to be the best reasons for the outcome they have chosen; but they cannot completely describe or justify it, for much of what they do lies below the level of explicit reasoning, beyond their capacity of articulation or even understanding.

This has consequences for the lawyer, namely, that in arguing to a judge you should speak to him not only as an ideal representative of an explicit mode of legal thought, but as a person with instincts, attitudes, deep commitments, styles of thought. You should make it your business to understand these as fully as you can, and speak to them too. You are arguing to a person who has power to decide the case, and you want to reach the springs of judgment and decision within him.

It also means that in his written opinion the judge is offering, as a writer, a text that has the odd quality of being at once committed and tentative: committed, because he has taken a real act in the real world behind which he must stand; tentative, because he knows, or should know, that what he has said is only one way of putting the case, and that the roots of decision and persuasion are in some sense beyond his conscious understanding. Moreover, he knows that the same issues will be thought about afresh in the next case, perhaps to a different resolution, or at least to a different understanding. For the same reasons, and in much the same way, the argument of the lawyer is also both committed and tentative.

For the legal mind, in both roles, writing thus becomes a way of creating instances of momentary order, asserted against a tide of ignorance and potential incoherence. We cannot fully comprehend the forces within us that lead to the judgments we make, as lawyers or judges, or those outside us that will give shape and meaning to what we say. In these respects the opinion or argument has more in common with poetry, as we saw Frost imagine it anyway, than one might have supposed: for the judge or lawyer also wants his work to end "in a clarification of life," nothing more so; but, like the poet, not necessarily a great clarification, "such as sects and cults are founded on," but "in a momentary stay against confusion." [10] And as is true of the poet, it may be the lawyer's or judge's capacity to do this—to create momentary coherences, at once committed and tentative—upon which his faith may most reliably rest that there are in the world coherences larger and more significant.

The Law as a Field of Life

The law is among other things a system for attracting our attention to difficult questions, and holding it there; for stimulating thought of a disciplined and often creative kind, and feelings too, especially—as I hope you felt as you worked through the graduation prayer case—the desire for justice that is called into existence by the questions the case presents, by the contrasting views of the lawyers on each side, and by our own inner sense of the reality and importance of what is at stake. The process of legal thought simultaneously resists simplicity and appeals to the side of us that wants to imagine the world, and ourselves and others within it, in a coherent way. A case is a bright moment, at which we have the opportunity to face at once the language we are given to use and the particulars of the case before us, and in both directions we are drawn into real struggles of mind and imagination. The object of law is justice; but the law teaches us, over and over again, that we do not have unmediated access to the pure idea of justice in the heavens, which we can apply directly and with confidence, but rather

---

10. Robert Frost, "The Figure a Poem Makes" in Robert Frost, *Collected Poems, Prose, & Plays* (New York: Library of America, 1995), 776.

live in a world in which everything has to be thought about, argued out, and reimagined afresh. It is a lesson in the difficulty of imagining the world, and the self and others within it, in such a way as to make possible coherent speech and meaningful action.

Think in this context once more of Frost and Herbert, who repeatedly bring to consciousness the deceptiveness both of their own desires and of the forms of language they are tempted to use. For both poets this deceptiveness works in two ways—in this is their extraordinary maturity of mind—for they see that one can be deceived into a denial as well as an affirmance of meaning. What, then, can be done by such creatures as we are, with such instruments as our languages? It is upon their own performances that both poets come in the end to rely: not upon creed, not upon denial, but upon their capacity, the human capacity, to make meaning in a universe that is deeply uncertain. The self exists in a world that it does not wholly understand, cannot wholly understand, and for which no language is adequate; the response they make, as Plato does too, is a specification and an elaboration of these conditions in the form of expression we call art. Something like this, I believe, is true of the judge and lawyer as well. The law can be seen as a collective enterprise the aim of which is to work out actual possibilities for thought about justice in the difficult conditions in which we find ourselves.

Frost and Herbert, and Plato too, discover that the language that they are given to use not only puzzles and constrains and misleads, but enables: it is a profound gift, a resource of meaning that asks only to be used in the right way. This is equally true of the material of Greek prose and English verse, and of the law as well. Here—in the sentence, in the poem, in the legal argument, in the momentary performances of language—can be found such truth and meaning and justice as it as given us to find. And when we turn from these performances of philosophy, poetry, and law to the rest of life, we may recognize that these writers have defined an activity of mind and imagination in which they invite us to engage in our own ways, with our own languages.

Think again what it would be like to be responsible for deciding the question in *Lee v. Weisman*. One line of cases point one way, the other a different way. You are in a sense free to choose whichever way you want to go, but that hardly helps, for the question remains: How should you exercise the freedom you have? It certainly ought not rest on whim or untutored reactions, but rather on a process of thought and reflection, as you seek to organize the material on both sides into a manageable whole, in light of what you take to be the central values expressed in the amendment itself and in the cases decided under it. The end of the process will not be a moment of perfect clarification, but an action on your part, a decision, with its roots in the world beyond words, ultimately a mystery even to you. It should be shaped and educated by the thinking and reading you do, by the arguments you hear, but it will not be dictated by them. For surely the process of argument and thought, as you test out your arguments and conclusions, must affect not only what you say, and sometimes what judgment you reach, but the workings and quality of your own mind. And in all of this you will be thinking, not only in the sense of propounding statements you can show to be true and that you can connect by logic into consistent wholes, but in a much deeper and fuller sense, in a whole-minded way that includes not only that kind of rationality but also the imaginative and ethical processes upon which all thinking rests. In this sense, the judge and lawyer too must learn to think and function as an artist.

Central to your own sense of confidence in your judgment, in many instances at least, will be your capacity to explain yourself; and your explanation or justification will satisfy you only if it is written not as an argument to a particular legal conclusion, like a brief, but includes what you think can fairly be said on both sides. Can this be done? In almost every case the good judge must in his heart be unsure until he has done it; and as he tries to explain, to his own satisfaction at least, what he thinks the true considerations are on both sides, and to organize them into a coherent statement, he must be constantly aware that he may fail. When he has finished he must know that what he has done is always imperfect, that there will always be more to say about the roots of the judgment in his own mind, about its effect on the parties and others, about its meaning to the world. Yet at the same time his capacity to do this not perfectly, but well enough, to reach and explain a judgment with which he can live, must be as good a way as there is to keep alive a sense of the possibility of justice in the world.

The faith on which such a judge will operate is that she will be able to cast her judgment in terms that will connect it both to the texts and ideas of the law and to her own instinct for justice, and that of her readers too. Her effort may be alive, full of tension, sincere—hence, as Thoreau would tell us, distant from the reader's mind, as it should be if she has thought deeply and originally about the case—or it can be empty, dead, without distinguishing energy, full of formula and cliché.

It is up to her, and a greater challenge to the education one can hardly imagine. She must have the perceptions of a Frost or Herbert about the language she is given to use and about her own proclivities for the false or sentimental or authoritarian; she must be able to remake her language, as Thoreau did; to confront her culture, including its most intractable possibilities, as Huck and Twain in their different ways did; to adapt to the ways her culture changes—say, from the time of the framing of the Constitution to the present day—as Odysseus did; she must in some sense know the souls of those to whom and about whom she speaks, as Socrates says the rhetorician must; and more than that, she must know, as Socrates says he himself must, her own soul. It may be surprising to discover it, but the case can work as a call to the side of the self that loves justice, loves the process of thinking about justice, not in the abstract but in the real world, where part of the task—but only part of it—is fidelity to decisions that have been made by others; a call to the side of the self that reads or hears the facts of a case and feels the feathers begin to itch and sprout.

❦

When I was on sabbatical leave in 1990, in Cambridge, I found myself thinking about the art of painting. I had seen quite a lot of paintings in my life, and they seemed somehow important, yet I did not really know how to look at them or think about them. So I took a train to London a few times in order to spend some time with a painting or two, chosen instinctively, to see what I might discover if I simply focused my attention in that way.

I found in the National Gallery a pair of portraits by Rembrandt, of Jacob Tripp and his wife, he on the right, she on the left, and this is what I saw.

Both people are old, but not ancient. He is sitting in a chair, facing the viewer; he is settled back a bit into the chair in fact, and resting his extended left hand comfortably upon a staff. His eyes are hooded, but they look directly at you; a soft beard hides most of his lower face, but you can see a piece of his lip, expressing you are not sure what. He looks prosperous and dignified and remote. The light comes largely from the left side (our left) so that one side of his face is in heavy shadow. The background is in warm tones, like his clothes and his face, creating a sense of harmony or comfort with context.

She sits forward in her chair, in a black dress with a large white collar like an awkward plate under her chin; she is holding in her right hand a white handkerchief, which she has perhaps twisted up. Her skin is lighter than his, mottled with red, lit more nearly from the front, and lit as well by the reflection from the collar. The background is mainly black, like her dress; the effect is one of contrast, black and white. Her face shows the flesh shrunken and skin sagged with age, hanging from the bone; his face shows changes too, but of a softer and heavier kind, a kind of incipient formlessness of flesh. She looks right out at you too, with black eyes, and much more energetically than he does.

What do these paintings mean? Surely, to begin with the obvious, they are more than mass and color and line and form; these are portraits of people, and they ask us to focus on who the people are. And who are they? What are we told of them by these paintings? If you look for an expression to tell you what they are feeling, whether happy or sad or angry or pleased, you see nothing; if you look for disposition, say whether they are kind or proud or sullen or cruel, you see very little. His hooded eyes and full lips could move into cruelty or warm good humor and kindness; her tight energy could equally express itself in repressive crabbing or in laughter. The point of the picture is not to capture a feeling or a disposition, even a dominant one, but to capture the soul at its point of widest feeling and capacity—the self that can be kind or cruel, sad or angry, the self at a level behind not only the present feeling but behind even the habitual disposition. Ambiguity and uncertainty about character is essential to the effect; it is what establishes the range.

What do we know of these particular people, then? A little: that he is hooded, perhaps quizzical, emotionally self-protective or guarded; slow, even stately, in movement and speech; his arm rests on the staff with a kind of ponderousness that can mean nothing else; his bearing bespeaks control.—She is energetic, quick, bird-like; her voice could be high or low, soft or harsh, but it could not be slow; she is engaged directly with life, just as she is with the viewer.

Or so I say: how are these things "known"? Part of it is through what could be called social iconography: his slightly raised right eye is a sign of quizzicality, we say. But is this a cultural universal in Western life or are we reading, wrongly, our own modern American social signs into that world? What of the hooded eye, the blacks and whites of her picture, the sense of contrast, of being on the edge? Are these unreliable?— Whatever the truth of it, we think this way and cannot help it.

These pictures represent human experience itself. Whatever else they are, these people are experienced in life: you don't know if she has lost three children or none, what diseases she has had, whether he has experienced robbery or betrayal or loss of goods at sea, or death of friends, but they have experienced life, suffering and satisfaction and the rest. Their flesh shows it, with its sags and hangings, and their dark eyes show it too. They have actual experience of life, as not everyone does, nor everyone in Rembrandt—think of the pictures of his wife, Saskia, for example. The great statement of these pictures is in fact the fundamental one that human beings are capable of experience. This promise is central to their meaning.

Another point: though two pictures, they form one composition, with certain touches carrying from one to the other, as for example the white shine on the staff in his picture mirrors the whiteness of her dress. These two experienced and experiencing people in some deep sense belong together, as a kind of music of contrast is set up between them, his hoodedness with her quickness, and so on. This is parallel to the kind of music set up within each of them, as perhaps always in Rembrandt, between the two sides of the face: his sculpted, hooded, fleshy right side, and shadowed, sketched, empty left side; and her two sides vary in intensity and solemnity too, creating both a tension between them and a sense of depth.

What of a young person? What could the point be there? Rembrandt's portrait of his mistress on another wall of the same room, young and round, swathed in white and light brown, is a place to look: her flesh is inexperienced, soft and white and plump; it has yet to mottle and detach itself from the bone, and hang. But her lips are open with anticipation; her gaze direct and full of life; she is a person looking forward to experience, and the promise is the same, of experience and therefore meaning in human life.

Finally and briefly, there are two self-portraits in the same room: one is young and confident, yet his eyes are insecure. His face is too soft for character yet. The older: patchy, bulbous-nosed, with troubled eyes, but with undeniable depth of inner life.

When I turn from the painting to the people in the gallery room, or to the mirror, what do I see? Is this painting by Rembrandt such a sacred object to us just because it catches and registers capacities for experience that were perhaps once common but are now, in a world of machines and consumption and mass politics, largely gone? And what of the sense one has that in some way the figures in the paintings are more real than those who walk by? This of course cannot be the case, yet one feels it, and feels it of literary figures too: of Huckleberry Finn, for example, or Odysseus, who have a kind of heightened reality that is not undone by the fact that they are fictional. In a related way Herbert and Frost achieve through their poetry an intensified presence in our lives, in my life at least, that is not undone by the fact that they are dead. And, to complete the circle, the creations of the law—the conception of a Constitution or of a judge, the ideal of due process or equal protection, the institution of the legal hearing, with its practices of proof and argument, all have a kind of force and value that is not undone by the fact that they are all human artifacts, fictions, never perfectly realized and often corrupted. Is Plato perhaps more right that we want to acknowledge in asserting the superior reality of essences, of ideas and ideals?

Looking at these paintings in this way made me feel that I had never looked at a painting before, that this was obviously how to do it, that I was only beginning.

NINE

The Depth of Meaning in Vermeer

In this book I have worked through a series of texts in which a mind can be seen trying to imagine the world, and the self within it, in such a way as to make possible coherent speech and valuable action. Thoreau takes the most crucial step, which is to see the problem as a real one—not everyone does—and to pour himself into the task of addressing it, making the claim at last to be a creator in a world of constant creation, and in this sense in harmony with it. As in our own way each of us ultimately must, Huck Finn confronts the constraints of culture, the force of the imaginings of others by which his world is shaped, and, in ways that we can at least partly trace, he overcomes them, if only for the moment. It is important that he could not do this alone, as Thoreau tries to do, but only as the beneficiary of the love and wisdom of Jim, who knew how to teach him. In his turn Odysseus faces with characteristic intelligence the fact that his world, like our own and every world, is in a process of constant change, and he adapts to two fundamental transformations with imaginative success. But his final achievement, with Penelope, is not his alone but at the center co operative, and the ultimate value the poem affirms is the relation of trust and mutuality they together attain. The chapter on the Greek language presents us with the reality and contingency of language it-self, and hence culture too, as a set of enablements and restraints that are always unique and particular. What you can do in one language you cannot do in another, for each language has its own way of imagin-ing the world and acting within it. And this is true not only in a general way, but at the level of the sentence, the smallest unit of meaning.

The *Phaedrus* combines all of these themes, representing at its cen-ter a conflict between different ways of imagining the world and the self, in intellectual and erotic life alike, and demonstrating a way of thinking about that conflict from a point within it—as we always must

do—in the performances both of Socrates, as he works upon Phaedrus, and of Plato, as he works upon us. For our purposes it is important that here, as in the other works we read, the movement of the
mind that seeks to understand itself and its world can end up finding
its most secure bearings in an activity of intellect, feeling, and imagination that it shares with another.

Like Plato, both Frost and Herbert find themselves in an uncertain
world, plagued and blessed by uncertain languages, with minds that
are themselves sometimes flawed and distorted; and, like Plato, for
both the greatest source of confidence that human life has value, that
the world makes sense, lies in their own capacity to engage in the activity of poetry (or philosophy) itself. For Frost and Herbert, it turns
out, to imagine the world is to imagine a way of living within it.

Perhaps surprisingly, much the same can be seen to be true of the
law, which, at least from the perspective of one who does it, can be
seen as an organized way of addressing conflicts between different
ways of imagining the world. It addresses these conflicts by creating a
language—a set of questions and ways of thinking about them—in
which argument and thought on these matters can proceed, and which
can itself be the object of critical thought and change. In slow motion,
as it were, and with others who disagree, in the law one engages in a
highly public version of the activity of imagination that is our subject.
The lawyer lives on the edge of language, where meaning is made,
and just like the poet and philosopher he must work constantly with
the inadequacies of his inherited ways of talking, the defects of his
own mind, the fundamental uncertainties of the world, the incomplete
knowability of the experience of others; and he may well find his most
secure ground of confidence and belief to lie in the activity of law itself,
which stimulates and works by a kind of love, less for another person
than for the possibility of justice itself.

I would like in closing to turn briefly to another kind of human
expression and action, in the form of certain paintings by Vermeer.[1]
Here we return to the point at which this book began: to the world
beyond words, to experience for which we know our language is inadequate yet of which we feel the necessity to speak. And, as we shall
see, these paintings school our minds, very much as philosophy and
poetry and law can do, in part by frustrating the very desires they

1. I will talk only about pictures I have seen and spent time with, mainly in the Netherlands and New York.

stimulate, by arousing hopes and desires that the world—or the paint-ing—cannot satisfy, leaving us at once more and less secure in our confidence in the working of our own minds and imaginations.

Five Paintings

The experience that Vermeer's paintings offer is I think both unique and uniquely puzzling. While he does have other subjects, in most of his paintings he presents a woman, often alone, at a moment of ab-sorption or engagement: beginning to read a letter, or just receiving one from her maid, or tuning her lute, or holding her pearls up before a mirror, or looking up from her writing desk, or pensively holding a pair of scales used to assay gold, or standing at a keyboard, or sitting at a table with a man, or opening a window, or sitting head in hand at a table, fast asleep.

Many people, including me, find these paintings utterly captivating, and the question is why: What is Vermeer doing here? How can we understand it? These paintings are full of mystery and charm and fas-cination; somehow they draw us inside the world they create, not just the physical but the spiritual or psychological world, so that we know of these women that they have deep and important inner lives. How do we come to feel this?

Such are my questions. My method in this chapter will be to build by graduated steps a sense of the way this art works, by attention to detail after detail, in a series of pictures. I do this partly for the sake of the intelligibility of my own conclusions, but partly because I think that much of the meaning of these pictures lies in the very process of attention they invite and reward. In all of this I assert my own sense of the paintings with some feeling because, as I later explain, I believe that one of the important themes they present is the tension between outer and inner experience, between surface and depth, and I wish to keep that issue before us.

Lady Standing at a Virginal

This is the famous painting of a woman standing at an instrument, looking out towards us (fig. 1), and it is a self-conscious and intellec-tual painting of enormous complexity.

The light comes through windows from the left; it is soft and uni-form. The woman, clad in silks rendered with extraordinary finish, stands at the instrument, looking out at the viewer, her face alive but at rest. Behind her are two paintings, a landscape and a Cupid; in front

FIGURE 1. Lady Standing at a Virginal

to her left, at an angle, on the inside of the cover of the virginal, is another painting, a largish landscape, rather crudely done. The landscape on the wall, itself a vaguely rendered hill, with clouds and sky behind it, has a gilt frame that is rendered with remarkable detail and realism, as if reminding us that the picture is only a picture while its frame is "real." The gigantic Cupid has a strong black frame, the painting on the virginal a thin black one. There is blue in the two landscapes, a bit washed out; in her dress, shiny and silky; and in a velvet-covered chair that dominates the front right of the painting. The floor is in regular black and white squares; the bottom level of the wall is a series of figured Dutch tiles.

This painting is in important ways about itself. There are, for example, the three paintings in the room with the woman (not very good either): they are "only paintings," we are necessarily told, while the woman is "real," and the extreme realism of the gilt and silk and velvet make us feel that to be true. But Vermeer's painting is in fact also only a painting, and it tells us that as well. So is it really just as unreal as the paintings it paints?

Or think of this: this is a picture of a woman at a musical instrument (as is the companion painting next to it at the National Gallery, and even more obviously so: in that one is a cello as well as the keyboard cabinet). Yet a musical instrument makes music, which a painting cannot possibly capture; in this way the painting draws our attention to what is outside itself.[2] This is done in other ways too: the black frame around the Cupid is a frame, really too heavy, reminding us that all pictures are a framing of life; this is even more true with the painting on the virginal, which is askew at a slight angle. (Both pick up the regular black and white markings in the floor.) And think of the source of light: the window is a bit brighter, I think, than the light in the room would warrant, and a little yellower too. This is a way of pointing to the source of light that lies outside the room, the source in a sense of everything: not in the frame, not in the picture. The Cupid, we know from its appearance in other pictures and from the presence of the same figure in a book of emblems, holds up a card bearing a written message, recommending a true and single love. What can this have to do with the experience of the woman? On this crucial issue question, which the painting itself invites, it is necessarily silent—as is equally true of the companion picture, which instead of the decorous Cupid has a dimly painted picture of a brothel scene on the wall behind the woman.

And the woman herself: What of her? She stands, posed and poised, at the keyboard, looking directly out at us, without, so far as I can see, any expression at all—no present feeling, no immediate anticipation, but a readiness for life. She is alive but closed to us: the only source of actual life in the picture is thus hidden from us.

---

2. On this point see Harry Berger Jr., "Some Vanity of His Art: Conspicuous Exclusion and Pastoral in Vermeer," in *Second World and Green World: Studies in Renaissance Fiction-Making* (Berkeley: University of California Press, 1988), 462–509.

FIGURE 2. A Girl Asleep at a Table

One might compare here the picture in New York of the young woman, usually thought to be a servant, asleep at a table (fig. 2). This picture too brings to our attention what is not represented in it: the door behind her is open to a room that has a picture, indistinct, on the back wall, and it reveals the edge of a window. The rug is rumpled up on the table in front of her, we do not know why; there is a carafe on its side, we do not know why; there is an object wrapped in filmy gauze that we cannot identify. The woman is asleep, in a sense, with her head on her hand; but to sleep sitting up is never stable, and who knows how long this moment of somnolence will extend? Someone has suggested that she is supposed to be drunken, pointing to the wine glass and to the openness of her collar, which is a deviation from propriety. But what is most striking to me is the face of the woman asleep: she is there, but not there; somewhere else, out of sight, is her mind and imagination, the source and reality of her life. The painting thus makes its viewer want to locate this woman in a narrative that will explain who she is, what she is doing, what will happen next, and so on. Yet this desire is utterly frustrated, for there is no way to know these things.

The idea is not that the picture of the woman at the virginal, or the sleeping girl, undoes itself as a painting by pointing to what it leaves out; far from it. Rather they are wonderful paintings in part because the painter finds a way, in using the materials and forms available to him, to recognize what they omit, or cannot say or do. This is a feature of some of the greatest art of other kinds: the kind of lyric poetry that says and unsays, capturing the sense in which things are true only when poised against their contraries; the drama, which sees the truth not in any speech or person but in the dynamic relations between them; or a great work like the *Iliad*, which uses a language of value and motive in such a way as to subject that very language to criticism. Here this quality of the art has a specific force, for both of these paintings make us feel simultaneously that the figure before us is a person with an inner life, and that that life is hidden from us. The paintings thus make us affirm what cannot be true, for there is no person here, and make us want to know what cannot be known, for it does not exist; but in doing so they affirm, or lead us to do so, the possibility of deep inner life in others and in ourselves, and beyond that the possibility that these lives can connect.

Woman in Blue Reading a Letter

In this painting, at the Rijksmuseum in Amsterdam, we see a woman standing in the light of a window, apparently pregnant, reading a letter (fig. 3). On the wall behind her is a map; in front of her is a table, heaped with nondescript cloth; in front of her, to our left, but out of sight, is a window, the only source of light in the room. She is dressed in blue; the chairs are blue, as is the cloth on the table; the map is light brown, as is her face; the wall a muted white.

FIGURE 3. Woman in Blue Reading a Letter

What strikes me first is her repose: her eyes are attentive, her mouth is open, as it were in unconscious anticipation; but there is no tension whatever in her face, at the corners of her eyes, or her cheeks, or the muscles of her lips. As with the woman at the virginal, as with the Rembrandt portraits, we have here not the representation of feeling but of a person capable of a range of feelings. The moment is one at which she has begun to read the letter, but has not yet begun to respond to it. The only tension I see is in her fingers, which are close together, as if on their way to making a fist.[3]

Behind her is a map, which also appears in many of Vermeer's other paintings. It is a map of the Netherlands, which in some paintings is presented with great exactitude, in others far more sketchily, as here. In this painting one effect of the map is to suggest a possible author and subject for the letter: it may come from her husband, perhaps a merchant on his travels, for example. The painting thus tells us that the event we witness is one stage of a narrative, and teasingly hints at possibilities, but it frustrates the very desire it occasions.

The map also marks a different kind of representation from Vermeer's own: quantitative, not qualitative; instrumental and utilitarian; a method by which the physical world may be reduced to understanding and control; yet also, in the seventeenth century, with a romance of its own. It is continuous with compasses and ships and sextants and cargoes and territorial claims and exploration, with wealth and war. Like the paintings on the wall behind the woman at the virginal, the map is also marked as artificial, in contrast to the woman herself. That is, although the woman is in fact not a real woman but only a picture, by contrast with the map she seems real: the map thus marks out a realm of the artificial, to be contrasted with the real and natural woman.

The map is masculine in another way, in the pointed pole that holds the map down. At the Metropolitan Museum in New York there is a painting of a woman playing her lute, or tuning it, by a window, where this effect is even more dramatically marked: there the map pole points directly at her temple, as if it were imprisoning her (fig. 4). In that picture the woman's face is full of expectation and excitement, as she sees something out the window or simply listens intently in connection with her tuning. The familiar lion chair, heaped with cloth, and the table, and the chair beside her, and the map on the wall are all rectangular shapes imprisoning her. The arrow of the pole at the bottom of the map nearly reaches her head; the lute nearly reaches the map; her

3. A school of thought in psychology takes the view that the first stage of emotion is a state of alert preparedness, of fresh attention to a discrepancy or change in the environment. See, e.g., Phoebe C. Ellsworth, "Some Implications of Cognitive Appraisal Theories of Emotion," in *International Review of Studies of Emotion,* ed. K. T. Strongman (New York: Wiley and Sons, 1991), 1:143–61. One can see a picture like this as capturing just such a state.

FIGURE 4. Woman with a Lute

elbow nearly reaches the table; all these show her almost filling the space, and in a sense hemmed in. She is overshadowed by the lion chair and the cloth.

Here, in *Woman in Blue,* the map is a rectangle, as the picture itself is too, of course, bounded by straight lines running up and down (north and south) or sideways (east and west). In this it is part of a pattern of rectangles, for the spaces on the wall that the map leaves open are of course rectangular too, as is the table before which the woman stands, and the seats of the chairs, and even their backs. Suddenly, one can see this picture as full of hard straight lines and edges at right angles to one another, including even the letter she is holding in her hand, which is not only rectangular itself, but creased sharply. Among these lines and planes rises something very different, the soft and three-dimensional figure of the woman herself. Her apparent pregnancy emphasizes this roundness, and also suggests the possibility that the letter—perhaps a kind of annunciation—is from the father of this unborn child, or about him, and that the news may effect the welfare of this unseen being. This is another instance of the way Vermeer's paintings are about what lies beyond their compass, in this case the future life and feelings of this as yet unborn child.

The woman's dress is quite roughly painted. It is a common feature of Vermeer's work that parts are painted with enormous clarity and precision, as if in a kind of superfocus, others with great roughness, as though hardly seen at all. It is not only Vermeer who does this, of course: Rembrandt is famous for having an extremely narrow focal plane. In his paintings sometimes only a part of a face will be in full focus, the rest of it slightly blurred, either because it is too close or too far. I think here particularly of Rembrandt's picture of his mother as a biblical figure reading the Bible, where her hand on the printed page is represented with the most extraordinary clarity and vividness, a mass of tiny wrinkles, the rest of her much less precisely. But in Rembrandt and Vermeer alike, it is not merely a matter of a precise focal plane: in the Rembrandt picture, the hand is in focus, but the page upon which it rests is not; likewise here, the face is in focus, but the dress that is virtually at the same depth is much more crudely presented. It is not, then, that either painter simply imagines a narrow focal plane in the real world, and then represents it; instead, his contrasts of focus are ways of directing the viewer's attention, and holding it on one place or object, here the face of the woman.

The woman's dress has strong upward markings, representing the folds, which add greatly to the sense that the figure is rising up, a bit like a flower.

What of the array of chairs and table? This woman is not as imprisoned by these objects as the woman playing the lute is, but they nonetheless bound her. In one direction is the wall, in another the table, behind her the chair; it is true that that chair is open and inviting, one that she might sit upon, or has perhaps just risen from; but it is still

there, and its lion heads, nearly universal in Vermeer's paintings of interiors, direct their somewhat threatening gaze towards her. On the
table is an object I cannot identify, which looks like a book of letters
or music or something like it. But it is marked with the brass nail heads
that appear on the chair upholstery too, creating a pattern that sur-
rounds her. Finally, on the table, barely sketched out, is some cloth or
similar stuff, painted with extraordinary crudeness. It is common for
Vermeer to show a rug or textile on a table in the foreground, sometimes painted with great care and clarity. Here it is of a nondescript
and somewhat ugly color, a kind of brown inscribed on blue; it has no
detail; and its form is threatening to her. It looks a bit like a lizard or
dragon or other beast, aiming itself directly at the middle of her body.

An important part of the life of this picture, then, derives from the
tension I am describing, between the appeal and warmth and naturalness of the woman, her roundness and vulnerability, all emphasized by
the focus on her face, and the various threats to which it is subjected,
by the straight lines and right angles, by the cloth on the table, by the
chairs that imprison her, and, of course, by the unknown news in the
letter. We are led to see and care about something, and to see it threatened at the same time. The balance of these emotional forces is the
fundamental source of meaning in this picture.

A similar tension animates the picture at the Frick, in New York, of
an eager young woman sitting at a table facing a soldier who by virtue
of foreshortening seems twice her size (fig. 5). He is clad in red, with a
large black hat, facing her. We cannot see much of his face at all; his
right arm is cocked on his hip, and he leans forward from the lion-
headed chair. His hat is black and enormous; it lies across the open
window, which is the brightest light in the room, creating a sense of
stark contrast, black on white, and of threat too. He is large and mysterious, assertive. She by contrast is small and open-faced, her face
glowing with a kind of eager excitement. She holds a carafe of wine
and sits in front of the usual map, this time drawn with great care. This
is a picture of eager and open femininity threatened or excited—or
both—by male swagger and power.

There is another feature of *Woman in Blue* that is difficult to talk
about yet nonetheless requires attention. Unlike the Rembrandt paintings discussed earlier, which are portraits in which a person chooses
to be represented to the world, this woman is seen, in imagination at
least, in her private life, unposed. Unlike the woman at the harpsichord, she is not even looking at us: we gaze upon her, but that gaze is

FIGURE 5. Officer and Laughing Girl

not returned. Is this fact, in some way, part of the meaning of this picture, and others like it?

Behind this question is a more general issue, namely, what is the significance of the male presentation of female beauty to male viewers? This is so much part of our aesthetic culture that it is hard to see it as a practice with particular significance, rather than as simply what is done. But one could regard it as an unhealthy practice, disrespectful of the women, especially when there is an element of eroticism in the way they are presented—most especially when they are naked— which needs to be accounted for. Think of Manet's famous *Olympia*, for example, who presents her naked body in a kind of self-conscious display on the couch and at the same time fixes the viewer with a fierce and challenging gaze.

In one kind of painting the woman seems posed, as if presenting herself for view as an erotic object; this kind of painting presents the danger of a certain form of pornography, which the model in *Olympia* is represented as simultaneously performing and resisting. In another kind of painting, the woman is represented as unconscious of her viewer, as she simply goes about her private life. This, as Edward Snow has argued, is the quality of the famous paintings of nude or half-dressed women by Degas: they are not presenting themselves but are relaxed, as they unselfconsciously go about their toilet or other activities.[4] Here there is a different psychosexual danger, that of voyeurism, that is, taking pleasure from observing while being unobserved. It is this kind of painting that Vermeer offers us here.

What of the ethics, as it were, of these two kinds of painting? The first can be seen to respect the capacity of the female form and face for a certain kind of beauty, and for its power in attracting and holding male attention; yet it seems profoundly reductive of the woman herself, and to affirm a certain kind of sexuality that is not, at bottom, mutual or respectful, however admiring it may be. It is against these facts that the model in *Olympia* is rebelling, as it were daring the viewer to respond to her nudity by denying the authenticity of the gesture—just as a prostitute maintains her self-respect by her contempt and anger towards her customers.

The second form of painting is from one point of view even worse, for it is a kind of unknown invasion of privacy; from another, however, it can be enormously respectful of the woman—who she is, and what she is feeling. It is significant that the invasion of privacy here occurs only in the imagined, not in the real world. The woman whose naked body is presented in a painting as an object of erotic desire does have an actual body that is so presented; the model who reads the letter, by

4. See Edward Snow, *A Study of Vermeer,* rev. and enl. ed. (Berkeley: University of California Press, 1994), 27–34. See also John Berger, *Ways of Seeing* (London: BBC and Penguin Books, 1972), 45–64, and Linda Nochlin, *Representing Women* (New York: Thames and Hudson, 1999). For further examples, consider the striking *Nude Girl* (1909–10) by Gwen John, expressing the model's sense of awkwardness and embarrassment at her nudity. This picture, at the Tate, can be usefully compared with another in the same collection, Lord Leighton's *Bath of Psyche,* which has much of the feeling of what is now called "soft" pornography, and with Jean Bonnard's *Woman on a Bed,* at the National Gallery in London, which seems even more openly meant to stimulate male erotic response.

contrast, is only acting, not really reading the letter. In this sense her own privacy is not invaded. Nonetheless, in its imagined world the painting may give rise to such a fantasy on the part of the viewer, and this should trouble us.

How far does the Vermeer painting invite the viewer to imagine that he is invading the privacy of another? At this point the fact I referred to above, that the woman has not yet responded to the news in the letter, becomes significant. She is in a sense not yet feeling anything, or showing her feelings, and the sense that we might otherwise have, of watching the unselfconscious revelation of emotion, is missing. In fact, you could see the enormous reticence of the Vermeer painting as highly respectful of the woman in the imagined world, and indeed of the model herself.

Another psychological point is suggested by a theme Michael Fried has developed in another context. The woman in the painting is reading a letter, reading it for its meaning and wholly absorbed in the task; we, as viewers of the painting, are reading *it*, for its meaning, and are wholly absorbed in the task. Her absorption makes manifest our own, making explicit what is otherwise implicit in our own experience, that we are standing looking at an object for its meaning; it thus makes conscious what is unconscious in our experience.[5]

Beyond that, since reading a letter and looking at a picture are different activities, yielding different sorts of meaning, it works as something of a challenge. What she is absorbed in will presumably yield meaning of a known and predictable kind—he will be coming home; he won't; the voyage succeeded, or it failed; and so on. The challenge is: What kind of meaning does this picture yield? It at once holds itself up to us a kind of mirror, then changes what is in the mirror, all as a way of presenting us with this question. By a kind of reverse ekphrasis, as a painting of someone reading, it invokes a world of meaning that it cannot replicate, in much the same way that *Lady Standing at a Virginal* invokes the art of music, which it cannot replicate either.

The Milkmaid

In the same room in the Rijksmuseum is one of Vermeer's most famous pictures, that of the peasant woman pouring milk from a jug into a bowl (fig. 6). The wall behind her is light, as is her hat; her jacket is

5. See Michael Fried, *Absorption and Theatricality: Painting and Beholder in the Age of Diderot* (Berkeley: University of California Press, 1980).

FIGURE 6. The Milkmaid

yellow, the pottery is red, her apron and the cloth material on the table in the foreground are blue. It is a picture of bold primary colors against a bright wall.

To begin with the wall, it is strikingly bright, lighter than would really be warranted by the brightness of the window to the left, through which all the light enters. What is more, the wall is not simply a background of smooth plaster, as it is in the painting just discussed, but is represented with enormous realism: full of checks and chips and nails driven in it and so forth. It is the ordinariness and actuality of the wall that stand out; likewise its size, for it extends further to the right of the woman than would be strictly necessary if she were our sole subject, and descends to the floor where, askew, lies a foot warmer and some other indeterminate object. If you put your hand over the woman, the background of the wall, in the shape of an inverted "L," fills a surprisingly large area of the painting itself. This is the painting that might have been; the ground upon which the act of creation takes place.

When you turn to the woman, what is striking is her stolidity and weight: she is physically present in an almost aggressive way—rounded, and fleshy, and palpable. She almost bursts her yellow jacket, and her arms are muscled, tensing slightly to hold the jug; they reveal a line between the part of her arm that is normally exposed to the sun and the part protected by her clothing, a line between dark and light. She is absorbed and focused on what she is doing, but it is not a private thing, and there is not the faintest overtone of voyeurism here, perhaps because there is nothing, like the letter, that promises to trigger important feelings in her.

The composition is based upon two diagonals, the first running from the upper left to the lower right, through the material objects in the room and ending with the foot warmer referred to above. This is a cascade. Cutting against it is another diagonal, from the woman's face down to the objects on the table in front of her, to her right, marked by the light reflecting from her face and body, as well as by her gaze, which directs our own to what she is holding in her hand.

When we do look where she tells us to look, we see a basket with a loaf of bread, a table piled with breads of various kinds, and a pitcher. The bread and pottery lie on the table in front of her and beside the bowl into which the milk is being poured. They are in extraordinarily crisp focus: bright, clearly delineated, marked with Vermeer's typical accent of small white dots. What is more, they form a perfectly composed still life. In a sense, then, there are here three pictures in one: the still life; the woman behind the still life, pouring milk into the bowl; and behind her the white plaster wall, flecked and checked, which serves as the background.

The still life is of course still, immobile; so is the wall, and the foot warmer, and the brass and wicker baskets hanging in the upper left; so indeed is the woman, who seems not even to breathe—the only sense of life is the tension in her forearms where she holds the jug. The jug and the bowl too are inanimate, immobile.

But right at the center of the picture, bright white against the circular black whole that is the mouth of the jug from which it flows, is the milk; and it is pouring. In *Woman in Blue* we had a background of

angles and rectangles and flat surfaces, against which her rounded figure rose, alive and sentient; here we have a background of still and
immobile objects, against which we see the pure and simple action of
the milk flowing from jug into bowl. Once more, it is a composition
based upon contrast.

The contrast is in fact at its most intense just at this point, where
the small splash of white is nearly encircled by the disk of black. As
I looked at the picture more and more, in fact, I came to feel that its
center was the black hole from which the milk issued. The blackness
works in part as a source of threat, of the kind we also saw in the other
picture, the threat here consisting of the combined sense that we are
looking at something real and that we cannot see it. For in a painting
whatever is represented is subject to imaginative and technical control;
the dark hole in a sense shows us unrepresentable reality.

There is another, related, point. I have said that in his other work
Vermeer's paintings constantly draw attention to what is outside of
themselves—the music, the voyage, the contents of the letter, the narrative leading up to the moment, the future of the unborn baby, and so
forth. What is present is defined in part by what is absent, and we feel
the absence. The milkmaid is for the most part a masterpiece of presence: we feel as a tactile reality the wall, the woman, her dress, the foot
warmer, the bread in the still life, and so forth. To achieve this, said
Bernard Berenson, is the main object of painting. And here there is
no mysterious letter, no musical instrument leaning against the wall,
no clothing of another person, no other person himself present, with
his back to us, no map on the wall referring to another scale of life
entirely; everything is immediate, vivid, present; everything, that is,
except that dark circle at the center of the painting, a purified representation of absence itself.

The painting at first looks direct and simple, as though its meaning
lies in its brightness, in its immediacy of its impact, in the tactile reality
of the objects it represents. But upon examination, it develops the same
kind of complexity as the other paintings, and its significance is similar
too—representing what it values, but subject to principles that challenge the presentation itself: a sense of limitation, of what the painting
leaves out; and a sense of vulnerability and threat as well.

The Letter

This picture also hangs in the Rijksmuseum (fig. 7). At its center it
shows a young woman, rather elegantly dressed, sitting perhaps on a

FIGURE 7. The Letter

stool. She holds a letter she has perhaps just received from her maid, who is standing to her right and a little behind her; she is looking anxiously up at the maid's face, who smiles down at her with somewhat enigmatic pleasure. In theme this is obviously related to *Woman in Blue,* where the woman is reading a letter she has received; here, by contrast, the letter is unopened and the recipient full of anxiety. Even more markedly than the other, this painting is about what it cannot represent: the imaginary letter is sealed; its imaginary sender is off-stage, somewhere else, and we shall never know anything about him.

Likewise, we shall never know what feelings the letter will inspire in the imaginary woman before us, when it is opened.

The center of this picture is dynamic, and in a more complex way than in *Woman in Blue:* while there our eye goes back and forth between the woman and the letter she is looking at, here it makes a circle, from the woman's face to the maid's face, then to the letter the woman is holding, and then back again to the woman's face. A circle of life at the center of the picture, like the circle of absence at the center of *The Milkmaid.*

What I have described is a complete picture, and it could have been offered as such. But in fact it fills an area at the center of the painting that is only a small fraction of the painting as a whole. The rest of it frames this central scene dramatically. To start with, we are looking at the woman and her maid through a doorway. On the left is a dark, roughly painted wall, and adumbrated upon it is our familiar map with the familiar rod pointing at the woman. All that takes up perhaps a quarter of the painting. In the center is the open doorway, over which hangs a heavy curtain, tucked up to the right but ready to fall. On the right, taking up perhaps a third of the picture, is a wall and against it a chair, roughly painted, with music and clothes heaped upon it. Both of the foreground panels are extremely dark; all the light is on the central scene.

The framing of the scene is not yet complete, however: behind the woman to the right is a door, beyond which we see an interior wall; apparently a passage goes off to our right behind her. On the wall directly behind the woman are a landscape and a seascape, in the usual simplified style Vermeer uses for such paintings. Once more they define themselves as artificial, the woman and the maid as real, and in a way that undoes itself, for the woman and the maid are of course only pictures too. The curtain hanging across the doorway covers part of the landscape, making more vivid its threat that it might fall across the entire scene, erasing it from view. On the floor beside the woman and the maid, on our left, is a laundry basket containing clothes; then, nearer us, and lying directly in the path from the doorway to a woman, are a pair of clogs or shoes and a large broom, leaning at an angle against the wall, as it were cutting off escape in this direction. Finally, the floor itself consists of black-and-white tiles, not arranged in checkerboard fashion, but with the black tiles forming the pattern of a cross; these crosses advance along the floor towards the woman.

People sometimes say that the effect of all of this framing is to create a sense of privacy, or interiority; but that is not how it works for me. Rather, it is all a cumulative threat or domination: the woman is framed and boxed in by the walls; by their darkness; by the blankness of the passageway behind her (which does not open out into other rooms, as happens, for example, in *A Girl Asleep at a Table*; and by the paraphernalia of the maid's work that clutters the floor. The map and chair and music in the foreground dominate the scene, reflecting other interests than her own. It is this sense of imprisonment, or threat, that makes the woman's anxiety emotionally appropriate; it also makes us want to interpret the smile of the maid: Is it in fact reassuring or perhaps rather superior or knowing? The maid is, after all, standing while the woman sits, looming large beside her. All this focuses attention dramatically upon the circle of life, of anxiety and perhaps reassurance, that lies at the center of the painting. Yet even here there is a qualification, for the object in clearest focus is the maid's laundry basket with its clothes.

Once more the painting makes us ask questions about what is happening that it simply refuses to answer. We want to place these events in a larger story that will make sense of them, but are prevented from doing so. All this works as an insistence on what is actually before us, the moment of anxiety itself.

The Little Street

This is a picture not of a woman but of a street scene: the viewer looks across a road, very fuzzily painted, to the facade of a building. Roof lines drop in an angle from the middle of the left side of the picture to a covered double alley, with a flat roof, beside the main building, which rises by steps to the top of the picture, thus making the shape of an irregular "V" against the sky (fig. 8).

People are depicted in three places: one woman is bending over a broom in the alley that divides the two buildings; another sits in the dark doorway of the building on the right, working with something in her hands; two others—one man, one woman, or perhaps two children—are on their hands and knees near a bench between the other two. The facade itself is all brick, the mortar lines sketched in, rather splotchily; the windows of the building, one or two of which are open, are opaque to us: ways of seeing out, not seeing in, like eyes. The roof line on the left has some vegetation cascading down it, perhaps like ivy. Through the irregular "V" made over the alley one can see other roofs and buildings of the city, implying still others behind them, dis-

Figure 8. The Little Street

appearing into the distance. Above it all is the sky, partly blue, partly bright and moving clouds.

What gives this puzzling picture its life? Part of it is the roof line, swooping down and then rising; part of it the contrasts between the world of the sky and the world of the city, between vegetation and brick; part of it—and in this it is like his full-face pictures of women— the contrast between the perfect accessibility of the surface of the building and the total opacity of its depths. We have no idea what goes on within; the open door and open windows do not help, for the interior is, to us, black and impenetrable, just like the jug in *The Milkmaid*. The human activities here establish a range of intelligibility: we understand the woman with the broom plainly enough; the woman sitting at her work is concentrating on something, but we don't know what; the two people on their hands and knees, near the bench, are pursuing something entirely hidden from us.

Compare *The Country Cottage* by de Hooch, also in the Rijksmuseum, in which every brick is delineated, where the activities are transparent, and where everything is beautiful, as if in a model city (fig. 9). Even though many of the elements are similar to those in Vermeer's work—the blank windows; the man and woman at a table; the woman to the side, engaged in solitary activity—there is here no mystery, no threat, no sense of inner life. Vermeer's women have depth, compared to those of de Hooch or, say, Nicolaes Maes; and his street scene has a mysteriousness, an opacity, that is missing in the others.[6]

In *The Little Street* there is an irregular line, running from left to right, where the brick wall has apparently been whitewashed. It is not clear why it has been whitewashed, nor why it remains so white; but when I stand away from the picture and half shut my eyes, letting my natural myopia take over, it is the jagged band of white bisecting the picture that is its most striking element. It is ugly, when everything else is beautiful. In particular, at the right, a newly painted red shutter lies across the whitewash, creating a moment of contrast like the black hat against the window.

The sky in this painting is not merely a background, as it so often is in de Hooch, but a skyscape like one by van Goyen or van Ruisdael. The sky thus dominates the city, at least in the sense that it is the background against which the city is made; but more than that, for the sky preceded the city and would exist without it. It marks the city as ephemeral.

6. For de Hooch, see Peter C. Sutton, *Pieter de Hooch, 1629–1684* (New Haven: Yale University Press, 1998). His pictures show domestic interiors, and sometimes exteriors, in moments of normalcy and peace. The people are not represented as having interior lives; the interest is in the physical interiors, which are often given great depth by the careful use of perspective. See, e.g., *A Boy Bringing Bread*, in the Wallace Collection, *A Woman and Young Man with a Letter*, in the Rijksmuseum, *A Mother and Child with Its Head in Her Lap*, also in the Rijksmuseum. For Maes, see his *Listening Housewife*, in the Wallace Collection, or *A Sleeping Servant and Her Mistress*, in the National Gallery, London.

FIGURE 9. The Country Cottage

As the sky dominates the city, the city dominates the building, for the series of roofs and walls we see add up to much more than this little street; in turn, the building dominates the people, who are dwarfed by them. It is hard to imagine that this mass of brick was made by people like these.

Like *The Milkmaid,* this painting contains several independent compositions: one could frame the woman at the doorway, or the woman with the broom, or the two people on their hands and knees, in such a way as to make a fine composition, standing alone; or one could expand the frame to include all three human actors, and create another composition; the same could be done with the sky and roof line on the left of the painting. One of the ways in which Vermeer creates a sense of life in his paintings is exactly this, by making it possible to frame them many ways, creating many compositions, for this is an aspect of the real world.

Finally, the last thing I saw in the picture, just off the center, where the "V" begins to rise toward the right, is an indistinct brown blotch, between the eye and the buildings behind; it is not clear at all what it is, but it is significant that one sees it so late. In this, as in its indistinctness and brownness, it recalls the threatening cloth material pointed towards the woman reading a letter in *Woman in Blue.*

The Art of Vermeer

What can we say, then, about the art of Vermeer as it is revealed in this set of paintings? First, that his paintings point constantly to what lies outside of themselves, to the eternally unknown: the contents of the letter, the ultimate reaction of the woman, the identity of the sender, the face of the man with his back to us, the source of light in *The Letter* and *Woman in Blue,* the music that is played at the harpsichord in the picture in London or from the sheet music in *The Letter,* the world of adventure and voyages and surveying and trade implied by the map, and so forth. Each of these pictures captures a moment that is defined as a moment, only a moment, in a world that cannot otherwise be known. It does this in part by suggesting that this scene is part of a story, and it invites us irresistibly to locate it in a narrative line; but we cannot do it. The painting frustrates the very effort it stimulates. We are full of questions without answers.

At the same time, each of these paintings presents something as valuable, yet as subject to threat: the pregnant woman, full of potential feeling, reading the letter, but surrounded by imprisoning rectangles, and perhaps about to read news of disaster; the eager young woman at the table in the painting at the Frick, facing the huge male figure, black and red; the anxious woman receiving a letter in *The Letter,* and so forth. What is rendered by the art of Vermeer is not simply the surface of life, stripped of merely human significance, as perhaps one version

of objectivity would have it, but a drama of the deepest human significance and value, the sense of life itself imperiled. These women—and
they are all women—have interior lives as rich and complex as the
interiors they inhabit, or more so. The tension and perplexities and
dangers of the interiors themselves all suggest it. Yet the particulars of
this interior life are withheld from us.

Compare, once more, the painting by de Hooch. It is executed with
extraordinary finish and polish, and represents an appealing and attractive life. But one has a sense of completeness of representation—
everything seems to lie before us, accessible to the mind—rather than,
as with Vermeer, a sense of the fragmentary or momentary. And in de
Hooch there is no sense of threat whatever: his figures belong comfortably in their world, as we are encouraged to feel that we do too. Not
so with Vermeer.[7]

Think back now to the pictures by Rembrandt discussed above.
These are portraits of real people, meant to represent their nature,
which must mean their inner nature, as that is reflected in their outer
appearance. But how is it that we perceive and judge these appearances? What connection is there or can there be between the inner state
of a person and what his or her features happen to be? From one point
of view, the physical is merely contingent, and there can be no connection; but from another point of view, or invoking a different capacity
of the self, we all know that we make judgments of this kind all the
time. She has a sweet and open face, or a sly and mistrustful one; he
looks shallow and dumb, or alert with intelligence, or alive with depth
of feeling. Sometimes of course we are misled or otherwise make a
misjudgment, but this fact merely confirms the power and accuracy of
our judgment as a general matter. Yet exactly how we read each other's
appearance is a mystery: no objective rules, say interpreting the shape
of the skull or the distance between the eyes or the fullness of lips, will

---

7. The painter who is closest to Vermeer is probably Gerard ter Borch, though he does
not seem to me to stimulate in the viewer anything like the same sense of value, of threat;
nor does he capture moments as precisely defined in a stream of unseen and unknowable
time. For a good brief analysis of ter Borch from a point of view congenial to my own, see
Zbigniew Herbert, *Still Life with a Bridle,* trans. John and Bogdana Carpenter (Hopewell,
N.J.: Ecco Press, 1991), 62–77; for an explicit comparison with Vermeer, see Albert Blankert
et al., *Vermeer* (New York: Rizzoli, 1988), 84–90. For particular pictures, see especially
A Lady Dressing Her Hair and *A Lady Reading a Letter,* both in the Wallace Collection, *A
Woman Writing a Letter,* in the Mauritshuis, and the striking *A Company in an Interior,* at
the Rijksmuseum.

work. This is a capacity we have and use, but one that is not wholly accessible to the conscious mind.

The gifted painter of human faces, here Rembrandt or Vermeer, draws upon this capacity both in himself, in making the painting, and in his viewer, in seeking to understand it. It is the essence of Rembrandt's mature self-portraits that they give you a sense of who he is; not as superficial, not as caught up in a momentary feeling, but as one who has experienced deeply and has a rich inner life. Likewise with Vermeer, who makes us feel that the women he paints are not simply handsome, or bourgeois, or engaged in a social practice we can understand—like folding linen, or buying fish, or weighing gold—but are individual people with important inner experience. In that, not the regularity of their features, is their allure, indeed their beauty. It is this that we are drawn to value, in a sense to love, and hence to feel in peril.

In its largest form, as the tension between the objective and the subjective, the question presented here is also at work in other art forms, including writing. Of course in literature we do not have the relation between physical appearance and inner life to puzzle us, but we do have a parallel one. In reading the poem or play or philosophic dialogue to what extent do we see just what anyone would mean by uttering these words, as though they were produced not by a person but by a machine, and to what extent do we rather perceive behind the words the person, the mind, the self at work, and see its meaning there? What exactly do we do when we read a poem by Frost or Herbert? If our reading does seek to detach the poem from the mind that made it, why would we read the poem in the first place? Or think of music, and the motions of the mind and feeling that it enacts: If it came not from a person but a machine, why would you listen to it? In literature and perhaps in music too, the idea of the voice to which one attends may capture the sense in which we want an objective thing, the words or sounds, to express the subjective reality of another.

With respect both to painting and to writing, and music too, the puzzle has still another dimension: To what extent is what I see or hear what you see or hear? Meaning has a subjective element in this dimension too, that is in the mind of the reader or viewer or listener. My own descriptions of these paintings, which express as well as I can manage what I see in them, may at certain points have seemed to you to contain highly arguable or personal elements, interpretations you could not share. The same is of course also true, but perhaps less obtrusively so, of the other readings I have offered in this book. I have foregrounded this problem here not with the idea that you or I could somehow go back and "correct" my readings to fit with yours, or vice versa, but rather with the thought of presenting this problem explicitly, for I think it is inherent in the process of reading and viewing and talking, inherent indeed in all human communication. Just as pure subjectivity would be opaque, impossible to comprehend, so too pure objectivity ultimately makes no sense either, and is also opaque. In all of life we seek contact with the mind, the self, or what Plato would call the soul, of another, and that contact is always imperfect. We begin in the world beyond words and end in it too.

ONE MIGHT EXPECT A PAINTER to try to record a stable reality—what that boat or person or river looks like, that bowl of fruit or vase of flowers—on the assumption that his aim is to represent his subject at the deepest possible level of truth, manifesting its internal structure. Something like this indeed seems to be the idea of the Rembrandt paintings I discussed earlier; it may even be built into the medium itself: the painting will not change, after all, and should therefore represent an unchanging reality.

But Vermeer does something close to the opposite of this: he represents a moment defined with such clarity and precision that it necessarily invokes what comes before and after it, locating us in a river of time in the imagined world. Like Rembrandt, he represents the value of the human capacity for experience, and for finding meaning in it, but he does so not statically but dynamically: by creating a sense of immediate expectancy. It is not just that the person we see is capable of experience: we are located right on the edge of its realization; our sense of this commits us to the reality of the imagined experience itself, and hence to the reality and value of such experience in our own world. It is the momentary quality of his paintings that makes them live.

It is a bit as though Vermeer discovered Impressionism three centuries ahead of time, except that Impressionist paintings usually strive to catch a moment that is detached from other moments, like a snapshot, not a moment implying the existence of a stream of experience that it is the aim of the painting to validate. To compare him again with de Hooch, you might say that de Hooch learned how to represent domestic interiors with a wonderful sense of spatial depth created by the art of perspective; Vermeer on the other hand learned how to present an image of psychological and emotional depth by an art without a name, which we might call inner perspective. I think this explains one of the sources of the astonishment and wonder one experiences in beholding Vermeer's paintings: they achieve just what one would think that this art, which is an art of surfaces, could not possibly attain—a depth of meaning.

As I have suggested both of Rembrandt and of Vermeer, the capacity for human experience that this art defines and values is ultimately not that of the subject, not in the imagined world of the painting, but our own, in our world. It is our experience of value and threat, created by Vermeer, that in the end confirms in us the human capacity with which he is concerned. This is why, when we turn from the paintings to the crowd in the museum, asking whether we have lost this capacity or still retain it, we can feel some hope for ourselves and others. Sometimes, indeed, I find myself looking at this person or that with something of the eye of a painter, wondering how they could be represented, either as Rembrandt does it, to catch their deepest capacities for experience and meaning, or as Vermeer does it, to catch them alive, at a moment, in a stream of significance.

One more picture, about which I will say almost nothing, the famous *Head of a Girl* in The Hague (fig. 10). Here the figure in the painting engages us, the viewers, directly. The moment that is caught and located in the mysterious stream of time that lies beyond the power of the painting, in the imagined world whose existence is made real for us, is thus a moment not only in the experience of the subject, looking up or over her shoulder, but in our own life too. We want the next thing to happen, the smile or frown or tightening of the eyes or lift of the head, but it will not, not ever. For the world of the painting is ultimately frozen, only a moment, only imagined. We turn away with regret, with a sense of loss; this has no doubt an erotic component, but that is not the main thing, which is the sense of the possibility of human contact, first made vivid, then disappointed.

Yet not disappointed after all: the contact with Vermeer is after all real—that is what happens in all this gazing at his pictures, one mind reaching another—and we turn away from the painting to what lies around us with a sense of possibility newly defined. The extraordinary sense we have that this woman, like the others in Vermeer's paintings, has a rich and valuable interior life is really a perception not of her life, but of what Vermeer has led us to feel about our own. The painting confirms, that is, the reality and value of our own interior experience.

Vermeer's paintings thus stimulate and sharpen a feeling of simul-

FIGURE 10. Head of a Girl

taneous value and threat, which is perhaps the deepest feeling appropriate to human existence; they intensify the tension between our sense of the momentariness of the scene represented and our simultaneous consciousness that the particular representation, like one of Keats's odes, exists almost out of time entirely; and they force upon us a double sense that the person in the painting is available to our perception, known to us, and our awareness that she is in another sense unknown and unknowable. In each of these respects, the extraordinary depth of meaning we experience consists in the intensification of a fundamental mystery of human life.

Vermeer makes us want to know what we cannot know; in so doing he focuses attention upon what we can know, upon the nature of the moment before us. He makes us want to connect with another person with whom we cannot connect; in so doing he focuses attention on the desire and capacity for connection of that kind, indeed for that kind of love. And similarly, he makes us desire perfection and security, at the same time teaching us that all that we can value is perpetually subject to threat. All of this may remind us of Plato and the famous myth: Vermeer stimulates in his viewer a kind of love, love for these images of women, which becomes not a love for any person—there is no person there at all—but of beauty itself, and of the vitality and volatility of human life.

In looking at paintings for their meaning, as in reading poems, we focus upon details, then shift to structure, then return to details, then shift our perspective, asking other questions, then return to where we began, and so forth, in an endless process. It is a search for meaning; it rests upon a faith that the picture, or the text, will yield meaning, in the form of its various readings and beyond them too. It is the same faith, I believe, with which the biologist studies the cell, the astronomer the stars; a faith that the universe has meaning and that we can apprehend it, seeing what is really there; even more, that as parts of the universe, parts of the creation, we too are bearers of meaning.

༄

I met with Elizabeth once a week for a couple of years, as part of a team of five people—one of us worked with her for an hour each day—in a program to help children who were having difficulty in school, especially with reading. Elizabeth was tall for her eleven years, ungainly, dark, and silent. When she read aloud it was in a whisper too soft to hear, and her eyes seemed perpetually downcast. She read as she seemed to do everything, listlessly and without caring whether she understood. She seemed to me depressed, or in some other way demoralized, or perhaps just miserable.

We kept at it, all of us, week after week. Gradually she seemed to relax, to come to life, until one day, after vacation, she was utterly closed, stone silent. I asked her whether she had

had a good vacation; she said, "Not really; two of my relatives were shot to death." I was stunned, and fumbled to say something. How do you respond to such a fact in a child's life?

I spoke to the program director, who said that she must be recalling a murder that had occurred in her extended family a year earlier, but it was not so. This was a second killing.

Here is this child beside me, I thought, suffering what no child should suffer. She is a fragment of God's presence on earth, as real and important as any other, calling out for what I cannot provide, what no one can provide. What can I give her? Not my mind, or my professional expertise, or my intellectual life; only my presence, for whatever it might be worth.

That and one other thing: it occurred to me that she might have trouble understanding what reading is because she had never been read to. So in our lessons I began reading to her from her book, then she would read, then I would read again. It became something we did together.

ACKNOWLEDGMENTS

I am grateful to many people for the conversations and friendships that lie behind this book, especially to Arthur Adkins, Huda Akil, Rudolf Arnheim, Milner Ball, A. L. Becker, Lee Bollinger, Homer Clark, John D'Arms, Kenneth DeWoskin, Thomas Eisele, Phoebe Ellsworth, Alice Fulton, Orit Kamir, L. H. LaRue, Sabine MacCormack, John Adam MacPhail, Ronald Mann, Bruce Mannheim, Alfred McDonnell, Jonathan Post, Sara Rappe, James Redfield, Michael Schoenfeldt, Ruth Scodel, Zoe Strother, Winnifred Sullivan, Helen Vendler, Joseph Vining, Christina Whitman, and, as always and above all, my wife, Mary.

I owe a special debt to my beloved friend Gerda Seligson, with whom I have been reading Greek once a week for fifteen years, and from whom I have learned much about that language, about reading and conversation, and about the possibilities of life itself. This book is dedicated to her with great gratitude and affection.

I am grateful as well to the following for permission to reprint material (often with considerable revision and rewriting) from the publications indicated: Washington and Lee Law Review, "Why I Write," 53 *Washington and Lee Law Review* 1021 (1996); Raritan, "The *Odyssey*," 8 *Raritan* 102 (1988); The George Herbert Journal, "Reading One Poet in Light of Another: Herbert and Frost," 18 *George Herbert Journal* 59 (1996); University of Michigan Press, *"This Book of Starres": Learning to Read George Herbert* (1994), copyright © by the University of Michigan 1994; Federation Press, "The Ethics of Meaning," in *The Happy Couple: Law and Literature*, ed. J. Neville Turner and Pamela Williams (1994); Karakters, "The Mystery of Meaning in Vermeer," 1 *Karakters* 9 (1996).

In addition I am grateful to Henry Holt & Co. for permission to reprint a passage from *Selected Letters of Robert Frost*, ed. Lawrance Thompson (1964), copyright © 1964 by Lawrance Thompson and Henry Holt and Co., reprinted by permission of Henry Holt & Co., LLC; and for permission to reprint Robert Frost's "The Road Not Taken," "Range Finding," "Design," and "Mowing" from *The Poetry of Robert Frost*, ed. Edward Connery Lathem, copyright 1936, 1944, © 1962 by Robert Frost, © 1969 by Henry Holt and Co., © 1964

by Lesley Frost Ballantine; reprinted by permission of Henry Holt &
Co., LLC.

I am also grateful to the following museums for permission to reproduce the paintings by Vermeer and de Hooch: Frick Collection, for
Vermeer, *Officer and Laughing Girl,* copyright The Frick Collection,
New York; Mauritshuis (The Hague), for Vermeer, *Head of a Girl,*
photograph © Mauritshuis; Metropolitan Museum of Art (New York),
for Vermeer, *A Girl Asleep at a Table* and *Woman with a Lute,* all
rights reserved, The Metropolitan Museum of Art; National Gallery of
Art (London), for Vermeer, *Lady Standing at a Virginal,* photograph
© National Gallery, London; and Rijksmuseum (Amsterdam), for Ver-
meer, *The Letter, The Little Street, The Milkmaid,* and *Woman in Blue
Reading a Letter,* and for De Hooch, *The Country Cottage.*

INDEX